Information Disclosure
and the
Multinational Corporation

Information Disclosure and the Multinational Corporation

S. J. GRAY
University of Glasgow, Scotland

with

L. B. McSWEENEY
Association of Certified Accountants

J. C. SHAW
Deloitte Haskins and Sells

JOHN WILEY AND SONS
Chichester · New York · Brisbane · Toronto . Singapore

Library of Congress Cataloging in Publication Data

Gray, S. J.
 Information disclosure and the multinational corporation.
 (Wiley/IRM series on multinationals)
 Includes bibliographical references and index.
 1. Financial statements—Law and legislation.
 2. Disclosure of information (Securities Law).
 3. International business enterprises—Law and legislation.
 I. McSweeney, L. B.   II. Shaw, J. C. (John Calman), 1932–
 III. Title.   IV. Series.
 K1335.G7   1984   346'.0666   84–3565
 ISBN 0 471 90424 4   342.6666

British Library Cataloguing in Publication Data:

Gray, S. J.
 Information disclosure and the multinational corporation.—
 (Wiley/IRM series on multinationals)
 1. International business enterprises.
 2. Freedom of information—Great Britain.
 I. Title   II. Shaw, J. C.   III. McSweeney, L. B.
 659.2   HF5549.5.C6

 ISBN 0 471 90424 4

Phototypeset by Input Typesetting Ltd., London.
Printed in Gt Britain by Page Bros (Norwich) Ltd,
Mile Cross Lane, Norwich NR6 6SA

Acknowledgements

The authors wish to express their appreciation to the Institute for Research and Information on Multinationals for financing the project.

In addition, a large number of officials and executives at all levels in national and international organizations and multinational corporations have given their time which is gratefully acknowledged.

Finally, thanks are due to colleagues and external reviewers for their many helpful comments and criticisms relating to earlier versions of this study.

S. J. GRAY
J. C. SHAW
L. B. McSWEENEY

University of Glasgow,
Scotland
December 1983

Contents

Preface

'European management faces an explosion of proposed legislation on corporate information disclosure. International bodies like the ILO (International Labour Organization), the UN (United Nations), the OECD (Organization for Economic Cooperation and Development) and the EEC (European Economic Community), indeed governments everywhere, are scrambling on to the disclosure bandwagon as fast as the legislation procedures will allow'.[1]

In general terms this 'explosion', referred to by Jack Peel, a former Director of Industrial Relations of the European Commission, is the result of a gradual building up of three sources of pressure. The first is an economic pressure. European companies are having to face rapid technological change in the face of US and Japanese competition, as well as new, bitter competition from the newly industrializing countries (NICs). Decisions resulting from these new structural developments are having to be taken within the context of the world's worst recession since the 1930s. Such restructuring decisions have an immediate effect on the future employment prospects of thousands of employees and for future employers it becomes increasingly difficult to deny the right of these employees to have their interests taken into account by management, to have an opportunity to receive full information about these decisions and also to be involved in the decision-making process itself.

A second pressure for information disclosure is the trade unions who have strengthened their power to the point where they are able to launch an assault on what for so long had been considered management prerogatives. Trade unions have been helped by legislation which, in many European countries, has given workers a role in the running of their companies. Moreover, allowing workers greater participation on the supervisory boards of all companies in the European Community has been on the legislative agenda since 1972.

Finally, new concepts of the role of employees do not just stem from economic change or the development of trade union power, they are also derived from social changes, which have taken place since the war. These are, especially, higher standards of living, increasing educational opportunities and social mobility. This has provoked a questioning of unaccountable power, an erosion of deferential attitudes and has given birth to demands for a more transparent society. Pressure for companies to disclose more information has therefore been produced as a result of these three changes.[2]

However, employees have not been the only groups wishing more information. Governments and investors have also joined in this chorus. Their desire is not only for more information but for more usable information, focusing their attention on the need to improve the comparability of financial and general data.

As a result, the OECD, EEC and the UN have been for many years attempting to standardize accounting methods. These attempts have run into protracted difficulties. However, the EEC, in 1983, did pass the seventh directive on group accounts which by 1990 will oblige companies to obey general EEC standards as opposed to national laws.

Undoubtedly, demands for more data and more comparable data have worried MNCS. However, it has been pointed out that these trends may work to their advantage.[3] The sharing of more information with their employees helps blunt the frictions that inevitably occur over the implementation of hard, but necessary decisions. Also, maximum norms of information disclosure in comparable formats can help employers compare their own performance against competitors, while disarming critics and reducing the hostility with which multinational companies are often perceived in developing as well as European countries.

The purpose of Professor Gray's book is to provide a review of the major issues, problems and trends relating to this process of information disclosure and the multinationals. His book discusses the evolution of accountability and information disclosure, the arguments for and against more disclosure from the viewpoints of all the actors and reviews information disclosure developments in practice on a world-wide basis.

IRM sponsored this work because it considered it an important issue concerning the nature of the multinationals. Through this promotion of serious and independent academic work, of which Professor Gray's work is a good example, IRM hopes to better inform trades unionists, managers, international civil servants and politicians involved in policy discussions on multinationals.

References

1. Jack Peel, *The Real Power Game*. (London: McGraw-Hill Book Company, 1979), p. 122.
2. See chapter 3. *Report of the Committee of Inquiry on Industrial Democracy*, Chairman Lord Bullock, Her Majesty's Stationery Office, 1977.
3. 'Multinationals become focus of moves to standardize company data'. Brij Khindaria. *International Herald Tribune*, November 28, 1983.

GEOFFREY HAMILTON,
Research Associate,
IRM

The Institute for Research and Information on Multinationals (IRM) promotes and finances independent academic research on multinational companies and their impact on society. This research is undertaken by academics of various disciplines from all over the world. The findings are made available to the widest possible audience through the publication of books, reports and bulletins, through the media, and through the organization of conferences, seminars and other activities.

1

Introduction

The power of multinational corporations (MNCs)[1] to control and move resources internationally[2]—sometimes to the apparent disadvantage of national interests—has recently given rise to demands, especially from governments and trade unions, for extensions in accountability and information disclosure.[3]

At the international inter-governmental level, the involvement of The United Nations (UN), the Organization for Economic Co-operation and Development (OECD), and the European Economic Community (EEC) in the development of accounting standards, with special reference to MNCs, confirms the politically sensitive nature of MNC operations and impact.[4] Apparently, the global reach of the MNC is to be countered only by global/regional regulation.

Pressures on MNCs are evident not just from inter-governmental organizations. A broad array of interest groups are demanding that MNCs improve the quantity and comparability of information disclosed. Deficiencies in current disclosure and measurement practices are perceived by international organizations of trade unions[5] and investment analysts[6] alike—albeit with some differences consistent with their own special concerns. The accounting profession, in the form of the International Accounting Standards Committee (IASC) is also striving to attain some measure of harmonization of accounting standards worldwide.[7] MNCs themselves would tend to support some degree of international harmonization, as a result of their concern with the multiplicity of national financial reporting requirements, while viewing with alarm the growing number and variety of international standard-setting agencies and their demands for extensions in information disclosure.[8]

The development of accounting and information disclosure by MNCs is thus taking place in a complex, multi-dimensional, and dynamic environment involving many participants, including governments, trade unions, investors, bankers, accountants, and managers.

1

1.1 PURPOSE AND SCOPE

The purpose of this book is to provide a review of major issues, problems, and trends relating to information disclosure and the MNC. This is an area of considerable controversy, and it is hoped that politicians, government officials, trade unionists, investors, managers, and other interested parties will be thereby better informed about the issues involved and recent developments. The discussion is also likely to be of particular interest to financial managers and accountants, though the analysis of specific accounting and reporting practices is limited to an overview of selected areas of significance to MNCs.

The main focus of the study is on information disclosure by MNCs in the context of corporate annual reports, comprising financial statements/ accounts and additional financial and non-financial information. These reports are usually referred to as general-purpose reports, i.e. they include information which may be used by a number of user groups for a variety of purposes. General-purpose reports may be contrasted with special reports designed for specific user groups, such as employees, and issued separately either on a confidential or publicly available basis.

While it is recognized that there is growing interest in the provision of special reports and that this is likely to be an important area for future development, given the diversity of users and information needs, the thrust of the current controversy is concerned with the content of general-purpose corporate reports. Indeed, much of the pressure to expand the content of such reports is aimed at accommodating the information needs of a wider range of users than hitherto envisaged. Thus the expansion of this type of report, with sections of special interest to specific groups, may be but a prelude to a widespread decentralization of corporate reporting.

It must also be appreciated that information is often disclosed to interested parties by means other than corporate annual reports, whether they be general-purpose or special reports. Financial and non-financial information is regularly, or occasionally, supplied to governments, bankers, works councils, trade unions, investment analysts, and others in a wide variety of contexts, formal and informal, on a confidential or publicly available basis. Thus corporate annual reports are not the only, nor necessarily the most important, source of information about MNC operations and impact. Nevertheless, it is widely recognized by governments, trade unions and the financial community in many countries that corporate annual reports are an important instrument of accountability, a public record, and a reliable source of information which may not be readily available elsewhere.

International inter-governmental organizations such as the UN, OECD, and EEC have recognized the significance of information disclosure in MNC annual reports, as have international organizations of trade unions, investment analysts, and accountants. Hence there would appear to be ample justification to focus our study accordingly while remaining aware of the limitations involved.

1.2 OUTLINE

The book begins with a historical review of the evolution of accountability and information disclosure, including a discussion of accountability in relation to MNCs with special emphasis on the differences between MNCs and domestic or uninational corporations (UNCs) which have given rise to recent pressures for more accountability and information disclosure.

Secondly, the demand for information from the major participants concerned is analysed with special reference to governments, trade unions and employees, and the financial community.

Thirdly, managerial perspectives concerning the supply of information are considered with some discussion of the likely costs and benefits that must necessarily be evaluated in decisions regarding disclosure, whether it be on a voluntary or regulatory basis.

Fourthly, the extent of regulation and information disclosure in practice is reviewed on a world-wide basis in respect to selected issues of significance to MNCs: consolidated financial statements, funds statements, segmental information, transfer pricing and related party transactions, accounting for inflation, foreign currency translation, and non-financial reporting, including value added statements and business forecasts. Problems and prospects for developments in each of these areas are briefly discussed.

Finally, an overview of the discussion is presented and some conclusions offered for consideration and debate.

2

The Evolution of Accountability and Information Disclosure

Accountability and Information disclosure[1] by corporations in the national context is influenced by a variety of economic, social, and political factors. The political system and type of economy, the stage of economic development, the social climate, the legal system, the management and ownership structure of corporations, the accounting profession, the tax system, and the nature and stage of development of the capital market, are all important environmental factors which determine both the accounting systems used and the extent to which information is publicly disclosed.[2]

The influence of these factors is likely to vary both between and within countries over time. Moreover, it would seem that there is an evolutionary process of some complexity at work with special reference to the growing number of cross-cultural and regional influences such as those arising from the activities of MNCs and international intergovernmental organizations such as the UN, the OECD and EEC. In the European context, the EEC is an especially significant influence in that any agreement on the harmonization of information disclosure becomes legally enforceable throughout the EEC countries. In figure 2.1 one attempt to formulate a model of the evolutionary factors involved is presented.[3]

While there are many differences in national environments, with corresponding differential effects on accounting systems, there are also many similarities. Attempts to classify countries, and identify clusters or groupings, are still very much at the early stages, but such efforts would seem to be useful in gaining a better understanding of factors influencing the development of accounting systems with consequent benefit in terms of predicting likely changes and their impact. Accounting systems in centrally planned economies such as the USSR are, of course, quite different from those developed in market economies such as in the USA and the EEC countries. So far as public reporting in

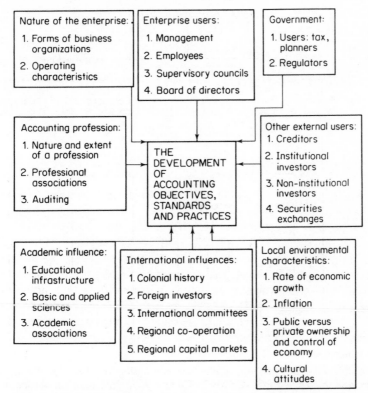

Figure 2.1. The evolution of accounting and reporting practices.
Source: *Lee H.Radebaugh, 'Environmental Factors Influencing the Development of Accounting Objectives, Standards and Practices in Peru',* International Journal of Accounting *(Fall, 1975)*

market economies is concerned, a number of empirical studies point towards the identification of four basic models, viz. British Commonwealth, Latin American, continental European, and United States.[4] There have also been attempts to classify national systems on a more judgemental basis as in figure 2.2 which is an example of a biological approach to systems classification.[5]

In all of these studies it would seem to be much more difficult to discern clear patterns relating to information disclosure as compared to asset and profit measurement practices which have perhaps been more stable over time.

Given the change factors at work it is not likely to be an easy task to predict future evolution. The current situation is highly dynamic in the context of the activities of a wide range of national and international organizations, as well as the changing nature of business and especially multinational operations. It may well be that new models or patterns

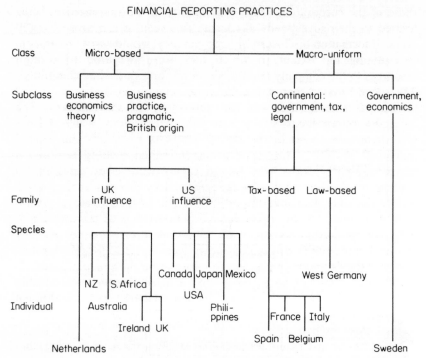

Figure 2.2. The classification of national accounting systems. Source: *C. W. Nobes and R. H. Parker (Editors),* Comparative International Accounting *(Philip Allan, 1981)*

of reporting are in the process of being formed, e.g. the UK and continental European models are in the process of co-ordination and some fusion following EEC developments in accounting harmonization.

Consider now some of the more influential factors in the development of information disclosure by corporations.

2.1 DEVELOPMENTAL FACTORS

A major factor influencing the development of information disclosure in the USA, UK, and other market economies was the recognition of corporations as legal entities with the public ownership of shares and the right of limited liability.[6] Two characteristics of these early corporations necessitated disclosure for the protection of two groups in particular. First, as a consequence of limited liability the resources available to creditors in the event of the corporation's liquidation were limited to those of the corporation itself. The liability of the shareholders being limited to their investment, disclosure was seen as a means of regulation. Information disclosure or 'transparency' would assist creditors in determining the extent to which they were prepared to commit resources to the company and the use of resources they had committed. The second major reason for the close relationship between limited liability and disclosure was the protection of shareholders. The emerging entrepreneurs often came from backgrounds which did not give them easy access to the capital necessary to launch and expand individual projects. The introduction of limited liability removed a major disability. Those who owned capital were often unwilling to become involved in what were frequently risky projects as they stood to lose not only their investment but the rest of their personal wealth as well. Limited liability restricted the potential loss to the investment in the corporation. As many of these investors were not directly involved in the running of the business, it was essential for their protection that they should have access to information on a regular basis.

Information disclosure to those with a direct financial relationship with corporations has been influenced by two additional developments—the growth of professional management and the emergence of stock exchanges.

Much has been written about the so-called separation of ownership and control which is supposed to have resulted from the emergence of professional management composed of individuals whose positions of power within corporations stemmed from their possession of administrative and/or technical skills rather than ownership of the corporation's capital.[7] The growth in size and increasing complexity of business is the basis for this growth of the managerial class. Whether, and to what extent, the separation of ownership from management and the division of the corporation into two essentially distinct groups results in corporation behaviour different from that of a corporation owned and controlled by the same persons is a matter of considerable controversy.[8] Whatever the general position may be, the fear of such deviance and the experience of individual cases were further reasons for maintaining and expanding disclosure as a means of checking that management was not behaving in a manner to the detriment of the owner's interests.

Corresponding to the growth in the number, size, and complexity of corporations was the demand for finance in the form of shares, or what is termed as equity investment, as well as loans. This gave rise to the development of capital markets where the raising of finance could be facilitated. A major factor influencing the disclosure of information was the emergence of stock exchanges which have their origins in the desire of shareholders to trade their investments without liquidating the company and the need for a mechanism for raising new finance in an efficient manner. The former reason, the exchangeability of shares, is that which preoccupies the major portion of the market's time and energy, especially in countries such as the USA and UK.[9]

The growth of stock exchanges necessitated the expansion of information availability to a wider audience, viz. potential investors interested in buying and selling shares. As most private shareholders were not capable of comprehensively analysing the financial disclosures of corporations, they tended to rely on specialist advisers/financial analysts.

It is these analysts who now act as interpreters of corporate reports for many investors, current and potential. It is in this way that the information needs of investors, and financial analysts in particular, have acted as a constant pressure on corporations to increase both the quality and the quantity of their disclosures. Thus the emergence of stock exchanges has served to both deepen and broaden disclosure.

The importance of information usage by potential investors and comments by financial analysts has meant that the financial disclosures of public corporations whose shares may be traded have become publicly accessible.[10] The availability of corporate reports to groups other than investors and creditors is not, therefore, a consequence of any pressure directly exerted by them but is a result of the necessity of public availability for unidentifiable potential investors.

The predominant influence of stock exchanges in determining the quality and quantity of publicly available information in corporate reports is indicated by the strong correlation between well-developed markets and the extent of financial disclosure in corporate reports. Countries with active and well-developed markets, e.g. the USA and UK, generally have a greater extent of public financial disclosure than those with relatively inactive ones, e.g. West Germany, France, Italy, Belgium.[11]

While the basis for this difference lies to some extent in national attitudes it is mainly due to the lower demand in some countries for public information disclosure. This is in turn a function of differences in environmental factors including especially the political system and role of government, the type of economy, the ownership of business, and the nature and stage of development of capital markets.

Why is it that stock exchanges appear to have been the predominant force in the emergence of *public* corporate disclosure? It has already been argued that the existence of an active market necessitates the publication of financial information for share-trading decisions by shareholders and potential investors. What distinguishes shareholders from other finance providers is that most shareholders are 'outsiders'. Despite being nominally owners of the corporation they have perhaps the least access to private information and arguably the least control. The bargaining power of *other* finance providers, e.g. bankers and lenders, is such that these participants do not have to rely on published reports exclusively if at all. In France and West Germany, for example, the public ownership of shares in corporations is much less widespread than in the USA and UK.[12] In France, it is the government which plays a major role in the provision of finance to corporations. In West Germany, the banks are a significant source of loan finance and are often major equity investors in their own right.

These 'other' finance providers generally have, as a result of their power, the ability to obtain considerably more detailed and up-to-date information than 'outsiders'. Therefore, disclosure to finance providers can be seen as a spectrum. At one end, that of least disclosure, are shareholders and investors (with the exception of those who are directly involved with the company). Beyond this point, information disclosure is less restricted and varies in its nature depending on the purpose for which it is required and the power of the finance provider.

The myth that shareholders control public corporations still persists nevertheless. While this may be the case for small private corporations where the number of investors is limited it does not apply to large public corporations. Private investors in public corporations, where there is usually a widespread dispersion of shareownership tend, except in exceptional circumstances, to exert little direct influence on the running of a corporation. These shareholders are usually passive, exercising their 'power' on the advice and initiative of management, i.e. the board of directors.

Even if share prices exert some indirect discipline on management, on account of their effect on financing potential and the possibility of take-over, this is unlikely to be significant in countries where there are few shareholders and where stock exchanges are of relatively minor importance.

Reinforcing the relative lack of influence of shareholders in many countries has been the influence of governments in the development and use of accounting systems which facilitate the provision of information for national economic planning and control. In France, for example, a uniform national accounting system has been developed as a basis for planning purposes and corporate taxation.[13] This is an entirely different orientation from the USA and UK where professional accountants have played a pre-eminent role in the development of accounting systems and forms of corporate reporting which have been directed primarily to those who do not have direct access to information about the corporation.[14]

2.2 A WIDER AUDIENCE

While accountability and information disclosure by corporations has historically developed in response to those with a direct financial investment, in recent years there has been an increasing acknowledgement that since finance providers, i.e. shareholders, bankers, lenders, creditors, are not the only group affected by the actions of a corporation, there is an obligation to report to a wider audience which includes employees, trade unions, consumers, government agencies, and the general public.[15] A variety of reasons has contributed to this widespread belief that companies should explicitly disclose information to groups other than finance providers, including:

(a) The development and growth of the influence of trade unions in most developed countries, both at the level of the corporation (through various methods of 'participation' and/or extensions of collective bargaining) and at national level.

(b) The increase in what has alternatively been called 'the challenge to authority' or the 'democratic imperative' with the demand for recognition of the view that those who are significantly affected by decisions made by institutions in general must be given the opportunity to influence those decisions. Business corporations are not immune to this changing attitude to institutions.

(c) The post-war attempt by many governments to implement Keynesian-type economics management was based on a rejection of some of the assumptions of classical economics, in particular the belief that the unregulated pursuit of private gain resulted in the maximum welfare of society, though this trend has been tempered somewhat in recent years by the swing to 'monetarism' and a more market-orientated approach, at least in the USA and UK.

(d) The potential gap between private gain and social gain, long referred to in economics textbooks, has become a source of public concern, especially in relation to so-called 'externalities', e.g. pollution.

(e) The substantial growth in industrial concentration has meant that some corporations are now large enough individually to exert an influence on macro-economic variables and national economic and social policies.

These developments, among others, have expanded the concept of 'accountability' and the desire of various groups in society to monitor/ influence the behaviour of business corporations. Wider corporate accountability has been of major interest to many writers in recent years. To what extent has it affected corporate reports? The development of information disclosure by corporations has been constrained by restrictions on both the supply and demand side.

On the supply side, the goal divergence, where it exists between corporation management and finance providers, e.g. investors, bankers, and creditors, operates within a common framework. Differences are usually measurable and controllable. However, explicit acknowledgement of the 'rights' of non-finance providers, e.g. trade unions, to information may, for some corporations, mean that they would be committed to pursue goals other than those which they have traditionally followed. From a managerial perspective, this could endanger the growth or survival of the corporation. The extent to which corporations have in practice been influenced in their behaviour by the goals of non-finance providers is another matter. But many corporations, regardless of what they actually do, have been reluctant formally to acknowledge the influence of other 'stakeholders'.[16]

Corporate reports may be used as a source of information useful for making decisions and reporting on management's stewardship. To the extent that the goals of finance providers and management are seen as not being completely compatible with those of non-finance providers, increasing information disclosure may, therefore, be seen as increasing the power of the recipients to influence the behaviour of the corporation as well as providing material for criticism of the corporation's performance.

A further constraint is that many of the expectations of non-finance providers are not clearly defined; the techniques to measure them do not exist. While the information requests of finance providers relate to the periodic financial resources and position of a corporation and the results of its operations, many of the information requirements of non-finance providers would seem to relate to a corporation's social as well as economic performance. Not only are measurement techniques often unavailable or underdeveloped but there is often not even general agreement on the broad elements of accountability involved.

On the demand side, to the extent that non-finance providers wish to use information, that which is made available for finance providers may in fact partially or even completely satisfy their information needs. Thus, in attempting to identify the special or unique information needs of non-finance providers, there has been a tendency to ignore the possibility that they may wish to obtain/use information aimed at finance providers.

The ability of non-finance providers to influence corporation behaviour varies considerably. Those with limited or no influence can exert little direct pressure for increased disclosure, whereas those with some power may be able to bypass the published corporate report and obtain information directly, and in greater detail, in special reports. In many European countries, especially West Germany and France, trade unions or employee representatives have, through various forms of 'co-determination' or collective bargaining, obtained access to information. In West Germany, for example, this right to disclosure is established in law with works councils given access to a wide range of financial and non-financial information.[17] The philosophy behind this is that such access will promote mutual trust between employers and employees. The availability of information for bargaining with corporations can be 'double-edged', however, in the sense that the information may not substantiate opinions previously held and could therefore retard rather than enhance the influence of the user group concerned.

An acknowledgement of a right of access to information implies certain political values—essentially those of liberal democracies, like those in Western Europe. In countries where democracy is not as well established, e.g. in some of the developing African countries, the conditions necessary for increased disclosure are considerably less developed.

In summary, public disclosure in corporate reports has in the main been a spin-off from the evolution, over a considerable period of time, of disclosure to finance providers. The major impetus has been provided by the growth of active and well-developed stock markets. In many countries such markets are not at all developed and while their limited maturity in this respect may not ultimately prevent wider disclosure, this would necessitate a disclosure development significantly different from that experienced in many of the developed countries.

2.3 ACCOUNTABILITY, INFORMATION DISCLOSURE, AND MULTINATIONAL CORPORATIONS

We have considered the evolution of information disclosure by corporations. However, corporations whose ownership and operations remain essentially in one country, i.e. UNCs have not been distinguished from those which operate simultaneously in a number of countries—MNCs. What differentiates MNCs from UNCs and how does this, or should it, affect the accountability of MNCs?

Before exploring the essential differences between MNCs and UNCs let us look briefly at the impact that the vast post-war expansion in the number of MNCs has had on the demand for a greater extent of information disclosure. The early expectations of rapid industrialization of the developing countries has not been fulfilled. The economic development theories of modernization of the 1960s, particularly those associated with Rostow, maintained that the path for development for these countries was simply to repeat the nineteenth-century Industrial Revolution of the West which would solve the problem of economic growth and through a 'trickle-down' process, that of income distribution.[18] To what extent this may or may not be possible in the longer term goes beyond the scope of this study and, therefore, does not concern us. What matters is that early expectations have not borne fruit, with a resultant increase in frustration and criticism. The contributions of MNCs are thus frequently analysed not on the basis of what they have achieved or what any alternative could have realistically achieved but rather compared with the immense needs of the developing countries. It is not difficult to find commentaries which blame MNCs for the ills of society which have their origins in past history or internal circumstances unrelated to MNCs. Foreign direct investment entails certain benefits and costs for host countries. The developing countries, many of them relatively recently independent, have increased their assertiveness. Within these countries, this process has been assisted by the establishment of MNCs and externally by the increase in the number of sources of foreign direct investment with subsequently greater competition between MNCs. In addition to arguments concerning the right of access to information, the demand for greater disclosure from MNCs may be viewed as a part of a bargaining process—an effort by host countries, and developing countries in particular, to improve their bargaining powers. The fact that MNCs operate in a number of different nation states has given them an opportunity to take actions in their own best interest which are not available to UNCs and also is the basis for a conflict of perspectives, viz. that of a national view of various groups within the nation state and the multinational view of the MNCs. While business activities in a single country may be for many MNCs but a part of their global operation, it is that part which is of primary concern for most of those affected in the host country.

The multinationality, size, and complexity of MNCs have enabled some to undertake actions to the detriment of a host country. Cases of tax avoidance bordering on evasion, political interference, discriminatory practices, and so on are well documented.[19] Whether these are aberrations, exceptions undertaken by a few deviants, or whether they represent more general practice is a matter of debate. The known cases, however, have been sufficient when combined with other factors to increase the pressure for greater disclosure.

The huge size and prominence of some of the largest MNCs perhaps explains why they have become the object of a wide range of criticism which rarely distinguishes between those aspects (positive or negative) of MNCs which they share also with UNCs and those which result from their uniqueness which is their multinationality. Much of the writing on MNC disclosure fails to make this distinction. What is it then that distinguishes MNCs from other companies, UNCs, whether large or small? The philosophy underlying this difference has been expressed as follows:

> For business purposes the boundaries that separate one nation from another are no more real than the equator. They are merely convenient demarcations of ethnic, linguistic and cultural entities. They do not define business requirements or consumer trends. Once management understands and accepts this world economy, its view of the market place—and its planning—necessarily expand. The world outside the home country is no longer viewed as a series of disconnected customers and prospects for its produce but as an extension of a single market.[20]

The existence of business organizations operating in a number of different nation states but with common ownership and/or control (i.e. MNCs) provide opportunities for activities which are not available to UNCs. The extent to which these opportunities are actually used and their effect on the welfare of individual nation states is the central question in the political debate on MNCs. We cannot nor do we purport to answer this question but rather we look at what MNCs have the opportunity to do, which we make somewhat more concrete by referring to some of the available evidence. Consider now the two related characteristics of MNCs: intra-group trading and centralized ownership/control.

2.3.1 Intra-group transactions—the flow of goods and services

Cross-frontier or (export) transactions by UNCs are mediated by the market. The prices paid are at arm's-length price agreed by unrelated parties. However, similar transactions between MNC units in different countries do not necessarily represent a free play of market forces.[21] The internalization of intra-group transactions means that prices are explicitly determined within the group (subject to the effectiveness of external constraints) rather than by the market. In aggregate terms, MNC intra-group trading is substantial, e.g. around 50 per cent of exports from the USA are on an intra-group basis.[22] Bypassing the market does not necessarily mean a decline in global efficiency. Indeed it has been suggested that the internalization of transactions by MNCs within the firm may increase efficiency by facilitating resource allocation and reducing costs.[23] Regardless of views on the impact of MNCs on global welfare, the operation of an international organization in a national framework may mean that the pricing policies adopted may harm or benefit individual countries.

Sensitive to national criticism, many MNCs have attempted to give their national entity a local image and have emphasized—indeed in many cases overemphasized—their autonomy. According to Vernon, 'some degree of co-ordination and control exists in the network of any multi-national enterprise that manages to survive'.[24] This view is qualified by evidence which suggests that while medium and large MNCs are centrally controlled and co-ordinated, smaller MNCs appear to allow their units greater autonomy of operation.[25]

The existence of national restrictions, e.g. limitations on repatriation of profit and of national taxes, provides MNCs with an incentive which may or may not be exercised, to determine the prices of the intra-group goods and services with the object of minimizing the total tax payable by the global group and/or bypassing national restrictions. In addition, intra-group transactions may be used to weaken or undermine local competition in order to attain or reinforce market dominance and make excessively high profits at the expense of the consumer. The latter category of objects, however, are not goals which may be pursued only by MNCs. They are a consequence of size and a position of market dominance rather than multinationality itself. However, the *combined* effect of the international operations of MNCs and their oligopolistic nature serve mutually to reinforce each other. The global objectives of intra-group transfer pricing include:

(i) reducing the total system's tax liability, corporate taxes, customs duty, etc.;
(ii) diverting of profits to tax haven jurisdictions;
(iii) reducing or eliminating the effect of certain restrictions imposed by host countries (e.g. through disguised repatriation of profits or capital);
(iv) circumventing exchange controls and hedging against currency changes;
(v) reducing reported profits to avoid or reduce pressure from various groups in the host country, e.g. governments, minority shareholders, and trade unions;
(vi) the attainment or maintenance of market power;

(vii) the lessening of the impact of price controls.[26]

These objectives are not always compatible. For example, a low import price to reduce customs duties will increase profits, whereas a high import price with correspondingly lower profits or a loss by the importing subsidiary may be desirable in order to reduce the group's net world-wide tax. The inducement to seek some or all of these objectives is likely to vary considerably and will be influenced by the specific conditions of each country within which the MNC operates and the industry, structure, and corporate personality of the particular MNC in question.

Two aspects of the value of intra-group transactions involving goods or services are influenced by pricing decisions. First, the total value involved which has a variety of consequences, positive or negative, e.g. on the balance of payments of a country and second, on the profit or loss made on the transaction. Profit and loss are residual categories so that comparatively small shifts in price will have proportionately a much larger impact on the residual, with obvious effects on reported profits and taxation (see figure 2.3).[27]

Aside from the pricing objectives outlined above there are often technical problems in determining the prices of intra-group transactions. These difficulties exist even if the MNC subsidiary is free to pursue a profit maximization objective and the aim is to determine arm's-length prices. The first problem is that of MNC specific goods where the goods are unique and where no equivalent market price exists.

The second problem relates to the pricing of intra-group services and the allocation of control (overhead) expenditures. In practice, a variety of pricing policies are followed and 'there does not appear to be any fixed pattern either industry-wise or country-wise'.[28] Determining an arm's-length price for such services may be difficult or impossible. National tax authorities faced with determining the acceptability of the pricing decision will have to ask a variety of questions including:

> If the services are provided on an 'on call' basis, should an enterprise be expected to pay irrespective of whether it uses the service over a given period?
> Can expenses incurred by a parent company in managing and protecting its investments be properly charged to members of the group?
> If services are performed or made available neither in the exclusive interest of the parent company nor in the specific interests of one or several subsidiaries, how should the various members of the group pay for such services?[29]

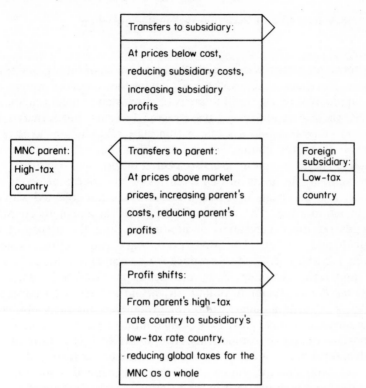

Figure 2.3. The impact of transfer pricing on profits and taxation. Source: *Jeffrey S. Arpan and Lee H. Radebaugh,* International Accounting and Multinational Enterprises *(Warren, Gorham and Lamont, 1981)*

The freedom of MNCs to utilize the cross-frontier relationship of their units to further their overall goals is not unlimited. There are both internal and external constraints. The main internal constraints are possible negative impact on the management of units whose 'real' performance is understated, the complexity in determining and evaluating appropriate strategies and, where they exist, minority shareholders in 'underrated subsidiaries'. The main external constraints are governmental monitoring and control. These constraints limit the flexibility of MNCs. The precise extent to which they do so is, however, a matter of controversy owing to the lack of empirical evidence on transfer pricing practices.[30] While the potential for manipulation is clear, there is some doubt as to whether this is necessarily widespread in practice.

2.3.2 Resource allocation—expansion and contraction

The above discussion was concerned with the price of intra-group transactions. Decisions must also be made about the source of production, the supply of services, and the areas of expansion and contraction. In a UNC these decisions may have a regional impact, but activity takes place in general within a single nation state. Production takes place there as does any contraction or expansion. Similarly, any services available within the group are also located in the same country.

In contrast, the decision of MNCs about the source of goods and services and the location of new investment are not confined within a single nation state. The amount of flexibility available to an MNC depends on the organization of production, and the nature of the products and markets. The MNC producing a product from a single source will find it difficult to produce from another source, at least in the short term. However, if the product is produced in a number of countries it has greater flexibility. In certain industries an increasing tendency towards homogenization of production has been observed. Even products that are extremely dissimilar may be composed of a large proportion of similar components. The ability of MNCs to terminate production is not as great as is popularly assumed, at least in the short run, but over time the source of existing or expanded production can be shifted and with it a shift in the location of new investment.

Decisions on the source of production and the location of new investment may affect a variety of countries. In aggregate, the impact on such matters as employment and economic growth may be no different than if such production/investment was made by UNCs, but the fortunes of individual countries will be affected none the less.

Multinationals frequently maintain that the restrictions on their freedom imposed by nation states reduce global optimization of growth and welfare. 'The critical issue of our time is the conceptual conflict between the search for global optimization and the independence of nation states.'[31]

The global market imperfections that exist do not, however, result exclusively from the actions of nation states. The oligopolistic nature of some MNCs and UNCs is also contributory to this situation. Whether or not MNCs are maximizing global growth and welfare and the extent to which a freer market might contribute to this goal are beyond the scope of this study. However, aside from any direct benefits brought to home or host countries by MNCs, the pursuit of global goals in a global framework through pricing, sourcing, and location decisions may result in additional profits and benefits for the MNC which are by the nature of the decision not evenly spread among the affected nation states.[32] From the perspective of a nation state and specific groups within that country, some decisions made by the MNC in its global best interest may not be in the interest of that nation state. Alternatively, of course, it may well be the case. But if it is, it is only because in that instance the objectives of the MNC and that particular nation state have coincided.

2.4 CONCLUSIONS

The evolution of accountability and information disclosure has been traced with the conclusion that the evolution of public disclosure in corporate reports has been largely a function of the growth of active and well-developed stock markets. More recently there have been pressures to provide information to a wider audience including governments, trade unions and employees, consumers, and the general public.

Accountability by MNCs may be differentiated from that by UNCs though both are business organizations with many features in common. A UNC's primary operations are in one country and its cross-frontier relationships are with unrelated parties. On the other hand, MNCs operate in a number of countries with different legislations and currencies, and there is usually a significant volume of transactions between its units located in different countries. The common control of these globally dispersed operations provides the opportunity to co-ordinate pricing, sourcing, and location decisions in a manner which, while increasing the net return of the group, may be detrimental or, alternatively, advantageous to individual nation states. It is this special impact of MNCs which appears to have given rise to much of the pressure for more accountability and information disclosure. Let us now consider the demand for information arising from the impact of MNCs in some greater depth, with special reference to the user groups and organizations involved.

3

The Demand for Information: Participants and Pressures

The demand for improvements in the quantity, quality, and comparability of information disclosures by MNCs is a manifestation of diverse interests and concerns by a wide range of participant groups and organizations. In support of these demands is the belief that improvements will facilitate a better evaluation of an individual MNC's performance and prospects; reveal more clearly their role and impact; assist in constraining aspects of their behaviour which are regarded as unacceptable; contribute to national and international policy making; or perhaps simply demystify, and make transparent, large and complex organizations. MNC disclosures in corporate annual reports are apparently viewed as an important current and potential source of information required for a wide range of purposes.[1]

Which groups of users and organizations are interested in the affairs of MNCs? The power and global reach of MNCs is such that most nations and many people are affected, directly or indirectly, by their operations. It is possible, however, to distinguish a number of groups who, while having some common concerns, have some which are unique. Why is that they want information relating to MNCs? What is the nature of the information that they desire or need to satisfy their decision requirements? Why do they wish to influence the behaviour of MNCs in respect to the disclosure of information?

It is our intention here to outline the information demands of what may be described as the major participant groups:

(a) governments;
(b) trade unions and employees;
(c) investors (including financial analysts);
(d) bankers and lenders;
(e) the general public; and
(f) accountants and auditors.

In particular, we will be concerned with the activities and influence of international inter-governmental, trade union, professional, and investment/banking organizations involved in the setting of international standards and accounting and reporting by MNCs. A simplified model of the participants and pressures in the demand for information disclosure by MNCs is set out in figure 3.1. National and international participant groups are distinguished, though clearly there is likely to be considerable interaction between these levels and also between and within groups at all levels.

While the focus of the discussion will be on major participant groups, broadly defined, it is also recognized that there will be differences in information needs not only between groups, but to some extent, within them as well. We will now briefly define the nature and scope of these groups as a prelude to a more detailed analysis.

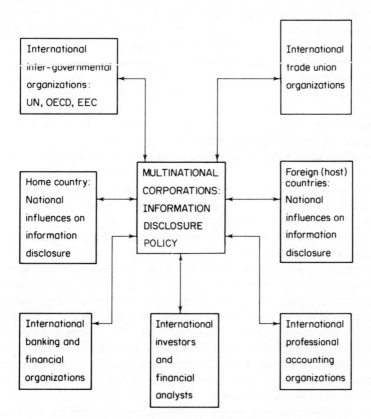

Figure 3.1. Multinational Corporations: The participants and pressures for information disclosure

(a) *Governments* exercise certain functions in each nation, viz. the control function (maintenance of 'law and order'); the ideological–cultural function (the fostering of consensus); the economic function (the regulation; protection, and encouragement of economic activities); and the international function (advancing and protecting the nation state in its foreign relations with foreign entities). The extent and manner in which these functions are undertaken by a government varies according to country, level of development and political system. Our concern is largely with information disclosures by MNCs which governments require/obtain to assist them in performing their economic function, though elements of the international function are also involved. An important distinction must be made between MNC home and host governments as this gives rise to different perspectives regarding MNC regulations. Included under the heading of governments are central and local government, governmental agencies, and international inter-governmental organizations such as the UN, OECD, and EEC. The dual role of governments as both a regulator of information disclosure and as a user of information is recognized.

(b) *Trade unions and employees* encompass a variety of layers of organized employees, ranging from committees of worker members at individual MNC subsidiary or plant level to international trade union organizations. The information requirements of each layer will depend upon its role, nature, and point of contact with an MNC or MNCs in general.[2] Such contact with MNCs may be direct, for example at the level of the subsidiary, or alternatively with the MNC's parent company (here the emphasis is on the attempt to influence the behaviour of individual MNCs). Alternatively, it may be indirect, either at national or international level, through attempts to influence government or inter-governmental organization policy.[3]

(c) *Investors*, including financial analysts, are those who have access to and use corporate reports and other publicly available information as a basis for making investment decisions. Investors are 'outsiders' to the MNC and range from the sophisticated to the lay-person, from the active to the passive and from the diversified to the non-diversified.[4] In the main, investors own or are potential owners of shares in the MNC parent corporation, though there may also be a limited number of investors of MNC subsidiaries. The interests of investors in obtaining more information from MNCs are represented by international organizations of financial analysts, and to some extent by the International Federation of Stock Exchanges.

(d) *Bankers and lenders* have information needs which are closely related to those of investors, i.e. they are concerned mainly with the financial performance and future prospects of MNCs. However, relative to investors, it is evident that this group is influential in that it has some access to internal information and does not have to rely solely on the publicly available information provided in corporate reports. MNCs enter into financial relations with bankers and lenders at the national, regional, and international levels, e.g. the Euromarkets.

(e) *The general public* embraces all other interested parties apart from accountants and auditors and, of course, managers and directors who are responsible for the information disclosed. While the members of this group may have overlapping interests, as shareholders/investors for example, it would seem useful to identify this group on the basis of an interest in the 'social' performance of MNCs.

(f) *Accountants and auditors* are involved with MNCs in a number of capacities, both internally as preparers and interpreters of financial and other information and externally as auditors and advisers. They are also involved at the level of national, regional, and international professional organizations concerned with the setting of professional standards of accounting and reporting. While accountants are major participants and an important influence on the process of information disclosure, they are also users to the extent that they are involved in take-over/merger activity or portfolio investment necessitating a study of information in corporate annual reports.

The information demands and pressures emanating from these groups will now be reviewed. Information disclosure, in terms of regulation and practice, including some detail of regulatory developments at the level of the UN, OECD, and EEC, will be the subject of later discussion in Chapter 5.

3.1 GOVERNMENTS

The role of government in determining the content and nature of corporate reports has been considered extensively in the literature, especially the extent of government involvement in the process.[5] It is comprehensive in some countries, especially those with a tradition of detailed prescriptive legislation, e.g. France and West Germany, in contrast to the Anglo-Saxon countries where the emphasis is on delegation to autonomous or quasi-autonomous private bodies. The literature on the role of government as an actual or potential user of corporate reports is, however, very sparse. Much of the discussion usually contains mere assertions that governments are users of such reports. The report of the UN's Group of Experts, for example, specifies governments, together with a long list of other users with little substantiation.[6]

The information required of corporations by government varies and is influenced, for example, by the extent of government planning and regulation. However, in any event, it is often vast and far too extensive to be included in a corporate annual report which would, if it contained all such information, be of enormous size. Moreover, in addition to the question of quantity, much of the information is mutually regarded by both supplier and receiver as confidential, and is thus limited to restricted special-purpose reports. While the relative power of corporations (and MNCs in particular) and governments is a matter of controversy, it is evident that governments usually have the authority to demand and receive whatever information they need from MNCs. The extensive, and mainly confidential, information needs of governments, both home and host, combined with their power to obtain such information, would thus seem to support the view that governments are not important users of published corporate reports. Yet, a great deal of the pressure for increasing the amount of information disclosure by MNCs has come from governments, e.g. through the participation in and support for the UN (1977) proposals.[7] This apparent paradox may be explained by identifying certain specific, rather than general, circumstances when governments may in fact be users. These circumstances reflect the transnational nature of MNCs, the role of inter-governmental bodies, the heterogeneous nature of government, the limited expertise of some governments, and the relative power distribution between MNC and host country.

Firstly, the interrelationship of an MNC subsidiary with other parts of the MNC group can mean that information required to evaluate the performance and prospects of that subsidiary should include information relating, in part at least, to operations of the MNC outside the jurisdiction of the government within whose territory the subsidiary exists. This extra-national, and indeed some national, information may not be available from the subsidiary but from outside the country, for example from the parent corporation or elsewhere within the MNC group. In such circumstances a government may have limited authority to obtain the information. While some MNCs may supply information where and when requested there may be others that do not or do so only to a limited extent. Where such information is not provided, governments may be unable or unwilling to press for it and may, therefore, in some circumstances, use MNC world-wide consolidated annual financial statements together with segmental information to provide an insight, albeit limited, into the performance of the local subsidiary.

Secondly, the important role of MNCs in world trade and development has meant that many governments directly, or through international inter-governmental organizations, wish to evaluate and monitor the performance, behaviour, and consequences of MNC operations as a whole.[8] A major source of such global information are the MNCs' annual financial reports. Information that is not drawn up on a similar basis as is the case with MNCs based in many different countries cannot be adequately aggregated. Thus, this governmental need is reflected in demands not only for increased availability of information, but also greater comparability of the information so that it can be aggregated.[9]

Thirdly, unlike investors, but to some extent like trade unions, governments are not single individuals or organizations. The varying roles of governments are performed by a large range of departments or agencies. Special reports supplied to one unit, e.g. revenue authorities, will usually not be available to other sections of government. The existence of discrete governmental units requires some such units to rely on corporate reports rather than on the more detailed information available only to other units. In some circumstances what is available in corporate records may be adequately comprehensive for the analytical purposes in question.

Finally, while governments are often characterized as having adequate power to require whatever information is needed from MNCs this power is not unlimited and is often overstated. There is no doubt that it is extensive in many countries.[10] However, in some host developing countries which are especially dependent on MNCs, requests for some types of information, e.g. social, may receive a negative response from the MNC. Increased availability of information in MNC corporate reports would mean that governments would have direct access to the information without having to bargain for it and possibly offend each MNC. Uniform disclosure requirements would also prevent MNCs from playing one potential host country off against another in the competition for investment, thereby bringing pressure on them to reduce their information disclosure requirements.

Governments would, therefore, seem to have an interest in access to a greater extent of information disclosure concerning extra-national operations, i.e. their concern is to place the operations of the MNC subsidiary into the context of MNC operations as a whole for accountability and predictive purposes. Accordingly, both world-wide aggregated and geographically disaggregated financial information is likely to be useful for this purpose. Moreover, the demand for greater comparability of MNC information disclosure would seem to be motivated by the desire of governments at national level especially in host countries, or through inter-governmental organizations such as the UN,

OECD, and EEC, to monitor the activities of MNCs in general as a basis for policy formulation.

In respect to the bargaining power of governments to obtain sufficient comparable information, there is clearly a perception that this is likely to be enhanced by involvement in intergovernmental organizations, in contrast to the scope for control over MNCs at national level.

The UN first became involved in the information disclosure debate in 1976 when a group of experts was appointed, in the context of the activities of the Commission on Transnational Corporations, to formulate proposals following a study of the impact of MNCs on development and international relations.[11] Not only did this study identify a problem of comparability of the information provided by MNCs but it also revealed an apparently serious lack of information, both financial and non-financial. As a result, the 'Group of Experts' concentrated on the development of lists of minimum items of financial and non-financial information to be disclosed by MNCs in their general-purpose corporate reports, both at the level of the MNC group as a whole and its individual member corporations.[12] The outcome of those deliberations was a comprehensive and detailed set of proposals incorporating, most importantly, world-wide consolidated financial statements, segmental or disaggregated information, and a wide range of non-financial and 'social' information. The relevant extract from the 'Experts' report is reproduced in Appendix I. These proposals were intended to be used as the basis for developing a set of international standards, in the context of a Code of Conduct for MNCs, and in 1979 this was taken a step further with the establishment of an *ad hoc* inter-governmental Working Group of Experts from 34 countries, including 22 countries from Africa, Asia, and Latin America.[13] It is the comprehensive spread of membership of the UN which ensures such a strong representation from the developing countries relative to those of the industrialized West and those from Eastern Europe. While the ultimate aim of this group would seem to be to recommend standards which member countries will agree to support and, if necessary, to enforce by law, there is little doubt that progress in reaching agreement on information disclosure has been slow and in some cases, with particular reference to non-financial information, impossible.[14] In October 1982, the majority of countries recommended that the group continue its work in a more permanent form. There was general consensus that any group established

> should serve as an international body for the consideration of issues of accounting and reporting falling within the scope of the work of the Commission on Transnational Corporations in order to improve

the availability and comparability of information disclosed by transnational corporations; the Group should review developments in this
field including the work of standard setting bodies; the Group should
concentrate on establishing priorities, taking into account the needs
of home and host countries, particularly those of developing
countries.[15]

This proposal was accepted by the UN, and 'The Intergovernmental
Working Group of Experts on International Standards of Accounting
and Reporting' held its first session in 1983.

The OECD has a much more limited membership of countries
compared to the UN. With only 24 members, as opposed to more
than 150, the OECD represents the interests of an industrialized and
substantially Western group of nations which includes the USA, UK,
West Germany, France, Canada, the Netherlands, Australia, and
Japan. In 1976, following consultations with business and trade union
interests, a set of 'Guidelines for Multinational Enterprises' was
approved with the aim of strengthening confidence between MNCs and
governments. The intention was to encourage the positive contributions
of MNCs to economic growth and social progress while minimizing or
resolving problems.[16] Governments agreed to recommend these 'Guidelines' to MNCs which related to financing, taxation, competition, and
industrial relations as well as information disclosure. The full text of
these 'Guidelines', including the 1979 revisions, is reproduced in
Appendix II. The recommendations relating to information disclosure
are, however, set out in Exhibit 3A for ready reference, from which it
can be seen that compared to the UN proposals the OECD 'Guidelines'
are very brief, general, and concerned with information disclosure by
the MNC taken as a whole.

While the information recommendations were left unchanged in the
revision of the 'Guidelines' which took place in 1979, it was decided
that the OECD should continue its efforts in this area by establishing
a working group as a basis for contributing to and participating in
the international standard-setting process.[17] In this regard, a survey of
accounting standards in OECD member countries was carried out in
1980 so as to assess the diversity of practice and the potential for
harmonization.[18] In the longer term it would seem that the aim is
to work towards promoting international agreement on a conceptual
framework as a basis for improving the comparability and harmonization of accounting and reporting standards.

The EEC has been involved in the harmonization of accounting and
reporting standards in the EEC since the middle 1960s as a necessary
part of the programme of company law harmonization introduced
consistent with the Treaty of Rome (1957).[19] Their activities have taken

---

Exhibit 3A

OECD GUIDELINES FOR MULTINATIONAL ENTERPRISES:

DISCLOSURE OF INFORMATION

Enterprises should, having due regard to their nature and relative size in the economic context of their operations and to requirements of business confidentiality and to cost, publish in a form suited to improve public understanding a sufficient body of factual information on the structure, activities, and policies of the enterprise as a whole, as a supplement, in so far as necessary for this purpose, to information to be disclosed under the national law of the individual countries in which they operate. To this end, they should publish within reasonable time limits, on a regular basis, but at least annually, financial statements and other pertinent information relating to the enterprise as a whole, comprising in particular:

   (i) the structure of the enterprise, showing the name and location of the parent company, its main affiliates, its percentage ownership, direct and indirect, in these affiliates, including shareholdings between them;

  (ii) the geographical areas where operations are carried out and the principal activities carried on therein by the parent company and the main affiliates;

 (iii) the operating results and sales by geographical area and the sales in the major lines of business for the enterprise as a whole;

 (iv) significant new capital investment by geographical area and, as far as practicable, by major lines of business for the enterprise as a whole;

  (v) a statement of the sources and uses of funds by the enterprise as a whole;

 (vi) the average number of employees in each geographical area;

(vii) research and development expenditure for the enterprise as a whole;

(viii) the policies followed in respect of intra-group pricing;

 (ix) the accounting policies, including those on consolidation, observed in compiling the published information.

Source: International Investment and Multinational Enterprises (OECD, 1976, revised 1979).

place in the context of promoting the goal of European economic integration and development whereby corporations, including MNCs, should have the freedom to become more international by being able to do business and compete within a common framework of law, taxation, and financial resources throughout the EEC. An important part of this process is perceived to be the public disclosure of reliable and comparable information to protect the interests of shareholders, lenders, suppliers, and other interested parties.[20]

The harmonization of accounting and reporting in the EEC is especially significant for MNCs because, in contrast to the UN and OECD, any agreement which takes the form of a 'directive' has the force of law throughout the Community countries as each country has the obligation to incorporate such 'directives' into its respective national law. 'Regulations', on the other hand, become law throughout the EEC without having to go through the national legislative process. The latest position (as at December 1983) in respect to relevant EEC 'directives' and 'regulations' relating to accounting and information disclosure is set out in Table 3.1. Directives of special relevance are briefly outlined below.

In 1968, the *First Directive* was approved, requiring publication of the annual accounts of limited liability corporations. In 1978, the *Fourth Directive* was approved, incorporating detailed requirements relating to information disclosure, classification and presentation of information, and methods of valuation.[21]

Inter-governmental agreement to the *Fourth Directive* involved a long and difficult period of consultation and negotiation especially in view of the fact that the UK and Ireland joined the EEC, along with Denmark, only in 1973, and with quite different traditions of accounting and information disclosure policy. The result was a compromise between the continental European and UK systems with perhaps the emphasis more on disclosing the nature and effect of differences between countries than on their removal. The intention was not in any case to produce uniformity necessarily, but rather to bring about a co-ordination or harmonization of existing legal requirements. However, the *Fourth Directive* does provide a uniform structure for the classification and presentation of information and incorporates disclosure requirements that are likely to increase significantly the level of information disclosure throughout the EEC countries.[22] Whether or not the concept of 'a true and fair view', taken from the UK and adopted as an objective which may require the disclosure of additional or, in exceptional circumstances, different information from that required specifically by the *Fourth Directive*, will have any significant impact in the continental European system remains to be seen.[23] So far, only Denmark, the UK,

Table 3.1. *EEC Harmonization of Accounting and Reporting*

Principal directives on company law and capital market harmonization	Draft dates	Date approved	Purpose
First	1964	1968	Publication of annual accounts, company statutes, and other basic information
Second	1970, 1972	1976	Distinguishes public from private companies, minimum capital requirements, restriction on dividend payments
Third	1970, 1973, 1975	1978	Mergers/fusions
Fourth	1971, 1974	1978	Annual accounts— minimum requirements for content, classification, presentation, also valuation rules
Fifth	1972, 1983		Structure, management, and audit of companies
Sixth	1972, 1975	1980	Information to be disclosed in prospectuses for issue of shares listed on stock exchanges
Seventh	1976, 1979	1983	Group accounts, consolidations, associated companies
Eighth	1978, 1979		Qualifications and work of auditors
—	1978	1979	Minimum conditions for stock exchange listing of shares
—	1980, 1983		Employee information and consultation (Vredeling)
—	1980, 1982		Information to be disclosed in prospectuses for unlisted shares
—	1981	1982	Interim reports to be published half-yearly
Regulations on company law	Draft dates	Date approved	Purpose
Statute for a European company	1970, 1975		A new form of company subject to EEC laws
European co-operation grouping	1973, 1978		A new form of business to facilitate joint ventures

France, and Belgium have implemented the directive by incorporating it into their respective national laws and even here it is still too early to judge its effect in practice.

Attention is currently being given to the newly adopted (June 1983) *Seventh Directive* on group accounts and consolidations which raises issues of special reference to MNC operations and which has become the subject of some controversy.[24] Of particular importance are issues concerning the definition of a 'group', where the UK approach based on share ownership and legal rights to control other corporations may be contrasted with the West German approach based on effective management control as well as share ownership criteria. In addition, there are issues relating to the method of consolidation or aggregation used in disclosing the performance and financial position of the MNC group. Other questions include the reporting requirement to be applied to MNCs based outside the EEC but with operations in one or more EEC countries. While the first proposal was issued in 1976, and revised in 1979, it was only in 1983 that agreement was reached following substantial further revisions allowing for some flexibility of interpretation between the member countries. In view of the importance of this directive, the full text is reproduced in Appendix III.

Another important, and highly controversial, proposed directive concerns employee information and consultation with special reference to MNCs.[25] This proposed directive, usually referred to as the 'Vredeling proposals', calls for the regular provision of information to employees in subsidiary corporations. Such information would relate to the activities of the MNC at group level as well as at the level of the individual subsidiary. The content of the information disclosed would cover areas such as organization structure; employment; the economic and financial situation; probable development in production, sales, and employment; rationalization plans; and plans for new working methods or other methods that could have 'a substantial effect' on employee interests. Furthermore, employees would need to be consulted when decisions proposed by management are likely to affect their interests, e.g. in the case of closure or any change in the activities of the subsidiary corporation. While this proposed directive, issued in 1980 and amended in 1983, is likely to emerge ultimately in a substantially revised form, it represents a major development in terms both of government involvement in the internal decision-making processes of MNCs and the extension of information disclosure to employees as a specific user group. In view of the significance of this proposal, the original and revised text is reproduced in Appendix IV.

Related to developments in company law harmonization are those concerned with the harmonization of stock exchange regulation and securities law with a view to ensuring that investors, both existing and potential, have sufficient access to information and to promote the development of a 'European' capital market with active and well-developed stock exchanges in all of the EEC countries. Directives concerning (1) the minimum conditions, and (2) the disclosure of information, for the admission of shares to official stock exchange listing were adopted in 1979 and 1980 respectively. The most recent directive, on interim reports, adopted in 1982, requires listed corporations to publish a half-yearly report of financial results together with information on trends and likely future developments in the current year of operations.

This brief review of the activities and influence of international inter-governmental organizations such as the UN, OECD, and EEC in the area of information disclosure indicates a developing if varying concern to monitor and, where necessary, to control the activities of MNCs. The disclosure of sufficient comparable information seems to be perceived as essential if policy-making is to be informed and control is to be exercised—and inter-governmental involvement is seen to be influential in this process. Such a process is not necessarily detrimental to the interests of MNCs as there is clearly a concern to promote international business and the growth of MNCs as much as to regulate their activities. There are, however, likely to be differences in emphasis and approach according to the membership and objectives of the inter-governmental organization concerned.

3.2 TRADE UNIONS AND EMPLOYEES

The term 'trade union' encompasses a number of different but related organizations. The trade union organizations which participate at inter-governmental level are the international trade union *confederations* (ITUCs), e.g. European Trade Union Confederation (ETUC), the International Confederation of Free Trade Unions (ICFTU), and the World Confederation of Labour (WCL). These represent the national central trade union organizations. The international trade union *secretariats* each concentrate on a specific industry, for example the International Metalworkers Federation, and represent internationally those trade unions involved with the relevant industrial category.[26] Their direct contact with MNCs, albeit limited, is with individual MNCs rather than inter-governmental organizations.[27] In the national context, trade union attempts to influence the behaviour of MNCs may take place at a variety of levels ranging from activities at shop-floor level to influencing national government policy. The relationships of trade unions with MNCs are considerably more complex and varied than, for example, those of investors in the context of stock markets. The perceived information needs of trade unions will depend upon the specific point of contact with MNCs and the purpose for which information is required.[28]

Trade unions are primarily grounded within the national territory within which they operate. It is within nation states that trade unions have developed, and where their power exists. While MNCs have grown beyond the limits of national territories, trade unions have done so only to a very limited extent. The growing gap between the location of international business and national trade unions is in the eyes of the latter a potential, and in some instances actual, disability for them.[29]

A substantial amount of literature relating to MNCs has been produced by trade unions. Its scope is wide-ranging, and it is unlikely that there are any socio-economic aspects of MNCs that trade unions have not commented upon. However, it would seem that trade unions are interested, before anything else, in, and therefore information relating to, the terms, conditions, scale, security and location of employment. A corporation is for them primarily an employer. These concerns are not exclusively relevant to MNCs. But the variation in terms of conditions of employment in MNC subsidiaries in different countries, the perceived ability of MNCs to switch production or disinvest to areas outside a national trade union's sphere of influence, and the possibility of transfers of goods and services at other than arm's-length prices with consequent distortions in reported results, introduces dimensions not relevant to UNCs.[30] Trade unions, similar to investors, clearly have an interest in the performance and future prospects of MNCs. But they are also concerned, directly, with the scale and location of production and employment. While investors may be interested in disaggregated information, in so far as it may provide insights into the performance and prospects of the corporation taken as a whole, a national trade union is primarily interested in those parts of an MNC that operate within that trade union's national territory. They are thus interested in the aggregate or total picture only to the extent that it may provide insights into that part of the MNC with which they are directly involved.[31]

Comparisons between MNCs which are of some concern for investors have less relevance for trade unions. However, comparisons between MNC subsidiaries may well be significant. There are useful comparisons, e.g. pay and working conditions, to be made between MNC subsidiaries in the same industry or with similar categories of employees within the same country or between subsidiaries of the same MNC in different countries.[32] Comparisons in the latter category are not infrequently invoked by MNC management to admonish or urge greater effort. National trade unions, not unnaturally, but often with little success, request extra-national information to evaluate such comparisons.[33]

International trade union organizations, reflecting the desires of their national trade union members, have emphasized the demand for increased availability of information, especially that relating to the interrelationship between the components of each MNC. International trade union organizations have also pressed for greater international harmonization of accounting standards.

In 1977, the ICFTU, WCL, and ETUC issued their own set of accounting and information disclosure requirements.[34] The focus of this document was on MNCs and the need for international harmonization, with recommendations relating to a more uniform approach to accounting as well as comprehensive and detailed disclosures of financial and non-financial information. The ICFTU also issued an earlier 'multinational charter' in 1975 which emphasized the need for MNCs to be more publicly accountable and called for legal regulation to require the disclosure of more information, including a report about matters of a social nature and information about future prospects, investment, and employment.

Their object in these proposals, however, is not to facilitate inter-firm comparisons, though such may be of some limited interest, but rather to provide a reliable basis for the formulation of policy concerning MNCs. Such policy development is inhibited not only by gaps in the available information about MNCs, but also by the impossibility of obtaining an accurate *aggregate* picture of their activities and impact based on existing information—the problem being the variation in methods of measurement used as well as a lack of what is perceived to be necessary information.

The main national trade union concern, reflected also by international trade union organizations, is with an increase in information disclosure relating to the operations of MNC subsidiaries. What is of particular concern to trade unions in relation to MNC information disclosures are the *consequences* of each MNCs subsidiary's transfer pricing policies.

The relationship of an MNC subsidiary with other units of the MNC, especially those outside that subsidiary's country of location, may affect the relevance and reliability of the financial position and performance reported by the MNC subsidiary.[35] While the impact of MNC intra-group transactions is of concern to a range of interested groups, many of them, e.g. revenue and taxation authorities, do not rely for their information on corporate reports, having access to greater amounts of information direct from the corporation concerned. For those who are interested in the affairs of MNC subsidiaries but who have to rely wholly, or mainly, on corporate reports for financial information, e.g. trade unions, the impact of transactions of such subsidiaries with related parties is of crucial concern. The primary concern of most regulatory bodies, and accounting commentators, with the information needs of investors has meant, however, that this matter has received little attention to date.[36]

There are two main problem areas in corporate reporting by MNC subsidiaries. These arise from the possibility of differences as between the operating and the legal entity, and between the form and economic substance of transactions.[37]

Firstly, as regards the reporting entity, in many MNC subsidiaries the legal and organizational structures are not identical, and indeed may in some cases differ substantially. National statutory requirements oblige MNCs to maintain separate legal entities in each country. A legal entity may contain within it several operational units, some related but others not. Alternatively, a single operational unit may span two or more legal units in one or a number of countries. What then should be the reporting entity at national level? For information disclosure to be meaningful it must relate to an entity that is distinguishable from others. Should the reporting entity be the operating units, or the legal units? While legal entities are identifiable with specific countries, MNC operational units are frequently integrated among other countries. In practice the legal entity has usually been taken as the appropriate reporting entity.[38] However, corporate reports based on the legal entity alone may not provide much information that is useful for predicting, comparing, and evaluating enterprise earning potential, being in many cases an accumulation of unrelated, or incomplete information from separate operating units. The legal entity may not, therefore, be an adequate basis for distinguishing it from the rest of the group.

Secondly, regardless of whether or not the operational and legal structures of an MNC are identical, there is the additional problem of whether MNC subsidiaries are independent entities, i.e. whether they have independent powers over their resources and transactions. International (or cross-frontier) transfer pricing has given rise to considerable interest and controversy because of the volume and nature of such transactions.[39] It has been estimated that approximately 40 per cent of all international trade consists of transfers between related MNC units and that national differences, e.g. different tax and custom rates, may provide significant opportunities to increase consolidated post-tax profits through valuing transfers at prices higher or lower than arm's-length prices, i.e. different from those operating between independent corporations.[40] The objectives of international cross-frontier transactions, conflicts between these objectives, the internal and external constraints on MNCs using non-arm's-length prices, the complexities of measurement, the impact on matters of national interest, and other features have been discussed earlier in Chapter 2. We are concerned here only with the relevance of related party transactions to corporate reporting.

The reporting and auditing implications of related party transactions, of which cross-frontier transactions between MNC units are a specific example, have received very limited attention from the accounting profession outside of the USA and Canada.[41] The impact of international transfer pricing on corporate reports is eliminated in the preparation of consolidated financial statements which may partly, at least, explain such indifference. When MNC intra-group transactions take place at a price determined by arm's-length bargaining, or an equivalent price, the form, i.e. the price paid, and the substance, i.e. the value transferred, as was or would be determined by the market, are identical. However, in cases where the prices are other than at arm's-length then the form and substance differ. As a result, where the proportion of such transactions represents a material amount of an MNC subsidiary's transactions the external financial report is unlikely to provide a reliable indicator of the financial performance of the subsidiary.[42] Even in circumstances where the transactions take place on an arm's-length basis the reported financial results may not indicate the costs and benefits to the MNC group as a whole, nor to the subsidiary either, in view of the incomplete picture necessarily given by any purely financial assessment.[43]

Differences between legal and operational structures, between the form and substance of transactions, and the impossibility of measuring and assessing many costs and benefits to the subsidiary and the group undermines considerably the value of MNC subsidiary corporate reports as measurements of results and indicators of future performance. This raises the question of whether, when some or all of these circumstances exist to a significant degree, there is any value in requiring the preparation of publicly available annual financial reports by MNC subsidiaries. However, the needs of certain groups, for example, trade unions and minority shareholders of the subsidiary, would seem to require the posing of alternative questions, i.e. what can be done to make such reports more meaningful, and how can users be made more aware of their limitations if they are not so aware already?[44]

It can be concluded then that while trade unions require information about the performance and future prospects of MNCs, just as much as do other groups, of special concern to them is information concerning the terms, conditions, scale, security, and location of employment. Their primary interest is at national level with regard to the situation of each MNC subsidiary and its relationship with other subsidiaries in the MNC group. International trade union organizations are concerned also to obtain information about related party transactions and transfer pricing practices as a basis for formulating overall policy towards MNCs.

3.3 INVESTORS

Besides additional information disclosure, especially information about the future prospects of MNCs on a world-wide basis including up-to-date measurements relating to earnings and asset values, investors and financial analysts appear to be concerned about the lack of comparability or standardization of much of the information that is currently provided.[45] However, some observers have recently detected a shift in emphasis towards an information approach whereby a wide range of relevant information relating to earnings prospects is provided, in contrast to an emphasis on the calculation and prediction of earnings on a standardized basis.[46]

Despite this apparent change in emphasis, with special reference to the needs of expert financial analysts in the context of well-developed and efficient stock markets, there is continuing concern with the lack of international comparability of corporate reports for investor purposes expressed by international financial analysts and professional accountancy organizations as well as by governments.[47] The perceived problem is that even in countries where extensive corporate reporting requirements exist, e.g. the USA and UK, the corporate annual reports of corporations based even in the *same* country may not be comparable—the variety of measurement methods usually permitted being a major factor thwarting effective evaluation of financial position and performance. Even in the EEC, the recently enacted *Fourth Directive* allows corporations a choice of accounting alternatives in a number of instances.[48] But the differences *within* countries are considerably less than those *between* countries, thus making MNC reports from different countries even less comparable.

What are the reasons for such concern with comparability between corporations? The purpose of comparison is to evaluate alternatives and is, therefore, especially relevant to those who wish to choose *between* corporations. Investor decisions are characterized by choice between alternative corporations in the context of changing or retaining their investments/portfolios. Buy, sell, or hold decisions require evaluation of the comparative performance and the likely future risks and returns of different corporations, though for the diversified investor holding a portfolio of shares it is a corporation's risk relative to the market as a whole and its effect on overall portfolio risks and returns that will be of special concern.[49]

To facilitate the analysis and comparison of MNC reports based on dissimilar accounting influences, at national level, and to enhance understanding of those from other than the user's country, investors and financial analysts, e.g. the European Federation of Financial Analysts Societies (EFFAS), support progress towards international accounting harmonization.[50] In this regard it is interesting to note that EFFAS, formed in 1961, has developed its own 'European method' of financial analysis which incorporates a standardized approach to financial statement classification and presentation. EFFAS has also urged a more uniform approach to measurement together with additional information disclosures including segmental information. While changes are expected to take some time there is, in the interim, a strong demand for information disclosure which will facilitate the desired comparisons and analysis, e.g. accounting policies concerning the measurement bases used, including those relating to inflation adjustments, consolidation, foreign currency translation, taxation, and so on.

It should be emphasized that this concern with comparability does not necessarily imply uniformity but at least a degree of harmonization or standardization, and in the short term a minimum of information disclosure concerning differences, sufficient to enable comparisons to be made. Evidence concerning the operations of well-developed stock markets such as in the USA and UK indicates that there is a tendency for such markets to be 'efficient' in the sense that expert or sophisticated investors will ensure that share prices will quickly reflect all publicly available information and in doing so will allow for the effect of differences in accounting methods, to the extent that this is possible with the available information.[51] Of course, even the experts will not be able to allow for differences which are not disclosed, or generally known about, nor will they be able to compensate for any absence of relevant information which is not otherwise obtainable from alternative sources. Even if the experts were able to unravel the differences there may well be a cost-saving if corporations were able to adopt a degree of standardization which did not entail any loss of information content.

As regards the information to be disclosed, it has been suggested that investors are only concerned with overall MNC results, as reported in world-wide consolidated financial statements, and thus are not interested in disaggregated information. However, an analysis of aggregate results often requires an understanding of the profitability, degree of risk, relative performance, and potential for growth of the component parts. As a diversified corporation's performance and future prospects are the sum of those of its various parts, investors are also likely to be interested in disaggregated, or segmental, information.[52]

Geographical segmentation is of special relevance to MNCs which are, by definition, diversified across national boundaries. Segmental information on an industrial, line of business, or product-line basis is also of relevance to those MNCs which are active in a number of industries, but it is not exclusive to them, as such a corporation may confine its operations to one national territory. This interest in segmental information is not to say that aggregate financial information is necessarily of any less importance to investors. On the contrary, knowledge of the total results of operations, including resources and obligations, of the MNC on a world-wide basis is also essential to an overall assessment of risks and returns. World-wide consolidations are, however, by no means the norm in many countries, including France and West Germany, which are the home bases of many MNCs.[53]

Accordingly, the kind of disclosure relevant to investors and financial analysts would appear to include information relating to the performance and future prospects of the world-wide operations of the MNC group and, in particular, geographical and line of business segmentation. In the absence of the international harmonization of accounting and reporting principles and practices, there is a demand for information which will assist in determining the validity and effect of the measurement bases used and so facilitate international comparisons.

3.4 BANKERS AND LENDERS

Similar to investors, the information needs of bankers and lenders would appear to be focused on corporate information relating to financial position, performance, and future prospects. There is, however, a difference in emphasis as there is likely to be particular concern with the security of loans advanced, i.e. the risk of default on obligations to pay loan interest and to refund the loans when due. It is evident that in countries where bankers and lenders are more significant than shareholders as financiers of corporations, including MNCs, as in France and West Germany, this is likely to have a conservative influence on the measurement of publicly disclosed financial performance and wealth.[54] At the same time, this group of information users is likely to have more direct access to information and does not, therefore, have to rely primarily on publicly available corporate reports.

In the context of international accounting harmonization, it would seem that international banking organizations are involved to the extent that they support the goal of requiring more comparable information from their clients who include governments, financial institutions, and corporations including MNCs. Of particular importance here are the international development banks, e.g. the Asian Development Bank, the International Bank for Reconstruction and Development, and the World Bank with special reference to the International Finance Corporation.[55] In addition, a host of banks are involved in international lending in the Eurocurrency markets and newly emerging international markets in Singapore, Hong Kong, and the Middle East.[56]

International banks often require special financial reports and the International Finance Corporation has gone so far as to issue detailed instruction booklets on accounting and reporting standards which are likely to have an impact on practice across countries. It is also evident that MNCs are often encouraged to increase the quantity of information disclosed in their corporate reports by the competition for funds in the context of the Eurocurrency and other markets.[57]

3.5 THE GENERAL PUBLIC

This group of information users and participants in the process of information disclosure could be taken to include all other interested parties apart from accountants and auditors, as both preparers, users, and verifiers of information, and managers, including directors, who are responsible for the information disclosed. Such other parties would include many who could be members of more than one group, e.g. consumers may also be shareholders. It would seem useful, therefore, to identify this group on the basis of a particular interest in the 'social' performance of MNCs. Those concerned with this aspect of the corporation's activities are likely to include governments, trade unions, investors, bankers, lenders, consumers, taxpayers, and others who may be influenced by the 'social' performance of MNCs instead of, or in addition to, its 'financial' performance.

'Social' performance involving issues of equity and the quality of life, may diverge from 'financial' performance to the extent that MNC activities may give rise to costs and benefits which are not fully reflected in its own transactions. These are known as 'externalities' and may be positive or negative, e.g. the MNC may provide benefits in the form of roads and communications, but also costs in terms of pollution of the environment.[58]

It seems likely, therefore, that the net social impact of MNCs will only correspond coincidentally with measures of 'financial' performance. This would suggest that the disclosure of additional information relating to 'externalities' could be useful as a basis for making judgements about social matters. Such information may well be qualitative as much as quantitative in view of the problems involved in attempting to measure 'social' performance.

3.6 ACCOUNTANTS AND AUDITORS

As preparers and users of information in MNCs it is evident that the accountant's role is an extremely important one in terms of technical skill, influence, and responsibility. This is reinforced by the role of the accountant as external auditor or verifier of corporate reports issued by MNCs to interested parties.

While international firms of accountants, which have grown primarily in response to MNCs,[59] are active in the context of the international harmonization of accounting and reporting, it is at the level of international professional organizations that most of the developments are taking place.

There are two major international organizations—the International Federation of Accountants (IFAC) and the International Accounting Standards Committee (IASC).

The IASC is itself incorporated within the IFAC but has retained an independent responsibility for the development of international accounting standards. The IFAC on the other hand, has concerned itself primarily with the promulgation of international auditing guidelines.

The IASC was established in 1973 by leading professional organizations in Australia, Canada, France, West Germany, Ireland, Japan, Mexico, the Netherlands, the UK, and USA. It now has a membership comprising organizations from more than 42 countries, including the founder members who constitute a majority of the governing board and thus retain a significant measure of influence. When compared with the membership of the UN, however, it is clear that the membership of the IASC is relatively limited and, of course, bounded by the need for a professional accountancy organization to exist—something which is often outside the experience of centrally planned and developing countries.

The stated objectives of the IASC are '(a) to formulate and publish in the public interest accounting standards to be observed in the presentation of financial statements and to promote their worldwide acceptance and observance, and (b) to work generally for the improvement and harmonization of regulations, accounting standards and procedures relating to the presentation of financial statements.'[60] The main aim of international professional standards in practice would seem to be to achieve a degree of comparability which will help investors in making their decisions while reducing the costs of MNCs in preparing multiple sets of accounts and reports. The IASC also sees itself as having a role to play in co-ordinating and harmonizing the activities of the many agencies involved in setting standards of accounting and reporting for MNCs.

The latest position (as at December 1983) regarding standards and exposure drafts issued by the IASC is set out in Table 3.2. A total of 22 standards have been issued so far, covering a wide range of issues including the disclosure of accounting policies, consolidated financial statements, funds statements, segmental reporting, accounting for changing prices, and accounting for leases. Taken overall, the emphasis of much of the work to date has been on matters relating to the harmonization of measurement practices and forms of presentation, in contrast to the UN where the prime concern has been with the disclosure of additional information by MNCs. The IASC's concern is, moreover, to develop world-wide standards for _all_ corporations which may well be unrealistic without widespread commitment to world-wide economic integration, in the context of objectives similar to the EEC, and also questionable in the light of perceived differences in national systems of accounting which are the outcome of particular environmental needs and circumstances.

In effect, IASC standards are in the nature of recommendations or guidelines which member bodies 'use their best endeavours' to follow where this is considered desirable and feasible. They are not mandatory requirements. This is especially the case in countries such as France and West Germany where professional accountancy organizations do not have the responsibility or authority to set accounting and reporting standards—such matters being largely the preserve of governments and the law. This may be contrasted with the position in the USA and UK where the accountancy profession is much more influential in the standard-setting process, and with Canada where professional standards receive legal backing.

Table 3.2. *IASC Standards (December 1983)*

	Issued
Preface to statements of international accounting standards	January 1983

International accounting standards issued

	Issued
IAS 1 Disclosure of Accounting Policies	January 1975
IAS 2 Valuation and Presentation of inventories in the context of the Historical Cost System	October 1975
IAS 3 Consolidated Financial Statements	June 1976
IAS 4 Depreciation Accounting	October 1976
IAS 5 Information to be Disclosed in Financial Statements	October 1976
IAS 6 Accounting Responses to Changing Prices	June 1977
IAS 7 Statement of Changes in Financial position	October 1977
IAS 8 Unusual and Prior Period Items and Changes in Accounting Policies	February 1978
IAS 9 Accounting for Research and Development Activities	July 1978
IAS 10 Contingencies and Events Occurring after the Balance Sheet Date	October 1978
IAS 11 Accounting for Construction Contracts	March 1979
IAS 12 Accounting for Taxes on Income	July 1979
IAS 13 Presentation of Current Assets and Current Liabilities	November 1979
IAS 14 Reporting Financial Information by Segment	August 1981
IAS 15 Information Reflecting the Effects of Changing Prices	November 1981
IAS 16 Accounting for Property, Plant, and Equipment	March 1982
IAS 17 Accounting for Leases	September 1982
IAS 18 Revenue Recognition	December 1982
IAS 19 Accounting for Retirement Benefits in the Financial Statements of employers	January 1983
IAS 20 Accounting for Government Grants and Disclosure of government Assistance	April 1983
IAS 21 Accounting for the Effects of Changes in Foreign Exchange Rates	July 1983
IAS 22 Accounting for Business Combinations	November 1983

Exposure Drafts issued	*Comments due by*
E 24 Capitalisation of Borrowing Costs	30 April 1983
E 25 Disclosure of Related Party Transactions	31 August 1983

In practice, the standards issued by IASC have tended to be flexible to accommodate country differences with special reference to the USA, UK and other influential countries.[61] At the same time, practices which many would consider undesirable have been identified as unacceptable. However, the response to IASC standards has not been as widespread as the IASC would have hoped and efforts have been made recently to urge more MNCs to comply and to consult more with other interested parties including international inter-governmental organizations, trade unions, and financial analysts with a view to increasing the IASC's influence.

The IFAC was established in 1977, a little later than the IASC, and now has a membership of professional organizations from more than 53 countries. The basic objective of the IFAC is 'the development and enhancement of a co-ordinated world-wide accountancy profession with harmonized standards'.[62]

While the IFAC is primarily concerned with the issuing of guidelines on international auditing it has also been concerned with matters relating to education and ethics. More recently, a discussion paper on management accounting has been issued indicating the expanding scope of IFAC activities. Table 3.3. sets out the latest position (as at December 1983) of IFAC guidelines and statements of guidance.

Table 3.3. IFAC guidelines and statements of guidance (December 1983)

AUDITING	
Preface to International Auditing Guidelines	July 1979
International auditing guidelines	
1. Objective and scope of the Audit of Financial Statements	January 1980
2. Audit Engagement Letters	June 1980
3. Basic Principles Governing an Audit	September 1980
4. Planning	February 1981
5. Using the Work of another Auditor	July 1981
6. Study and Evaluation of the Accounting System and Related Internal Controls in Connection with an Audit	July 1981
7. Control of the Quality of Audit Work	September 1981
8. Audit Evidence	January 1982
9. Documentation	January 1982
10. Using the Work of an Internal Auditor	July 1982
11. Fraud and Error	October 1982
12. Analytical Review	July 1983
13. The Auditor's Report on Financial Statements	October 1983

Table 3.3—continued

Exposure drafts

E 14	Other Information in Documents Containing Audited Financial Statements	October 1982
E 15	Auditing in an EDP Environment	October 1982
E 16	Events after the Balance Sheet	January 1983
E 17	Computer-Assisted Audit Techniques	March 1983
E 18	Related Party Transactions	July 1983
E 19	Using the Work of an Expert	July 1983
E 20	Audit Sampling	October 1983
E 21	The Effects of an EDP Environment on the Study and Evaluation of the Accounting Systems and Related Internal Controls	October 1983

EDUCATION

Guidelines

1.	Prequalification Education and Training	February 1982
2.	Continuing Professional Education	February 1982

Exposure Drafts

Core of Knowledge	December 1982
Test of Professional Competence	December 1982

ETHICS

Guidelines

Professional Ethics for the Accountancy Profession	July 1980

Statement of guidance

1.	Advertising Publicity and Solicitation	September 1981
2.	Professional Competence	September 1981
3.	Integrity, Objectivity, and Independence	September 1982
4.	Confidentiality	September 1982
5.	Ethics Across International Borders	January 1983
6.	Conditions for Acceptance of an Appointment when Another Accountant in Public Practice is Already Carrying Out Work for the Same Client	September 1983
7.	Conditions for Superseding Another Accountant in Public Practice	September 1983

FINANCIAL AND MANAGEMENT ACCOUNTING

Discussion paper

Definition and Scope of Management Accounting	June 1982

In addition to IASC and IFAC, there are a growing number of regional professional organizations which are involved in accounting harmonization at the regional and wider international levels to varying degrees. These organizations include the Asociacion Interamericana de Contabilidad (AIC) or Inter-American Accounting Association (established in 1949), the Union Européenne des Experts Comptables, Economiques et Financiers (UEC) (established in 1951), the Confederation of Asian and Pacific Accountants (CAPA) (first established in 1957), and the ASEAN Federation of Accountants (AFA) (established in 1977).[63]

While regional professional organizations are to some extent supportive of the world-wide harmonization efforts of IASC and IFAC there would also appear to be some concern to retain a measure of regional identity and to influence developments at the wider international level.

3.7 CONCLUSIONS

Irrespective of the merits of the various interests and claims of the many participants in the process of setting international standards of accounting and reporting for MNCs, there is clearly a well-articulated demand for additional as well as more comparable information by a wide range of organizations and user groups. These include governments and international inter-governmental organizations, trade unions and employees, investors and financial analysts, bankers, lenders, and creditors, the general public, and, last but not least, accountants and auditors.

While there are some similarities between groups there are at the same time a number of significant differences concerning the quantity of information which should be disclosed, the basis upon which the information should be measured, the degree of uniformity such information should have, and the extent to which information disclosures should be mandatory. Furthermore, the power to influence MNC information disclosure practices varies considerably, ranging from the legal force of EEC directives to the guidelines of the OECD and recommendations of the IASC.

This situation is dynamic in that international inter-governmental organizations such as the UN have the potential to be highly influential if, for example, national governments decide to implement any international agreement by incorporation into national law.

A major objective of information disclosure so far as international inter-governmental and trade union organizations are concerned appears to be to monitor and, where necessary, control MNC operations. At the very least, it would seem that information disclosure is perceived to be relevant to improving the competitive bargaining power of those involved in economic and social relationships with MNCs. From the standpoint of investors, financial analysts, bankers, lenders, and creditors, it would seem that the prime concern is for additional information about the financial position, performance, and prospects of MNC operations as a basis for investment and lending decisions. The interests of the general public, on the other hand, which embrace many participants, often acting in more than one role, are characterized by a concern with the 'social' as well as the 'financial' performance of MNCs. Accountants and auditors also have a vital role to play as preparers, users, and verifiers of information disclosed by MNCs and are, in the form of the IASC and IFAC, themselves involved in the standard-setting process which influences MNC accounting and reporting behaviour.

The development of information disclosure by MNCs is thus taking place in the context of a wide range of participants at national, regional, and international level. This is an extremely complex and essentially political process, with a variety of organizations, both public and private, involved in standard-setting affecting MNCs and all of them with differing objectives, scope, and powers of enforcements. At the end of the day, it seems likely that international inter-governmental organizations such as the UN, OECD, and EEC will be more influential relative to professional accountancy organizations, though there seems little doubt that the latter group will always have an essential role to play in terms of providing technical development and assisting in the practical implementation of desired standards of accounting and information disclosure.

However, the demand for information, with special reference to the participants and pressures involved, is but one side of the coin. Consider now the supply side to information disclosure by MNCs. What is the nature of the managerial perspective and response?

The Supply of Information: Managerial Perspectives

The amount of information disclosed by MNCs has expanded considerably since the 1950s. Until recently, the major source of effective demand was the financial and investment community. Both MNCs and standard-setting bodies in countries with well-developed stock markets, such as the USA and UK, have been concerned primarily with responding to pressures from this direction. Now there would seem to have been something of an explosion in the demand for information by a wide range of participant groups including, most importantly, governments, trade unions, employees, and the general public as well as investors, bankers, lenders, creditors, accountants, and auditors.

4.1 THE INFORMATION EXPLOSION

It is not surprising that MNCs are concerned about the manner in which apparently ever-increasing requirements for information disclosure are determined by regulatory bodies at governmental or professional level. The pace at which regulation has accelerated since the early 1970s is such that it is sometimes suggested that only a time-lag separates a request from its eventual declaration as a required disclosure. Such a view may vastly over-simplify the process, technical and political, through which standards are established—a process in which many companies directly or indirectly participate. But the ultimate result, albeit at times postponed or slowed down, has been increased disclosure requirements.

The acceleration in the demand for information for investment purposes might well appear to be unsustainable and hence eventually to decline. However, the increasing internationalization of share ownership, combined with a concurrent growth in awareness of the considerable diversity of accounting principles and practices in different countries, has fuelled the demand for additional information disclosures aimed at increasing both the quality and comparability of MNC reports.[1] Segmental information, for example, analysed by both line of business and geographical area is likely to be an important element of disclosure demands for some time to come.

Apart from the investor group, there is the growing belief among other groups such as governments and trade unions, that both an increased availability and an improved quality of information is a necessity.[2] It may be argued that many of these demands are general, vague, and imprecise. However, as the demand has grown so too has its precision, at both national and international level, including international inter-governmental organizations such as the UN, OECD, and EEC and international trade union organizations issuing lists of information requirements. These 'shopping lists' were at first quite short, identifying what was then perceived to be key items of information. Over time, the lists have grown as have, albeit slowly, the ability of such user groups to identify more precisely their information needs. The UN proposals which especially reflect the influence of developing countries and trade unions are probably the most extensive list yet drawn up.[3]

At a time when some may have thought that, for MNCs headquartered in countries with well-developed stock markets, the demand for information might have eased, there is now a growing and articulated demand from a range of non-traditional information users for more information, some of this being already available to and directed at investors—others uniquely demanded by emerging user groups.

Users with the ability/power to obtain 'tailor-made' reports, such as trade unions at national level with adequate bargaining power and organizational ability, are apparently learning the limitations of corporate annual reports and are increasingly concentrating their energies on obtaining special-purpose reports more in line with their specific information needs. The emphasis here is on timely, future-orientated, and disaggregated information. While this has the effect of reducing the demands on the annual publication of the general-purpose corporate report, it increases the pressures on corporations to improve the availability of more comprehensive information through other channels.

Thus the increased supply rather than reducing the demand for additional information appears in some respects to have actually increased it. If the demand for information were fixed, corporations could include its reduction and, indeed, ultimate satisfaction among the benefits to be matched against the costs of information disclosure. However, this is clearly not possible in the dynamic context of the demand for information now evident. But to what extent is the information demanded likely to be used and understood—and by whom?

4.2 USER COMPREHENSION AND INFORMATION OVERLOAD

The decisions of corporations and/or regulatory bodies as to which groups have a right to or should be provided with information is a major determinant of the content of corporate reports—particularly influencing the *range* of information. Equally important is the decision to whom within these groups the information is aimed at. This determines its *depth*. Despite the long history of information disclosure by corporations it is only very recently that systematic efforts have been made to assess the ability of supposed users actually to use corporate annual reports. There is now growing evidence that these reports are neither read nor understood by a considerable proportion of those whom they are supposed to inform, especially the lay-person investor.[4]

The direct users are apparently the relatively small number of experts who have the necessary ability and experience to do so.[5] No group is without its information analysts.[6] Many investors and shareholders do not make investment decisions alone, but rely on the advice of experts. They may do this by buying advice, or consulting the financial press or other sources of interpretation. Similarly, when trade unions use corporate reports they are increasingly provided with an analysis of the information by their own experts or research departments.

Why do a minority only directly use corporate reports? Is this because such reports are of necessity complex or because they have been made unnecessarily so by regulatory bodies? The fact is that corporations, of even a moderate size, are complex organizations. A comprehensive corporate analysis necessitates not only the use of financial information but additional data as well in order to assess current and future trends. In the main, MNCs are especially complex and thus so too are their corporate reports. Not only do they produce a variety of products but, most importantly, they operate in a number of countries and, therefore in different operating environments with a variety of risks, opportunities, and pressures. Accordingly, MNC corporate reports have some characteristics rarely, and sometimes never, found in those of UNCs. Their world-wide consolidated financial statements in the main are drawn up according to the accounting standards and practices of one country only, usually that of the MNC's headquarters. Users familiar with the accounting practices of more than one country are few, and there is thus an inevitable tendency by many users to interpret MNC corporate reports as if they were drawn up according to the practices of their own, rather than the source country.[7]

Limiting or reducing (by simplifying) the information in annual accounts may make them superficially more intelligible to a wider audience, but it may well result in the omission of essential information useful to the direct users—the experts. To suggest otherwise is to confuse corporate annual reports with the underlying reality they attempt to portray. That is not to say that the clarity of such reports cannot be improved, nor that some information provided may be superfluous. However, if corporate reports were to be pitched at the level of the lay-person they would have to be reduced substantially in size, thus forgoing important elements in the accounting and information message, and lowering the standard of analysis of those who actually, rather than ideally or hypothetically, use them.

In order to make informed decisions about corporations, an ability to analyse information is essential—those who cannot do so are precluded from making such decisions. The US Financial Accounting Standards Board (FASB) was quite definite about this when it stated: 'Clearly investors . . . have varying understanding of matters such as security markets, business enterprises and financial statements, and financial statements cannot directly help investors and creditors who know little about those matters. . . .'[8]

The tension between the need for more detailed and complex information for decision-making purposes and information which can be readily understood by the lay-person for stewardship purposes has led to much ambiguity. The US Trueblood Report, for example, stated: 'Accounting information should be presented so that it can be understood by reasonably well-informed, as well as by sophisticated, users. In effect, presenting information understandable only to sophisticated users establishes a bias . . . no valid users' needs should be ignored. Information that can be understood, and is needed, by sophisticated users should not be diluted to eliminate what less able users cannot understand.'[9]

However, this means trying to achieve the impossible—something for everyone. This ambiguity, and lack of consensus, while possibly acting as a constraint on increasing disclosure requirements has not in practice prevented regulatory bodies from requiring extensions in disclosure. The effective demand has come from those who actually use and desire more information, i.e. the experts, especially investment analysts active in the stock market, and not from those whom some may wish did so. Many MNCs would nevertheless appear to regard widespread usage of their reports as desirable and would view the current level of complexity, and the additional information now demanded even more so, as inhibiting or preventing this. Demanding expanded disclosures, often in the name of greater accountability, is to them contradictory. Increased information means greater complexity, thus making corporate accounts and reports even less accessible than before to all but a few.[10] A minority argument is to regard corporate reports as information which of necessity is, and can only be, appropriately used by experts. Accordingly, no amount of reduction, or alteration, would compensate for the absence of adequate analytical skills, knowledge, and experience of lay-persons.

Just as the majority of information providers consider questions of comprehensiveness of information within the ambit of the conventional wisdom of 'information for all with a legitimate interest', so too on the demand side there is a failure to appreciate the difference between actual users of information and those on whose behalf the information is so used. The OECD, for example, refers to information which should 'improve public understanding'.[11] Such a distinction is unnecessary, as what ultimately matters, from the user perspective, is the expanded *availability* of relevant information. Ironically, what might appear élitist, aiming information at the experts, is likely to be the most democratic, as it is in this way that the information needs of the many groups affected by the operations of MNCs are perhaps best served in practice. At the same time, there is presumably some limit to the quantity of information that can be conveniently analysed even by experts.

The view that does not differentiate between different levels of interpretative abilities within groups, but views them as homogeneous, has tended to dominate the disclosure debate. A major objective of corporate reports may well be, or perhaps should be, to 'serve primarily those users who have limited authority, ability or resources to obtain information and who rely on financial statements as their principal source of information'.[12] As suggested above, however, this is probably best achieved through the medium of expert users as they are likely to be able to make the most effective use of the information disclosed. While attempts to help the unsophisticated *directly*, by simplifying corporate reports may be worthy of investigation, the danger is that this may be less than effective, misleading, and hence a waste of resources. On the other hand, the provision of simplified information on a *supplementary* basis as a means of improving firm–participant communications could prove to be a worthwhile alternative which will not in any way diminish the supply of information for the expert user.

4.3 MANAGERIAL INCENTIVES TO DISCLOSE INFORMATION

There may well be incentives for the management of an MNC to disclose information voluntarily if it perceives it to be in its own interests and that of the corporation to respond to the information demands of users/participant groups, e.g. where corporations are competing for finance from investors.[13] Further, managers' and shareholders' interests may coincide to the extent that managers hold shares too and are concerned that share prices fully reflect the performance and prospects of the corporation. Where governments and trade unions exert an influence over the environment within which the MNC operates then there will also be strong influences on the MNC to disclose information in order to compete with other MNCs for investment opportunities, or in exchange for the maintenance of existing rights or the avoidance of potential constraints on their operations. In this regard, the legitimacy of MNC operations may be achieved by abiding by codes of conduct. In the late 1970s many MNCs have endeavoured to show that they are complying with the OECD guidelines largely in an effort to stave off a harsher code—possibly from the UN. Economic, social, and political pressures may thus operate to achieve an appropriate disclosure equilibrium. If management decides, on the other hand, that the information demands are unreasonable or inimical to their interests or those of the MNC, e.g. when the information is unfavourable or contains 'bad news', then they must either achieve some compromise or accept the consequences, if any, of non-disclosure.

Information disclosure is unlikely to be neutral. The relative power of either side in the bargaining process may be positively or adversely influenced by the use of information disclosed by the corporation. Such information may be used to a large or negligible extent. It may alter or strengthen preconceived ideas or may be used selectively to justify or rationalize the views expressed. Conflicts of interest, the uncertainty of the future, and different perspectives ensure that the information disclosed is unlikely to be interpreted in an impartial, uniform, or 'objective' manner.[14]

The benefit of disclosure to a corporation is in any resulting reduction in uncertainty about financial performance and future prospects and in any weakening of the bargaining powers of participants or increase in their belief/recognition of mutual interest with the corporation. The converse is the negative impact on the corporation that may result from participants being informed of any 'bad news' and the increase, if any, in the bargaining powers of such groups, especially governments and trade unions.

The benefit of an enhanced mutual interest has been the focus of much attention in recent years—often characterized by such terms as 'communications' and 'education', i.e. those with fallacious views of the role or condition of the corporation will through receipt of information become aware of the mutuality of interests, and through this be spurred on to greater efforts or increased co-operation.[15] However, this would appear to display a naïvety about the relationship of business with diverse groups and individuals, presupposing first, a 'unitary' view of the firm, i.e. assuming that all interests are essentially the same, and secondly, aside from whether such unity exists, that information disclosure can be effective in making recipients aware of the commonality of interests.[16]

Referring to disclosure the Confederation of British Industry (CBI), an employers' organization, suggested that information in corporate reports might assure the 'doubters' that all was well and discredit the 'critics'.[17] On the other hand, the USA Business Industry and Advisory Committee (BIAC), also an employers' organization, takes quite a different view, stating that: 'It is also doubtful that the mere increase in data can ever resolve several . . . issues that are in question. The reason for this is that often the two sides of the argument do not belong to the same logical set.'[18] The more pessimistic view by the US BIAC probably reflects a more realistic assessment of the experience of MNC disclosure in recent years despite the hopes expressed in the CBI's report.

MNCs are only too well aware of the increasingly critical and regulated environment in which they have to operate. They have become the object of criticisms of business in general, as well as those arising from their multinationality.[19] Certainly, international intergovernmental organizations such as the UN, OECD, and EEC do not believe that the free play of market forces between the participants can be relied upon to ensure the provision of sufficient comparable information by MNCs.

While many MNCs undoubtedly hope that increased disclosures, voluntary or compulsory, will ease the pressures on them through greater recognition by recipients of common interests between them and MNCs, it would seem that few see it as necessarily making a significant contribution. Their position is defensive rather than reflecting the enthusiasm that may be expected from the possessors of a major panacea.

4.4 COSTS OF INFORMATION PRODUCTION

The disclosure of information has a direct monetary cost. MNCs are understandably unwilling to incur increased costs through expanded disclosures unless they are required to do so, or the potential benefits exceed the estimated costs.[20] The direct cost to a corporation of information disclosure is the value of the resources used in gathering and processing the information and in its audit and communication.

Disclosure may be of information already used for internal purposes, or may be compiled wholly or partially for external communication alone resulting in significantly higher disclosure costs.[21] An example of disclosure required/requested which for some MNCs falls into the former category, but for others the latter, is segmental information on a geographical basis. There is a considerable demand that MNCs should, if they do not do so already, disclose information about their operating performance and financial position in specific geographical areas.[22] These proposals have met, as did earlier proposals, with considerable opposition from many MNCs.[23] The main stated objections are 'cost' and 'competitive disadvantage'. The opposition in some cases is to the concept itself, while in others it is to the amount of detail requested. The direct costs of such disclosures will pre-eminently depend upon the internal organization structure of an MNC. The nearer an MNC's internal structure is to the basis of segmentation required then the lower the cost. Conversely, the further away it is the higher the cost.

As the information needs of management are not always identical with those of others, the absence of complete harmony between internal and external information needs is inevitable. Many MNCs stress the differences, and the consequent high costs of gathering information exclusively for disclosure purposes.[24] Some users, however, have criticized this apparent constraint on disclosure. There are two grounds for this. First, that the legitimacy of external users' information needs should be recognized even when such information is not also used for managerial purposes. Secondly, that such differences are considerably overemphasized by MNCs, as much of the information requested is required by the corporations themselves for planning and control purposes.[25]

While information disclosure is not a market transaction in that the recipients do not *directly* pay for the information, it does represent a use of real resources which is paid for by the corporation and its shareholders. As there is no direct payment by users many MNCs complain that most users underestimate or ignore the costs of existing, let alone expanded, disclosures. Ignoring such costs is equivalent to attributing a zero cost to them. The argument that society must ultimately pay for the cost of disclosure, however, has little, if any, constraining influence on groups desiring more information. User groups, especially investment analysts, while acknowledging that costs are incurred, tend to consider that users' needs should, in the main, override cost as a disclosure veto.

The costs of disclosure, subject to some difficulties, are measurable in contrast to the elusiveness of benefits whether to supplier or user. However, no independent and published study of the cost of disclosure is available. A few MNCs have published estimates of the cost to them of certain additional disclosures. Compliance with the UN proposals would, according to one large MNC, cost it $US 250 million, while another large MNC has suggested that its costs for complying with the same proposals would be between $US 10 and 12 million. Without questioning the good faith or accuracy of the estimates above, an evaluation of these figures is not possible without knowing the assumptions on which they are based. For example, are the costs total or marginal; do they include fixed as well as variable costs; are they setting-up costs or the recurrent costs; how are the costs associated with information which has both an internal and an external use divided? An assessment of the costs of disclosure, whether existing or potential, by independent parties is desirable but problematic, as such a study would require considerable expertise and access to information which most corporations would, understandably, be unwilling to provide. Yet without such measurements, questions relating to the cost of disclosure remain as imprecise and unquantified in the public arena as the benefits. Such uncertainty and imprecision, however, does not make either costs or benefits the less real.

Apart from the direct costs of disclosure there are the indirect costs relating to competitive disadvantage, with its associated disincentives to innovate or invest, and the costs resulting from interference or regulation by governments.

4.5 COMPETITIVE DISADVANTAGE

The most frequently cited objection to increased disclosure requirements is probably that of 'competitive disadvantage', i.e. the use of the additional information by competitors to the detriment of the corporation disclosing the information.

It is a major basis for resistance to expanded disclosures.[26] This has been the case for some considerable time even when disclosure requirements were miniscule in contrast with current standards, e.g. even the disclosure of a profit and loss statement was once considered competitively disadvantageous.[27] Few, if any, disclosure proposals have not been opposed for this reason. Competitive disadvantage is a cliché or slogan in the disclosure debate. Regardless of its validity, it is rarely elaborated on or substantiated but merely cited. In the polemical language of the controversy it is often a synonym for 'no' by the corporation as information supplier.

In some circumstances, disclosure of information could be damaging to MNCs.[28] As a general rule, the more specific or future-orientated a disclosure is, the greater the potential competitive disadvantage for the disclosing corporation.[29] However, as an objection to disclosure expansion it tends to be used a little too readily and the number of items of information identified as such have probably been exaggerated.[30] Much of the information in corporate reports is too general and out of date ever to competitively disadvantage the information provider.[31] The ability of competitors to obtain more detailed and relevant information from other sources than is disclosed in corporate reports should not be underestimated.

What of the relatively small proportion of possible disclosures which hypothetically could cause damage to the discloser? Should this definitively rule out their release? Information which allows a competitor to increase his well-being at the expense of the discloser is damaging for the latter but profitable for the former. This is undesirable for the disclosing corporation, but does not necessarily mean that the welfare of the economy as a whole has diminished—on the contrary it may have gained as a result of the increased overall economic efficiency resulting from the higher level of competitiveness.

This argument is well-expressed as follows:

> It is fundamental that a market economy functions properly only in an atmosphere of extensive knowledge concerning financial and other aspects of corporate behaviour. Contrary to the assertions of many corporate spokesmen, corporate secrecy—not corporate disclosure—is the great enemy of a market economy in a free society.[32]

A number of MNCs, while supporting the philosophy of competition, simultaneously oppose greater disclosure. In such instances is there an element of 'having one's cake and eating it too'? Of course competition could, if carried to its ultimate conclusion, destroy the market economy through undermining the will of managers to invest, innovate, and take risks. On the other hand, the acceptance of restraints on disclosure may result in overall inefficiency and the perpetuation of monopolistic tendencies. It may also encourage enterprise but at the cost of enabling the rewards of invention and innovation, e.g. new products, sales in new markets, to be retained for a longer period than would otherwise be possible. However, the great majority of current and proposed disclosures seem unlikely to confer any significant competitive advantages or disadvantages—though no evidence is yet available to establish the case either way. In circumstances where information *is* competitively disadvantageous for the information discloser, then the economic welfare of society may be enhanced or diminished according to the specific circumstances involved, including the type of information disclosed, the nature of the economy and the competitive environment already prevailing, and the ability of management to exploit market opportunities. The extent of information disclosure required is also likely to vary according to the political and social values of the country in which the corporation is located, as these values will determine the accepted level of competition and hence the extent to which the regulation of information disclosure is considered necessary.

Another concern by MNCs is that proposed expansions in disclosure (for example, those of the UN) would be required of them alone and not of all companies, i.e. UNCs as well, providing the latter with a competitive advantage over MNCs. However, an alternative view put by international inter-governmental organizations and trade unions is that disclosure requirements/proposals, particularly relating to geographical segmentation of sales and profitability, would merely require MNCs to disclose information equivalent to that which is already provided by UNCs, but which is currently unavailable from some MNCs as a result of the aggregation of information relating to their activities in a number of countries. Far from UNCs having a competitive advantage it is more likely to be the case that some redress will be given to their position of competitive disadvantage relative to MNCs. A related concern by MNCs is that any regulation of disclosure should apply equally to all MNCs wherever based, thus providing support for international as opposed to national or regional initiatives, so as to limit competitive disadvantage, for example, by US MNCs relative to European MNCs.

The dilemma is to distinguish between disclosures which, for the economy as a whole, result in aggregate competitive advantages exceeding aggregate competitive disadvantages, i.e. in increased growth through competition—from the reverse result. What is detrimental or beneficial to the economy in the short term may in some circumstances have the opposite effect in the longer term. Increased competition through disclosure could lead to a greater vigour in the economy, or a decline in business incentives as a result of the appropriation of rewards by competitors facilitated by expanded disclosures.

The frequent public reference by corporate spokesmen to 'competitive disadvantage' as a major basis for opposition to increases in information disclosure contrasts with its frequent dismissal by MNCs as a real threat in practice. The potential gain from a greater extent of information disclosure may not, in fact, be to competitors but to other groups such as governments and trade unions, and indeed in some circumstances to the information providers themselves. However, objections which are legitimated by a supposed challenge to competition are apparently perceived to be more likely to obtain greater support than many other objections. The competitive disadvantage resulting from expanded information disclosures, while being the most frequently referred to, is therefore likely to be less real than is generally supposed.[33]

4.6 GOVERNMENT INTERFERENCE

The 1950s and 1960s were periods of considerable freedom for MNCs, but increasing concern, and indeed often hostility, towards them has in recent years led to an acceleration in attempts to monitor, regulate, and control their activities.[34] Some MNCs have operations in host countries which extensively control their activities. Their operations are evaluated against national requirements as perceived by the government. A variety of controls requiring adherence to centrally determined goals are imposed and may include: requirements to purchase specified proportions of local imports; restrictions on income and capital repatriation; requirements to employ local managerial staff; control over location of operation; control of the destination and quantity of exports; monitoring of cross-frontier transactions, and so on.[35]

Proposals for increased MNC disclosures are seen by many corporations as both a part of and a prelude to even greater regulation and interference, though recent experience suggests that the extent of this has probably been overestimated. At the same time it is recognized that an unwillingness to disclose information voluntarily may increase criticism of MNCs and thereby expand pressure for even further control of their activities.

Another view is that much of the increased demand for information from MNCs is emanating from 'hostile' sources who would not be placated by additional information. MNCs in this category are not inclined to increase their disclosures, unless compelled to do so.

If the principle of non-discrimination between MNCs and UNCs were to be strictly adhered to, then the MNCs would have no greater, or less, reason to fear control than UNCs.[36] However, in some countries the equality of treatment is not accepted and control is considered to be especially relevant to MNCs on the grounds that certain of their activities necessitate this and/or, simply, that they should not be treated in the same manner as UNCs as they are 'foreign'.[37]

Increasing information disclosure requirements are feared by some MNCs as a direct manifestation of increasing governmental control of their activities or would be a stimulant to such. In addition, such information could indirectly enlarge such interference by providing ammunition for groups which desire and press for increased governmental control of MNCs. Alternatively, disclosure may be a form of self-regulation which inhibits the pressures for governmental interference. Furthermore, such voluntary disclosure may also be beneficial to management through an increase in investor confidence and, therefore, an enhanced ability to raise finance for investment purposes. Another important factor from a social standpoint is the cost of governmental regulation, relative to self-regulation, in the development and enforcement of disclosure standards.

4.7 EVALUATING COSTS AND BENEFITS

A benefit of disclosure for the MNC is any positive contribution to the attainment of its goals. This contribution can only result from the positive influence the information has on the disclosee's, or third-party's, behaviour. The cost of disclosure may be direct or indirect. Indirect costs result, like benefits, from the change in behaviour resulting from disclosure but are negative rather than positive. Direct costs are the value of the resources used in obtaining and communicating the information.

Calculating the direct costs of past and current disclosures is relatively straightforward. However, estimating those of *proposed* disclosures, like all estimates, is a less precise process than the measurement of past expenditures. Nevertheless, some degree of accuracy is possible. Aside from this relative accuracy in measuring direct costs, it seems clear that disclosure decisions and consequences are characterized by imprecision and uncertainty.

The benefits and indirect costs of disclosure cannot be so easily identified and measured. If behaviour does alter as a result of disclosures, how can the changes attributable to the availability of new information be isolated from the multitude of other influences? In the few circumstances where the influence of disclosure may be identified can this be quantified, even if only approximately? How can it be measured if it is not directly manifested through the market? How, for example, could the effect be measured of disclosure, or non-disclosure, on a corporation's potential to raise capital; on its employees' increased/decreased bargaining power or increased awareness of the decline/improvement in company profitability; on the praise/criticism of the financial press and academics; and on the competitive advantages obtained by other corporations? The effect of information disclosure on share prices may indicate, for example, an influence on investor perceptions of the prospects of individual corporations, but changes in share prices can be no more than surrogates for those economic consequences which are of ultimate concern. Moreover, the effect of information disclosure on other participants, e.g. employees, is not at all assessable by this means.

Except in unusual circumstances a company cannot make an objective nor precise disclosure cost–benefit calculation in quantitive terms. While the direct costs can usually be measured with some degree of precision, the indirect costs and benefits cannot. The consequences of many *past* disclosures may be unknown. The imponderables of the future make the results of *proposed* disclosures even less determinable.

The uncertainty and imprecision of the consequences of disclosure means that in many instances no MNC can be sure of what advantages or disadvantages, for itself, can be gained from increase in information disclosure. The location of MNC participant groups in more than one country, and the volatile attitudes to MNCs means that the outcome of their information disclosure is even more uncertain than for UNCs. However, those MNCs which voluntarily are increasing their disclosures are apparently doing so in the belief that they will benefit from such a course of action or that they will at least diminish the negative consequences of non-disclosure.

4.8 CONCLUSIONS

There is no objective, verifiable economic calculus by which the costs and benefits of disclosure can be measured. This is not unique to the information disclosure debate. There are many other areas where, without quantification or certainty of costs and benefits, decisions are made and legislation enacted (for example, health and safety at work requirements). Information disclosure is determined either through the direct relationship of discloser and disclosee (through bargaining, consultation, persuasion), each making implicitly or explicitly their respective arbitrary cost–benefit calculations, or indirectly through the decisions of regulatory bodies, governmental and professional. The cost–benefit calculations of such bodies will of necessity be 'in ordinal rather than cardinal terms . . . rough rather than precise . . . always subject to revision, rather than fixed in store'.[38] The relative weights they give to the costs and benefits of both the discloser and the disclosee will depend on both the information concerned and the 'political' values they have or are required to adopt. Thus disclosure policy necessarily involves value judgements and the selection of what should be disclosed involves a process of political or social choice which will be resolved through the interaction of MNC participants.

Information Disclosure:
Regulation and Practice

From the foregoing discussion of the demand for information by a wide variety of user groups and the factors influencing its supply by management, it is evident that there are a number of significant issues in the context of information disclosure by MNCs.

Major areas of specific interest and concern include group accounts and the consolidation of financial statements, incorporating funds-flow statements, on a world-wide basis; segmental information, especially on a geographical basis; transfer pricing and related party transactions; accounting for the translation of foreign currency financial statements; accounting for inflation; and non-financial or 'social' information relating in particular to employment conditions and prospects, company organization, production, investment plans, and the environment.

But what is the current situation as regards the regulation and practice of information disclosure? We will now briefly review the position in each of these selected areas, indicating problems and likely developments where appropriate. In doing so, reference will be made to the prevailing regulatory framework, both governmental and private/self-regulatory. Special attention will be given to developments and proposals at the international level of the UN, OECD, EEC, and IASC.

While there have been few studies with a specific focus on the reporting practices of MNCs,[1] there have been a number of comparative international surveys of accounting and reporting practices which are relevant for our purposes here, including the *Price Waterhouse International Survey* (1979), the *OECD Survey* (1980) and the *Financial Times World Survey* (1980).[2] All of these surveys are concerned with large public corporations. Of particular interest is the *Financial Times World Survey* with its comprehensive analysis of the reporting practices of 200 of the world's largest corporations, most of them being MNCs.[3]

5.1 CONSOLIDATED FINANCIAL STATEMENTS

All MNC participants would appear to be interested in the financial performance and future prospects of the MNC as an economic entity. It is in this context that a report on the group of subsidiary corporations controlled and co-ordinated by the MNC parent corporation is relevant. In addition, the MNC parent may have interests in associated corporations which are not controlling interests but which are nevertheless significant to its overall situation.

While the demand for information about the MNC on a world-wide basis is evident, it is a matter of some controversy as to how best to present this. Consolidation is currently accepted in practice as the means of aggregating, on a 'line-by-line' basis, information about the assets, liabilities, revenues, and expenses of the MNCs many individual legal entities into income, financial position, and funds statements relating to a single economic entity. An example from the Du Pont (USA) report is given in Exhibit 5A. At the same time it is increasingly recognized that the complexity of MNC operations is such that consolidations are likely to be less than revealing without some disaggregation of the information accumulated. Hence the corresponding demand for segmental (disaggregated) information by line of business and geographical area. Consolidated and segmental statements are thus complementary forms of reporting—each would seem to be necessary for an informed appraisal of MNC operations. Paradoxically, just as consolidations are now becoming accepted in practice as appropriate in the international context, so are their inadequacies becoming apparent.

5.1.1 Regulation

The United Nations gave special emphasis in its 1977 proposals[4] to the need for world-wide consolidated financial statements together with information about group corporations including associates. Such consolidations should include all subsidiaries, but exceptions may be made provided that they are justified and accounted for by the equity method, i.e. the ownership share of earnings and shareholders' equity are included on a 'one-line' or lump-sum basis as opposed to a 'line-by-line' basis. Associated corporations, where the investor corporation holds a substantial interest, are similarly to be accounted for by the equity method. A special feature of the proposals is the provision for sub-group consolidations at country level where the MNC has an

Exhibit 5A. Du Pont (USA)

FINANCIAL STATEMENTS

E. I. DUPONT DE NEMOURS AND COMPANY AND CONSOLIDATED SUBSIDIARIES

Consolidated Income Statement

(Dollars in millions, except per share)

	1981	1980	1979
SALES	$22,810	$13,744	$12,650
Other income	282	149	131
Total	23,092	13,893	12,781
Costs of goods sold and other operating charges	15,420	9,659	8,428
Selling, general and administrative expenses	1,668	1,341	1,135
Exploration expenses, including dry hole costs and impairment of unproved properties	203	—	—
Research and development expense	631	491	420
Depreciation, depletion and amortization	1,144	777	763
Interest and debt expense	476	111	143
Taxes other than on income	1,369	406	371
Total	20,911	12,785	11,260
EARNINGS BEFORE INCOME TAXES AND MINORITY INTERESTS	2,181	1,108	1,521
Provision for income taxes	1,074	392	564
EARNINGS BEFORE MINORITY INTERESTS	1,107	716	957
Minority interests in earnings of consolidated subsidiaries	26	10	18
INCOME BEFORE CUMULATIVE EFFECT OF CHANGE IN ACCOUNTING FOR INVESTMENT TAX CREDIT	1,081	706	939
Cumulative effect for years prior to 1981 of change in accounting for investment tax credit	320	—	—
NET INCOME	1,401	706	939
Dividends on preferred stock	10	10	10
EARNINGS ON COMMON STOCK	$ 1,391	$ 696	$ 929

Consolidated Income Statement—continued

(Dollars in millions, except per share)

	1981	1980	1979
EARNINGS PER SHARE OF COMMON STOCK			
Before cumulative effect of change in accounting for investment tax credit	$ 5.81	$ 4.49	$ 6.07
Cumulative effect for years prior to 1981 of change in accounting for investment tax credit	1.74	—	—
Net income	$ 7.55	$ 4.49	$ 6.07
PRO FORMA—with 1981 change in accounting for investment tax credit applied retroactively			
Net income	$ 1,081	$ 744	$ 965
Earnings per share of common stock	$ 5.81	$ 4.73	$ 6.23

Consolidated Balance Sheet

(Dollars in millions)   December 31

	1981	1980
ASSETS		
CURRENT ASSETS		
Cash and marketable securities	$ 790	$ 228
Accounts and notes receivable	4,370	2,129
Inventories	4,500	2,018
Prepaid expenses	361	153
Total current assets	10,021	4,528
PROPERTY, PLANT AND EQUIPMENT	21,562*	12,366
Less: accumulated depreciation, depletion, and amortization	8,840	7,900
	12,722	4,466
INVESTMENT IN AFFILIATES	362	276
OTHER ASSETS	724	380
TOTAL	$23,829	$ 9,650

Consolidated Balance Sheet—continued

(Dollars in millions)   December 31

	1981	1980
LIABILITIES AND STOCKHOLDERS' EQUITY		
CURRENT LIABILITIES		
Accounts payable	$ 2,536	$ 830
Short-term borrowings	445	399
Income taxes	527	259
Other accrued liabilities	1,386	582
Total current liabilities	4,894	2,070
LONG-TERM BORROWINGS	6,403	1,079
CAPITAL LEASE OBLIGATIONS	176	34
OTHER LIABILITIES	1,309	254
DEFERRED INCOME TAXES	518	198
DEFERRED INVESTMENT TAX CREDIT	—	320
MINORITY INTERESTS IN CONSOLIDATED SUBSIDIARIES	71	71
STOCKHOLDERS' EQUITY	10,458	5,624
TOTAL	$23,829	$ 9,650

* Includes oil and gas properties accounted for by the successful efforts method of accounting.

Consolidated Statement of Stockholders' Equity

(Dollars in millions, except per share)

	1981	1980	1979
PREFERRED STOCK, without par value—cumulative			
Authorized—23,000,000 shares			
Issued at December 31:			
$4.50 Series—1,672,594 shares (callable at $120)	$ 167	$ 167	$ 167
$3.50 Series—700,000 shares (callable at $102)	70	70	70
	237	237	237
COMMON STOCK, $1.66 2/3 par value			
Authorized—300,000,000 shares			
Issued at December 31:			
1981—234,434,093 shares;			
1980—155,207,354 shares;			
1979—154,332,900 shares	391	259	258

Consolidated Statement of Stockholders' Equity—continued
(Dollars in millions, except per share)

	1981	1980	1979
ADDITIONAL PAID-IN CAPITAL			
Balance at beginning of year	438	406	405
Changes resulting from common stock issued in connection with			
Conoco acquisition	3,784	—	—
Remington merger	—	9	—
Compensation plans	26	23	1
Balance at end of year	4,248	438	406
REINVESTED EARNINGS			
Balance at beginning of year	4,690	4,399	3,869
Add—net income	1,401	706	939
	6,091	5,105	4,808
Less—dividends:			
Preferred stock			
$4.50 Series	8	8	8
$3.50 Series	2	2	2
Total preferred dividends	10	10	10
Common stock (1981, 1980, and 1979—$2.75)	499	405	399
Total dividends	509	415	409
Balance at end of year	5,582	4,690	4,399
LESS—COMMON STOCK HELD IN TREASURY, at cost (1,060,406 shares at December 31, 1979)	—	—	42
TOTAL STOCKHOLDERS' EQUITY	$10,458	$ 5,624	$ 5,258

Consolidated Statement of Changes in Financial Position
(Dollars in millions)

	1981	1980	1979
CASH AND MARKETABLE SECURITIES—beginning of year	$ 228	$ 377	$ 341
SOURCE OF FUNDS			
Income before cumulative effect of change in accounting for investment tax credit	1,081	706	939
Depreciation, depletion, and amortization	1,144	777	763
Increase in deferred income taxes— non-current	320	60	83
Dry hole costs and impairment of unproved properties	93	—	—
Other non-cash charges and credits—net	86	85	88
Funds provided by operations	2,724	1,628	1,873
Increase (reduction) in borrowings (including capital lease obligations):			
New long-term borrowings in connection with Conoco acquisition	3,850	—	—
Consolidation of Conoco debt			
Short-term	351	—	—
Long-term	1,598	—	—
Other			
Short term	(305)	163	(28)
Long term			
New borrowings	128	199	52
Reductions	(110)	(194)	(47)
Common stock issued in connection with			
Conoco acquisition	3,915	—	—
Remington merger	—	46	—
Compensation plans	27	29	22
Miscellaneous—net	69	21	(30)
	12,247	1,892	1,842

Consolidated Statement of Changes in Financial Position—continued
(Dollars in millions)

	1981	1980	1979
USE OF FUNDS			
Increase in net assets (excluding working capital and borrowing)—Conoco acquisition	6,688	—	—
Increase in working capital (excluding cash, marketable securities and short-term borrowings)			
Consolidation of Conoco	2,005	—	—
Other	148	148	285
Capital expenditures:			
Additions to property, plant, and equipment	2,389	1,297	875
Investment in affiliates	67	72	65
Dividends	509	415	409
Increase (Decrease) in other assets	(121)	64	172
Reduction in minority interests in consolidated subsidiaries resulting from Remington merger	—	45	—
	11,685	2,041	1,806
CASH AND MARKETABLE SECURITIES—end of year	$ 790	$ 228	$ 377
INCREASE IN WORKING CAPITAL			
Increase (Decrease) in current assets:			
Accounts and notes receivable	$ 2,241	$ 154	$ 341
Inventories	2,482	11	298
Prepaid expenses	208	32	(135)
Decrease (Increase) in current liabilities			
Accounts payable	(1,706)	(56)	(205)
Income taxes	(268)	40	50
Other accrued liabilities	(804)	(33)	(64)
Less: increase in connection with consolidation of Conoco	(2,005)	—	—
	$ 148	$ 148	$ 285

Source: Du Pont Annual Report, 1981.

intermediate parent in a foreign country which controls other group corporations in that country.

The OECD guidelines[5] are consistent with the UN proposals to the extent that they recommend disclosure of information about the MNC as a whole. However, they do not deal specifically with the issue of consolidation but recommend only the disclosure of accounting policies used. Information should nevertheless be given about 'the structure of the enterprise, showing the name and location of the parent company, its main affiliates, its percentage ownership, direct and indirect, in these affiliates, including shareholdings between them'.

International Accounting Standard No. 3 (IAS 3) entitled 'Consolidated Financial Statements', issued in 1976, appears to be entirely consistent with the UN proposals and if anything is a little more comprehensive. Criteria for the exclusion of subsidiaries from the consolidation are specified, i.e. if control is temporary or severe long-term restrictions on the transfer of funds impairs control by the parent. A subsidiary may also be excluded if its activities are so dissimilar as to warrant the presentation of separate financial statements. Uniform accounting policies for all corporations consolidated are recommended or, at the least, disclosure of any differences in policy.

At the EEC level, the *Seventh Directive* on consolidated accounts[6] has now been adopted (June 1983). This is a major event in the European context. In contrast to the pronouncements of other organizations this will be *legally* enforceable throughout the EEC countries following its introduction by 1990 into the respective national laws. This directive requires the world-wide consolidation of financial statements and is broadly consistent with IAS 3, based largely on USA and UK practice. At the same time, it is evident that some compromise so as to accommodate French and West German practice has been found. A major problem has been that the UK approach to defining a group is to emphasize the legal power to control another corporation through share ownership whereas the West German approach is to emphasize the existence of effective management control.[7] The *Seventh Directive* permits both approaches to be used to the extent that the latter approach may be employed as an additional criterion for consolidation.

In addition, West German law currently requires only domestic subsidiaries to be consolidated. A change of practice will be necessary here. It also effectively prohibits the 'equity' method of accounting for associates, i.e. the ownership share of earnings of an associate may not be included in the consolidated profit and loss statement. The *Seventh Directive* is permissive on this point in that associates may be accounted for either on a cost or equity basis. In France, in contrast, the absence of any legal requirement to consolidate has given rise to a diversity of practice including the innovation of proportional consolidation, i.e. the ownership share of assets, liabilities, revenues, and expenses are consolidated pro rata on a 'line-by-line' basis.[8] This is often used in accounting for joint ventures and is expressly permitted by the *Seventh Directive*.

Apart from the USA and UK, legal requirements relating to group accounts are not perhaps as comprehensive or widespread as might be expected, especially in countries with a significant number of MNCs. As already noted, in West Germany the law does not require foreign subsidiaries to be consolidated, and in France there are no current legal requirements relating to consolidations in corporate annual reports, though the Stock Exchange Commission (Commission des Opérations de Bourse), which requires all corporations making new issues to provide consolidated financial statements, and the National Accounting Council (Conseil National de la Compatabilité) are increasingly influential in persuading a growing number of corporations to comply. The EEC *Seventh Directive* will, of course, change this situation entirely with its mandatory impact on all EEC countries.

Other countries with legal requirements include Australia, Belgium, Canada, Denmark, Japan, The Netherlands, South Africa, and Sweden. However, there are no legal requirements in many other countries including Argentina, Brazil, Greece, India, Italy, Portugal, Spain, and Switzerland.[9] Japan, which in 1977 introduced a requirement to disclose consolidated financial statements, provides an example of the difference such disclosure requirements can make. Toshiba's 1976 earnings of $US 30 million on a non-consolidated basis became a $US 13 million loss when its foreign and other subsidiaries were consolidated.[10]

5.1.2 Reporting practices

While the reporting practices of MNCs must comply with legal requirements, it should be recognized that they are often changed voluntarily in response to professional recommendations and other influences of a private/self-regulatory nature, or as a matter of policy by management. Thus many corporations disclose information without any compulsion to do so.

The *Financial Times World Survey* (1980) revealed that of the world's 200 largest corporations, 86 per cent published consolidated financial statements in some form.[11] At the same time, the quality and quantity of disclosure varied considerably both between and within countries. In certain cases, notably the voluntary disclosures by some Italian and Swiss corporations, only summarized information was presented. In the UK a parent company balance sheet was always provided in addition to a consolidated balance sheet and income statement. In the USA, only consolidated financial statements were provided.

Around a third of the corporations publishing consolidated financial statements disclosed subsidiaries that had not been consolidated. However, the majority of these were accounted for by the equity method which incorporates the ownership share of earnings. As regards the treatment of associates, only 57 per cent of corporations accounted for them using the equity method. The cost method, whereby only dividends receivable are included in the results for the year, was most commonly used in Australia, South Africa, France, Sweden, and of course, West Germany. 82 and 74 per cent of corporations disclosed the names and ownership in subsidiaries and associates respectively. However, names only were given in the case of 6 and 8 per cent, and no information at all in the case of 12 and 18 per cent of corporations respectively.

Other surveys, including the *Price Waterhouse International Survey (1979)* and the *OECD Survey (1980)*, reveal that there are also some considerable differences between countries in the techniques of consolidation used, apart from the equity and proportional methods already referred to.[12] For example, the acquisition method of consolidation is normally used whereby assets are revalued as at the date of acquisition of the subsidiary and the difference between the purchase cost and the revalued net assets is described as goodwill on consolidation. However, in the USA and the UK, the merger or pooling of interests method is also permitted in certain circumstances, where assets are not revalued, no goodwill emerges, and where there is no distinction drawn between pre- and post-acquisition earnings.

The treatment of goodwill or the difference on consolidation also varies especially as between the continental European and Anglo-Saxon countries.[13] Goodwill may be amortized against income over a period, as in the USA, written off immediately, as in the Netherlands, or treated in various ways including leaving it at its original amount, as in the UK. However, in West Germany, and to some extent in France, the practice is quite different in that a consolidation difference is calculated at the date of each balance sheet rather than just at the date of acquisition. Accordingly, the size of the consolidation difference will change from year to year.

5.1.3 Problems and prospects

While there has been a growing demand for MNC consolidated financial statements, there has been by no means a rapid response. Many large MNCs do not provide *world-wide* consolidated information and are as yet under no general compulsion to do so, with special reference to France, West Germany, Italy, Spain, and Switzerland. On the other hand, many MNCs are voluntarily disclosing this information, e.g. Volkswagen in West Germany, Saint-Gobain in France, and Ciba-Geigy in Switzerland. In Italy, Fiat produced consolidated financial statements for the first time in 1982. Further developments must be expected with the continuing involvement of the UN, OECD, and IASC in the setting of international accounting standards, though the EEC will be the more influential in the short term with the *Seventh Directive* having legal sanction throughout the EEC countries.

Just beneath the surface, however, there are many problems to be resolved internationally, especially those relating to determining the appropriate concept for group identification and the relevant techniques of consolidation, including the treatment of associated corporations. Further issues include the disclosure of details of ownership in, and activities of, members of the group. Given the wide variety of participant groups interested in MNCs, there would seem to be pressure to develop disclosure and measurement practices that will provide information to satisfy a number of perspectives. From a governmental and trade union standpoint, for example, additional sub-group consolidated financial statements at 'country' level, as proposed by the UN and international trade unions, or at EEC level, as proposed by the EEC, may be useful, whereas investors who may be more concerned with the MNC as a total economic entity may well be satisfied with a group consolidation on a world-wide basis.

A final issue concerns the relevance of consolidation itself in the context of MNC operations, with its variety of geographical locations with differential rates of inflation, exchange rates, and political risk. Hence there would seem to be scope for experimentation with alternative forms of presentation and disclosure, including the further development of segmental reporting.

Consider now the funds-flow statement or statement of changes in financial position. This statement may be viewed as one of the required consolidated financial statements, but because it is something of an innovation in many countries it will be discussed separately.

5.2 FUNDS STATEMENTS

The funds statement, or statement of changes in financial position, is becoming increasingly recognized as an important and integral member of the consolidated financial statements. It provides an analysis of the sources and uses of funds accruing to the corporation during the period. The statement shows the inflow of funds from operations and from items such as new loans, equity capital, or the sale of assets, together with the outflow of funds for dividends, loan repayments, and new investment. It should be emphasized that the term 'funds' does not necessarily imply 'cash' flows, though some presentations emphasize the net change in cash/liquid balances as opposed to changes in working capital, i.e. stocks, trade debtors and creditors. An example from Nestlé (Switzerland) given in Exhibit 5B illustrates the former approach.

The purpose of the funds statement is to provide further insight into the financial performance, stability, and earnings prospects of the MNC—matters of common concern to all user groups. However, in the context of MNCs the usefulness of a consolidated funds statement may be extremely limited without additional information on a disaggregated basis. Of special interest here is the geographical location of the sources and uses of funds—information about which is effectively denied by a consolidated statement.

While there is nothing new about the use of funds statements, especially by financial analysts and bankers, they would appear to be something of an innovation so far as public regulation is concerned despite voluntary disclosures by a significant number of large corporations.

5.2.1 Regulation

The United Nations (1977) proposals would elevate the funds statement to the status of a primary financial statement at group and individual subsidiary level. Items to be included in the funds statements are indicated. But the focus of the statement is left flexible, i.e. either a change in working capital or cash/liquid funds approach is acceptable. In contrast, the OECD guidelines (1976) and International Accounting Standard No. 7 (IAS 7) entitled 'Statement of Changes in Financial Position', issued in 1977, do not go much beyond recommending the

Exhibit 5B. Nestlé (Switzerland)

**Consolidated statement of source
and application of funds for the year 1981**

Nestlé and Unilac Groups combined

In millions of Francs	**1981**	1980
Source		
Net consolidated profit	**964**	683
Depreciation of fixed assets	**911**	763
Cash flow	**1,875**	1,446
Less: dividends and directors' remuneration for the previous year	**(257)**	(250)
Sales of fixed assets and of participations	**116**	69
Increase of provisions	**197**	297
Decrease of working capital (excl. net liquid resources) and sundry movements	**822**	—
	2,753	1,562
Application		
Increase of working capital (excl. net liquid resources) and sundry movements	**—**	887
Investments in fixed assets	**1,111**	1,208
Purchases of new companies and increases of participations	**172**	42
	1,283	2,137
Surplus/(deficit)	**1,470**	(575)
Adjustment of total working capital due to modification of exchange rates	**(125)**	42
Increase/(Decrease) of the net treasury situation (cash in hand and at banks, securities and other deposits, less short-, medium-, and long-term bank and other financial creditors)	**1,345**	(533)

Source: Nestlé Annual Report, 1981.

presentation of a funds statement. IAS 7 does not specify the items to be disclosed, nor how the statement is to be presented, stating only that: 'Each enterprise or group of enterprises should adopt the form of presentation for the statement of changes in financial position which is most informative in the circumstances.'

At the EEC level, however, requirements or proposals relating to funds statements are conspicuously absent. This is perhaps not particularly surprising as there are no existing legal requirements in any of the EEC countries. On the other hand, in France a funds statement is recommended by the National Accounting Council in accordance with the Plan Comptable Général, and in the UK there is a mandatory professional accounting standard in the form of SSAP 10.

In other countries, legal requirements exist, for example, in Austria, Brazil, Canada, Norway, the Philippines, Sweden, and the USA.[14] In addition, there are professional requirements in a number of countries including Hong Kong, New Zealand, and Spain. Interestingly a few countries, including Fiji, Nigeria, and Singapore have adopted IAS 7 in the absence of national requirements. Stock exchange requirements are also influential, for example, in Australia. But in many countries there are no requirements to present a funds statement. Most notably, these include, Belgium, Denmark, West Germany, Italy, Netherlands, Japan, and Switzerland.

Clearly the disclosure and presentation of funds statements in published corporate reports has yet to be widely accepted as necessary of regulation. Even where legal requirements or professional standards exist they are generally limited to specifying the main items to be included. Matters of presentation are left to the corporations themselves.

5.2.2 Reporting practices

Despite the relative lack of regulation governing funds statements, it is evident that they are provided increasingly in practice and in particular by large corporations, including MNCs, on a voluntary basis. The *Financial Times World Survey* (1980) revealed that 87 per cent of the 200 largest industrial corporations disclosed funds statements, though 13 per cent of these were parent corporation funds statements only.[15] A significant number of large corporations in France, West Germany, the Netherlands, Australia, Japan, and Switzerland provided funds statements despite the absence of regulation. While the UN, OECD, and IASC recognize the funds statement as a primary financial statement, in practice 25 per cent of the disclosing corporations included the statement in the notes to the accounts and 8 per cent in the directors' report. Of more importance however, is the concept of funds used as the focus of the statement. Of corporations, 57 per cent adopted a working capital focus, i.e. with changes in such items being the end result of the calculation of inflows and outflows, whereas only 18 per cent adopted the other major alternative of cash/liquid funds; 7 per cent of corporations used other approaches, while 21 per cent did not disclose their definition of funds at all. There is also a wide variety of practice as regards the items included in the funds statement, the measurement of funds from operations, and the form of presentation.

5.2.3 Problems and prospects

While the funds statement is a relative newcomer to published corporate reports and is considered to be an innovation in many countries, it is rapidly becoming accepted as an essential and primary financial statement. There is growing pressure from the UN, OECD, and IASC for its publication. On the other hand, it has been omitted from EEC requirements and proposals, presumably because funds statements do not as yet feature in any of the laws of the member countries and thus the question of harmonization does not arise from a legal perspective. Regulation, looking at the world as a whole, is in fact relatively sparse and even where it exists it is minimal and highly flexible. Despite this, many large MNCs are voluntarily providing funds statements, especially in France, West Germany, Switzerland, and Japan. However, the funds statement is not well developed in practice, with much confusion and doubt about its purpose, effective presentation and use. There is considerable variation in the definition of 'funds' used, in the items disclosed, in the measurement of funds from operations, and in the form of presentation of the statement. The use of funds statements for comparative purposes is thus likely to be limited. It would seem also that existing forms of the funds statement need to be critically evaluated in the light of potential uses. Certainly the consolidated form is of limited usefulness in the context of an understanding of the complexity of MNC operations where the geographical location of sources and uses of funds is essential information. There is also the question of whether a cash-flow statement incorporating cash receipts and payments could be more useful than one based on accrual data incorporating obligations owed and owing as well as cash flows.

5.3 SEGMENTAL INFORMATION

The counterpoint to consolidated financial statements, including funds statements, is the disclosure of disaggregated or what is usually termed 'segmental' information.[16] An example from Nabisco Brands (USA) is given in Exhibit 5C.

Exhibit 5C. Nabisco Brands (USA)

Segment information—The Company's products are classified into six world-wide business segments: US Bakery, composed of US cookie and cracker products; US Confectionery; Other US Food, composed of nuts, margarines, dessert mixes, snack foods, cereals, pet and frozen food products; International Food, composed of cookies, crackers, nuts, confectionery, snack foods, cereals, pet foods, and other grocery products sold outside the US; Food Ingredients (US and International) composed of corn wet milling products, vinegar, and yeast; Other Consumer Products (US and International) composed of beer, wine, and spirits, toiletries and pharmaceuticals, plastic and cloth shower curtains, knitted curtains, tobacco, and other non-food products.

Corporate consists primarily of the following:

Operating Income—General and administrative expenses of headquarters' functions, including unallocated research and development and corporate engineering expenses.

Identifiable Assets—Corporate cash and short-term investments, headquarters' property and facilities, investments in and advances to unconsolidated affiliates, and, in 1981, the purchase price of Life Savers, Inc.

Capital Expenditure—For headquarters' administrative and research facilities.

Depreciation Expense—On depreciable headquarters' administrative and research facilities.

Business Segments
(Dollars in millions)

1981	Net Sales Amount	%	Operating income Amount	%	Identifiable assets Amount	%	Capital expenditures Amount	%	Depreciation expense Amount	%
US Bakery	$1,412.8	24	$219.0	35	$ 551.5	19	$ 59.1	25	$26.9	29
US Confectionery	265.9	5	25.0	4	91.7	3	8.4	4	3.4	4
Other US Food	1,299.0	22	140.0	22	448.8	15	32.8	14	13.5	14
International Food	1,745.4	30	140.2	22	994.4	34	68.6	30	26.3	28
Food Ingredients	514.9	9	54.0	9	358.8	12	47.2	20	16.2	17
Other Consumer Products	581.2	10	48.3	8	477.3	17	16.0	7	7.3	8
Total segments	5,819.2	100	626.5	100	2,922.5	100	232.1	100	93.6	100
Corporate	—		(73.4)		506.7		19.9		3.1	
Total	$5,819.2		$553.1		$3,429.2		$252.0		$96.7	

1980										
US Bakery	$1,266.5	23	$189.4	33	$ 496.0	18	$ 47.3	23	$23.7	27
US Confectionery	272.7	5	26.1	5	95.3	3	11.5	6	2.4	3
Other US Food	1,272.6	23	114.7	20	414.2	15	22.7	11	14.6	17
International Food	1,737.0	31	129.6	23	969.6	35	72.6	36	24.3	28
Food Ingredients	495.4	9	60.9	11	333.7	12	32.8	16	14.8	17
Other Consumer Products	543.0	9	44.7	8	489.4	17	16.3	8	7.0	8
Total segments	5,587.2	100	565.4	100	2,798.2	100	203.2	100	86.8	100
Corporate	—		(64.4)		233.4		9.7		2.5	
Total	$5,587.2		$501.0		$3,031.6		$212.9		$89.3	

Business Segments—continued
(Dollars in millions)

1979	Net Sales Amount	%	Operating income Amount	%	Identifiable assets Amount	%	Capital expenditures Amount	%	Depreciation expense Amount	%
US Bakery	$1,164.3	24	$181.2	39	$ 444.1	18	$ 46.3	33	$22.1	28
US Confectionery	217.9	4	24.9	6	77.3	3	7.1	5	2.3	3
Other US Food	1,244.0	25	101.7	22	464.8	19	16.4	12	14.3	18
International Food	1,502.3	30	98.3	21	836.1	33	39.4	29	20.4	26
Food Ingredients	388.7	8	17.4	4	304.9	12	20.9	15	12.9	17
Other Consumer Products	458.1	9	36.5	8	376.3	15	8.7	6	6.1	8
Total segments	4,975.3	100	460.0	100	2,503.5	100	138.8	100	78.1	100
Corporate	—		(42.6)		178.6		13.3		1.6	
Total	$4,975.3		$417.4		$2,682.1		$152.1		$79.7	

Geographic Areas
(Dollars in millions)

1981	Net sales Amount	%	Operating income Amount	%	Identifiable assets Amount	%
United States	$3,836.8	66	$449.3	72	$1,711.7	59
Europe	867.6	15	59.9	10	545.5	19
Canada	606.8	10	56.6	9	348.3	12
Latin America	345.9	6	53.6	8	221.2	7
Other	162.1	3	7.1	1	95.8	3
Total segments	5,819.2	100	626.5	100	2,922.5	100
Corporate	—		(73.4)		506.7	
Total	$5,819.2		$553.1		$3,429.2	

1980						
United States	$3,629.1	65	$405.0	72	$1,623.8	58
Europe	951.4	17	69.5	12	541.8	19
Canada	558.6	10	46.3	8	322.6	12
Latin America	307.5	5	39.7	7	214.3	8
Other	140.6	3	4.9	1	95.7	3
Total segments	5,587.2	100	565.4	100	2,798.2	100
Corporate	—		(64.4)		233.4	
Total	$5,587.2		$501.0		$3,031.6	

1979						
United States	$3,284.7	66	$338.9	74	$1,455.2	58
Europe	837.9	17	53.3	12	497.8	20
Canada	477.4	10	38.4	8	301.3	12
Latin America	261.6	5	26.7	5	168.4	7
Other	113.7	2	2.7	1	80.8	3
Total segments	4,975.3	100	460.0	100	2,503.5	100
Corporate	—		(42.6)		178.6	
Total	$4,975.3		$417.4		$2,682.1	

Source: Nabisco Brands Annual Report, 1981.

Segmental information is especially relevant to MNC operations which have grown more complex as corporations have ventured into different lines of business and new countries. Consolidated financial statements have become correspondingly opaque and thus likely to be of declining usefulness without additional information. Even at individual subsidiary level the complexity of MNC operations may become a problem where the legal entity financial statements no longer correspond with the activities of the entity as an economic unit. Segmental information is, therefore, increasingly viewed as essential to a more informed evaluation of MNC financial performance and future prospects, especially risks, by all major user groups. There seems to be a commonality of general interest in segmental information, but as the perspectives of investors and trade unions, for example, are different it also seems likely that there will be differences as to the level of disaggregation considered appropriate and the nature and detail of information content required. While segmental information would seem to be of special interest to MNC user groups it is still in the relatively early stages of development and would be considered an innovation in many countries.

5.3.1 Regulation

The UN (1977) proposals place special emphasis on the disclosure of segmental information by geographical area and line of business. The information to be disclosed would relate to both the MNC as a whole and its individual subsidiaries. Information disclosures include sales, transfers, operating profit, assets, new investment, and employees, together with the disclosure of the accounting policies used for transfers, and exposure to exceptional risks of operating in foreign countries. The proposals are general so as to allow for further development and to avoid a situation where 'segmentation of information could lead to a crossing of the line at which disclosure touched on sensitive data and could thus damage the company from the point of view of competition'.[17] A major problem recognized by the UN concerns the identification of geographical areas and lines of business. These have been defined in fairly broad terms so as to provide sufficient flexibility for segmentation to be adopted to suit the circumstances of each corporation. However, the need for more specific criteria especially relating to geographical areas is also recognized.

The OECD guidelines (1976) are consistent with the UN proposals except that the disclosure of operating profits by line of business and transfers between segments are not included. Only general guidelines are given for the identification of geographical segments. It is suggested that

> while no single method of grouping is appropriate for all enterprises or for all purposes, the factors to be considered by an enterprise would include the significance of operations carried out in individual countries or areas as well as the effects on its competitiveness, geographic proximity, economic affinity, similarities in business environments and the nature, scale and degree of interrelationship of the enterprise's operations in the various countries.[18]

On the other hand, International Accounting Standard No. 14 (IAS 14) entitled 'Reporting Financial Information by Segment', issued in 1981, offers no guidelines at all for the identification of segments, requiring only disclosure of the activities and composition of each business and geographical segment identified by management. In contrast to the UN and OECD, there are no recommendations to disclose new investment or employees on a segmental basis.

At the EEC level, both the *Fourth Directive* (1978) on annual accounts and the *Seventh Directive* (1983) on consolidated accounts are relatively modest. Only sales information by line of business and geographical area is to be disclosed. Again, little guidance is given regarding the identification of segments apart from the need to take account of how the corporation is organized.

These developments and proposals at the international level are far in advance of regulation, at least in terms of comprehensiveness, in most countries excepting the USA and Canada.[19] Apart from these countries, only in the UK, the Netherlands, Spain, Ireland, Japan, Sweden, Argentina, India, Pakistan, and South Africa are there any legal or mandatory professional/stock exchange requirements.[20]

These requirements are mostly restricted to line of business segmentation. However, geographical disclosures are also required in the UK, the Netherlands, and Sweden. The development of these requirements/proposals can, of course, be explained to some extent by the significant presence of MNCs based in these countries. However, a major problem with many of these regulations is that they tend to be so loosely framed as to permit a lack of, or possibly misleading, disclosure.

As already mentioned, by far the most comprehensive requirements at national level are those of the USA, closely followed by Canada, but even here considerable flexibility in the identification of segments is permitted, despite the application of quantitative criteria to determine the segments to be disclosed. Statement of Financial Accounting Standards No. 14 issued by the FASB in 1976 employs a 10 per cent criterion to determine reportable segments in the case of both line of business and geographical segments. But the prior identification of these segments is left flexible, with the consequence that segments may be inadvertently or consciously misidentified or aggregated to an extent that little useful information may be revealed. Thus a fundamental problem concerns the development of effective criteria for identifying segments.

The nature and detail of the information to be disclosed is another significant issue. At national level, everything proposed by the UN and OECD apart from analyses of new investment and employee numbers is already required in the USA by FASB 14. In contrast, in the EEC, where a more cautious approach to information disclosure is evident, only sales data will be required to be disclosed in the 10 member countries.

5.3.2 Reporting practices

Just as regulation varies from the comprehensive to the non-existent so does the extent of disclosure vary in practice. However, many MNCs disclose segmental information in countries where there is no compulsion to do so, e.g. in France, Australia, and Switzerland. The *Financial Times World Survey* (1980) of the 200 largest industrial corporations revealed, as might be expected, that the most comprehensive disclosures were provided by USA corporations.[21] Apart from the USA, examples of comprehensive disclosures were found in France, e.g. Rhône-Poulenc, Saint-Gobain; in the UK, e.g. BAT Industries, British Petroleum, and Rio Tinto Zinc, and also the UK–Netherlands corporations, Royal Dutch/Shell and Unilever; in Canada, e.g. Northern Telecom and Seagrams; in the Netherlands, e.g. Philips, and in Hong Kong, e.g. Hong Kong Land.

Looking at the overall extent of disclosure, however, a different pattern emerges. In respect to line of business segments, only 70 per cent of consolidating corporations (or 60 per cent of all corporations surveyed) disclosed sales and 64 per cent (51 per cent) disclosed profit results (variously defined). Geographical segment disclosures were even less in evidence. Only 57 per cent of consolidating corporations (or 49 per cent of all corporations surveyed) disclosed sales and 41 per cent (35 per cent) disclosed profits. Countries with apparently very low levels of disclosure overall include Belgium, Brazil, West Germany, Italy, and Japan. Evidently, Australia and South Africa were especially weak in the area of geographical disclosures.

While regulation in the USA is undoubtedly effective in securing a greater extent of quantitative disclosure than in other countries including the UK, which in turn exhibits a greater extent of disclosure than in the continental EEC countries, there are reasons to believe that the quality of disclosure is defective mainly on the grounds of lack of interpretability of the segments disclosed.[22] Regulation, in the USA may, therefore, be achieving little more in terms of usefulness than the relatively limited and more flexible approach prevailing in countries such as the UK. One problem concerns the diversity of segments identified by firms operating in the same industry. The major problem, however, is that USA corporations are disclosing, in general, information about relatively few segments.[23] This indicates a fairly high level of aggregation which is especially the case for geographic segments where continents are sometimes combined to form multi-continental segments. Exxon, for example, reported on OECD and non-OECD countries. Coca Cola reported only on foreign operations as a whole, and IBM reported on Europe/Middle East/Africa and America/Far East as its geographical segments. In the UK, while nearly twice the number of segments are often disclosed, the basis of reporting is usually by continent which still provides only limited insight into risk/return differences significant to an evaluation of the business strategy and future prospects of MNCs.

5.3.3 Problems and prospects

Despite the growing body of requirements and proposals relating to segmental information, especially at the international level of the UN, OECD, and IASC, this is an innovation in information disclosure which has yet to be fully developed. Few countries have regulations governing segmental information, but to the extent that they exist they have tended to be framed very broadly and enacted relatively recently. The major exception in terms of comprehensiveness is the USA, now closely followed by Canada, but even here geographic disclosures were required for the first time by FASB 14 only in 1976. International Accounting Standard No. 14 was also only recently approved and became effective in 1983.

The lack of disclosure requirements in many countries has not, however, prevented a number of MNCs from providing segmental information. Nevertheless, taken overall, the extent of disclosure at present suggests that there is scope for further innovation and development in what is likely to be an area of growing significance to MNC user groups.

Experience in the USA and UK indicates that a major problem

of regulation in practice is that many corporations are reluctant to disaggregate to any great extent, usually on the grounds of cost or competitive disadvantage, and that disclosures have tended to be of limited usefulness. Hence the need to develop effective criteria for the identification of both line of business and geographical segments. There are many difficulties to be resolved in this respect, especially those relating to the issue of competitive disadvantage. Materiality criteria also need to be developed to determine when a segment should be reported. Preferably, this should be relevant to an assessment of risk and return differences as opposed to the somewhat arbitrary 10 per cent significant criterion used in the USA. Further problems concern deciding on the information content to be disclosed, the measurement of profit results by segment which involves the special difficulties of transfer pricing and overhead cost allocation, and the form of presentation. On the question of presentation, the possibility of developing a matrix approach combining both line of business and geographical analyses could also be explored as these are interdependent aspects of MNC operations. The Bowater (UK) and Swedish Match presentations in Exhibits 5D and 5E indicate the potential here.

It is also interesting to note that the development of segmental reporting has been limited to the disclosure and presentation of analyses of summary information such as sales, income or earnings, assets, new investment, and so on. The presentation of financial statements in full, disaggregated by country, for example, as suggested by the UN in the context of sub-group consolidations is a possibility that has received little attention. Yet such a form of reporting may have the potential to meet more particularly the concerns of governments and trade unions who not only wish to evaluate the MNC as a whole and the contribution of its segments to overall risks and returns, but also require more comprehensive information at country level than can be given either by the financial statements of individual subsidiaries (or legal entities) or by the content of segmental information currently disclosed in practice.

5.4 TRANSFER PRICING AND RELATED PARTY TRANSACTIONS

The disclosure of information about transfer pricing and other transactions between related parties or corporations in the MNC group is an issue of prime concern to governments and trade unions.[24] There is a growing awareness of the potential impact of such transactions on

Exhibit 5D. Swedish Match

Corporate Sales, 1981
Amounts in SEK m.

Sales per market	Tarkett	Match	Åkerlund & Rausing	Doors	Kitchens	Other activities	Total	Total corporate exports from resp. country
SWEDEN	**460**	**46**	**463**	**306**	**396**	**419**	**2,090**	**1,181**
EEC								
Belgium	4	32	5	1		78	120	56
Denmark	14	35	77	51	9	10	196	7
France	25	378	13		10	239	665	100
Italy	5	20	2			24	51	
Netherlands	10	53	23			29	115	22
Great Britain	25	65	55	35	7	177	364	12
West Germany	46	120	189	70		662	1,087	468
Other EEC countries	4	2	1			1	8	
TOTAL, EEC	**133**	**705**	**365**	**157**	**26**	**1,220**	**2,606**	**665**
REST OF EUROPE								
Finland	79	4	11	64	1	4	163	25
Norway	137	25	48	167	86	114	577	24
Portugal	1	22				61	84	11
Switzerland	6	44	60	4	1	13	128	22
Austria	29	11	15			7	62	4
East Germany						30	30	
Other countries	4	33	11	2	1	79	130	13
TOTAL, REST OF EUROPE	**256**	**139**	**145**	**237**	**89**	**308**	**1,174**	**99**
OTHER COUNTRIES								
Morocco		25					25	
Rest of Africa	1	73	6			7	87	
Argentina		87				8	95	
Chile	7	67			2	6	82	7
Dominican Republic		12	74				86	1
United States	167	185	3		6	61	422	67
Rest of Americas	17	113	1			50	181	2
Philippines		82	35			4	121	27
Rest of Asia	5	102	7	1	8	64	187	
Australia, Oceania	14	3	2			2	21	
TOTAL, OTHER COUNTRIES	**211**	**749**	**128**	**1**	**16**	**202**	**1,307**	**104**
TOTAL	**1,060**	**1,639**	**1,101**	**701**	**527**	**2,149**	**7,177**[1]	**2,049**[2]
Less internal sales	21		12	23	10	94	160	616
TOTAL	**1,039**	**1,639**	**1,089**	**678**	**517**	**2,055**	**7,017**	**1,433**

[1] Includes sales between but not within groups.
[2] Includes exports of products manufactured in the respective countries, including total internal export sales.
Source: Swedish Match Annual Report, 1981.

Exhibit 5E. Bowater (UK)
Analysis of sales and trading profit

		Total 1981 1980	United Kingdom	North America	Europe	Australia and Far East
		£ million				
Sales	Paper and pulp	**594**	**164**	**409**	**12**	**9**
		441	127	302	12	—
	Packaging and other paper conversion	**199**	**187**	**12**		
		197	194	3		
	Tissue products	**230**	**155**	**19**		**56**
		192	141	12		39
	Other manufacturing	**130**	**38**	**8**	**50**	**34**
		106	41	5	53	7
	Merchanting, freight, and other services	**275**	**107**	**4**	**114**	**50**
		184	69	4	97	14
	Discontinued businesses	**300**	**138**	**69**	**15**	**78**
		640	328	74	67	171
		1,728	**789**	**521**	**191**	**227**
		1,760	900	400	229	231
Trading profit	Paper and pulp	**106.4**	**(0.7)**	**105.4**	**0.8**	**0.9**
		80.8	(1.8)	81.5	1.0	0.1
	Packaging and other paper conversion	**7.9**	**8.6**	**(0.5)**	**(0.2)**	
		12.2	12.4	(0.2)	—	
	Tissue products	**22.8**	**15.0**	**0.7**		**7.1**
		19.3	15.5	—		3.8
	Other manufacturing	**—**	**(4.2)**	**(0.3)**	**1.8**	**2.7**
		2.4	(2.1)	(0.3)	2.8	2.0
	Merchanting, freight, and other services	**7.3**	**0.6**	**—**	**3.0**	**3.7**
		4.1	0.8	(0.1)	2.8	0.6
	Discontinued businesses	**(5.0)**	**(4.2)**	**—**	**(1.1)**	**0.3**
		(10.2)	(11.8)	0.2	0.5	0.9
		139.4	**15.1**	**105.3**	**4.3**	**14.7**
		108.6	13.0	81.1	7.1	7.4

Commodity trading companies raise finance for specific contracts and regard the interest arising as direct expense; accordingly their trading profits are stated after interest of £5.4 million (1980: £9.2 million).

The above analysis includes the attributable results (but not sales) of associated companies.

Source: Bowater Annual Report, 1981.

national interests. Information relevant to an assessment of the degree to which MNC operations may have been affected by related party transactions is thus of considerable interest. However, it is an area of disclosure that is not well developed. All related party transactions are, of course, eliminated in the process of preparing world-wide consolidated finincial statements. Hence, this issue must be considered in the context of financial information relating to segments or individual corporations comprising total MNC operations. It is at this level, or through the disclosure of supplementary information, that developments will take place if the extent and impact of internal flows of funds, resources, and services are to be reported. Much of the detailed information that will be necessary in this context may be considered confidential, and as such it seems likely that it may often be more appropriate to provide it in special reports directly to the specific user group concerned, as opposed to the publicly available general-purpose corporate report. Depending on the context, such special reports could also be made available for the use of other interested parties.

5.4.1 Regulation

The UN, in its 1977 proposals, recognized that in many areas, including related party transactions, the detailed needs of trade unions and especially governments would be best served by special reports often confidential in nature. Areas distinguished as more appropriate for special reporting as opposed to general-purpose reporting included information relevant to the balance of payments, development planning, tax laws, employment policy, collective bargaining, future prospects, environmental impact, and corrupt and doubtful payments. While information of a general nature may be disclosed in a general-purpose report this would in most cases require to be supplemented by more detailed information disclosed in special reports.

As regards transfer pricing, the UN Group of Experts commented that it felt that 'while the description of the policies followed in such arrangements fell within the category of general purpose reporting, actual transfer prices of products or parts fell into the special purpose category'.[25]

The UN proposals recommended disclosures concerned with transfer pricing and related party transactions, most importantly, in the context of segmental information both for the MNC as a whole and its individual subsidiary corporations. For the MNC as a whole, the amounts of transfers between geographical areas and lines of business would be disclosed, including the accounting basis or policy used. At the level of the individual corporation, transfers between lines of business would also be disclosed together with the policy used. There would be in addition a general requirement at all levels to dislcose the accounting policies used for transactions between corporations within the MNC group as well as with associated corporations. Also relevant here are the proposals to disclose information about the members of a group. The names of all individual corporations would need to be given, unless voluminous, in which case only the principal corporations would need to be listed. The ownership percentage and the country of location would also be required. Similar disclosures are suggested for associated corporations.

At the individual corporation level, balance sheet and income statement disclosures are recommended. Investments in group and associated corporations would be disclosed together with the amounts of inter-corporation long-term receivables, current receivables, loans, and current payables. In the income or profit and loss statement, related party transactions would be disclosed for revenue and expense items either in the statement itself or in the notes. A description of the transactions would also be given when they are deemed significant.

The provisions of the OECD guidelines (1976) are, by way of contrast, minimal. It is stated only that disclosure should be made of 'the policies followed in respect of intra-group pricing'. While segmental disclosures are recommended the amounts of transfers between segments are not. Additionally, information about the names, locations, and percentage ownership of the MNC's principal subsidiary corporations should be disclosed.

At the EEC level, the *Fourth Directive* (1978) and *Seventh Directive* (1983), while requiring segmental information, albeit more limited in content, similarly do not require transfers between segments to be disclosed. Nor do they require the disclosure of the transfer pricing policy used. There are, however, requirements similar to the UN proposals as regards balance sheet and income statement items but more precisely specified, e.g. interest payable and receivable. Information about associated corporations is also required.

The IASC in contrast, has yet to issue a standard concerning related party transactions, though an exposure draft on the subject has now been published (March 1983) which proposes disclosure of the parties concerned, the amounts and the pricing policies followed. However, International Accounting Standard No. 5 (IAS 5) on 'Information to be Disclosed in Financial Statements', issued by the IASC in 1976, requires significant related party transactions to be disclosed in the income statement. More importantly, IAS 14 (1981) on segmental information requires the disclosure of revenue transfers between segments including the transfer pricing policy used.

At national level, legal or professional requirements in this area are somewhat sparse, especially as regards disclosure of the amounts of transfers and the accounting policies used.[26] However, in the USA and Canada, for example, disclosures of these items are required in the context of requirements governing segmental reporting. Information about foreign subsidiary and associated corporations is also required, as it is in a number of other countries including the UK, France, and West Germany. Balance sheet information about receivables, payables, and loans with related parties is much more widespread, and in fact is a legal requirement in a large number of countries including Australia, Brazil, Canada, West Germany, India, Italy, the Philippines, the UK, and USA.[27]

5.4.2 Reporting practices

Assessments of disclosure practices in this area are relatively few but there is no doubt that balance sheet disclosures of receivables, payables, and loans to related parties are widely required and disclosed with the exception of countries such as Greece, Spain, Morocco, Ecuador, and to some extent Switzerland.[28]

Disclosure of the names, percentage ownership, and location of subsidiary and associated corporations is, however, not so widespread. The *Financial Times World Survey* (1980) revealed that 82 and 74 per cent of the 200 largest industrial corporations disclosed the names and percentage ownership of significant subsidiaries and associates respectively. Apparently many corporations do not provide useful information in this respect, especially corporations based in Japan and, surprisingly, Canada.[29]

When it comes to information about transfer pricing policies and amounts of transfers between segments or subsidiaries, disclosure in practice apparently becomes almost minimal apart from the USA, Canada, and to a lesser extent the UK. A recent comparative USA–UK study showed that only 52 per cent of US corporations disclosed inter-segment transfers by geographical area, despite FASB 14 requirements, compared with a mere 2 per cent of UK corporations disclosing on a voluntary basis.[30] However, a further 16 per cent of UK corporations disclosed the total amount of transfers and 16 per cent disclosed their transfer pricing policy albeit in general terms.

5.4.3 Problems and prospects

Information disclosures in respect to transfer pricing and related party transactions pose many problems, but the crucial issue concerns the extent to which such obviously sensitive information should be disclosed in general-purpose corporate reports as opposed to more detailed special reports, publicly available or confidential, designed specifically for the user groups concerned whether they be governments or trade unions. While there is scope for a certain amount of information of wider interest to be disclosed in general-purpose reports, e.g. transfer pricing policy, amounts of transfers, inter-corporation indebtedness and financial flows, ownership of subsidiaries and associates, incidence of foreign taxation, and so on, it is evident that for many purposes such information will not be sufficiently detailed. More detailed information, much of it confidential from a competitive standpoint, seems likely to be dealt with more appropriately in the context of special reports. One possibility is to consider providing such information in the context of a special 'country' report by MNCs.

Existing regulation and practice in this area is not well developed and further research is necessary regarding the type of information that is likely to be relevant and the costs and benefits involved. Information about the extent of inter-segment transfers may be useful to assess the dependency of segments on internal trade and the potential for transfer price manipulation. But a general statement about transfer pricing policy is perhaps not very helpful without further information unless it is expected that the requirement to make such a statement is likely to influence MNC policy towards more socially responsible behaviour.

5.5 INCOME AND ASSET MEASUREMENT: ACCOUNTING FOR INFLATION

Inflation is a world-wide phenomenon and there has been increasing concern in countries most affected to adopt accounting systems which will remedy the defects of historical cost accounting by revealing the impact of inflation on income and assets. Under inflationary conditions, historical cost profits tend to be overstated, as conventional accounting systems do not incorporate the impact of changes in prices on costs. Conversely, assets tend to be understated as they are usually not updated to reflect current values. The result is likely to be very mislead-

ing for all concerned. The situation is made even more confusing by
the fact that historical cost accounting is applied in different ways in
different countries according to the influence of users and corporation
financiers. Continental European countries, such as France and West
Germany, tend to adopt a much more conservative approach to profit
measurement as a result of banker/lender emphasis, compared to a
relatively less conservative or more optimistic approach in countries
such as the USA and UK with well-developed stock markets and hence
an investor orientation.[31]

The type of accounting measurement system used and its interpretation is clearly an essential issue to all user groups in that the measurement of income or profits is relevant to a wide range of concerns
including share prices, business stability, wages, job security, and economic growth. In the context of the MNC, this concern is heightened
by the existence of user groups with constituencies located in different
countries with different traditions of accounting measurement.

While there may be some recognition of the necessity to introduce a
system of 'inflation accounting', except in countries such as West
Germany where it is considered likely to institutionalize inflation, the
term covers a variety of possible methods. The major alternative
approaches are 'general purchasing power accounting' and 'current
value accounting'.[32]

General purchasing power accounting includes all systems designed
to maintain the real purchasing power of capital or shareholders' equity
in the corporation by accounting for changes in the *general* level of
prices, i.e. the general purchasing power of money. This is the strict
meaning of the term 'inflation', though the term 'inflation accounting'
is generally used in a very broad sense. Variations on the term 'general
purchasing power accounting' include 'constant dollar accounting' or
'general price level accounting' in the USA and 'current purchasing
power accounting' (CPP) in the UK.

Current value accounting on the other hand, includes all systems
designed to account for current values or changes in specific prices.
These include 'current cost accounting' and 'replacement value accounting' which aim to maintain the physical capital, productive capacity, or
operating assets of the corporation; and 'selling price accounting' which
aims to maintain shareholders' equity but in terms of selling prices of
the corporation's net assets.

While there is a wide range of alternatives proposed within each of
these broad classifications, together with systems which combine
elements of both, the use of 'inflation accounting' systems in practice
is not well developed.

5.5.1 Regulation

The UN (1977) proposals incorporated a disclosure approach to the 'inflation accounting' issue. It was recommended only that the measurement policies used should be disclosed, with reliance placed on the IASC for future developments in this area. In formulating this recommendation there was, however, some discussion of the 'replacement value accounting' system with some consideration of the arguments both for and against such a system as follows:

> Concern was voiced that the method of replacement value, open as it was to subjective judgement, could, for example, place labour at a disadvantage in negotiations. On the other hand, it was also pointed out that replacement value might give a more realistic view of financial position and results of operations. The Group noted that the problem of inflation accounting was still being discussed in many countries and that, so far, no consensus had emerged as to the appropriate method to follow. However, the Group emphasized that the policy decided should be fair to all concerned.[33]

While the OECD guidelines (1976) make no mention of inflation accounting, the EEC *Fourth Directive* (1978) is permissive in that member countries may authorize (Article 33) alternatives to historical cost accounting including 'replacement value accounting', 'general purchasing power accounting', or other methods including periodic revaluations to reflect changes in prices. If an alternative method is adopted then historical cost information must also be given.

Contrary to the reliance placed by the UN on the IASC for standardizing developments in inflation accounting, International Accounting Standard No. 6 (IAS 6), issued in 1977, states only that if an inflation accounting system has been adopted by a corporation then this should be disclosed. IAS 15 issued in November 1981 and entitled 'Information Reflecting the Effect of Changing Prices' goes further in stating that corporations should disclose information showing the impact of inflation on earnings but without specifying any particular method to be used.

At national level, substantial experience of inflation accounting has been gained in South America where there are requirements most notably in Brazil and Argentina.[34] In Brazil, legal requirements to adjust accounts to a general purchasing power basis were introduced in 1964; but in 1976 a new Corporation Law required all corporations to prepare their *primary* financial statements on this basis. In Argentina, on the other hand, professional standards issued in 1972 recommended the presentation of supplementary general purchasing power financial statements. The very high rates of inflation experienced by South

American countries would appear to explain the relatively rapid adoption of inflation accounting systems compared to other countries. In the UK, the accounting profession introduced a requirement (SSAP 16) in 1980, after a long period of debate, to publish 'current cost accounting' financial statements either as supplementary statements or as the main accounts with the proviso that historical cost accounts must also be provided. The current cost accounting system provides for four adjustments—depreciation, cost of sales, monetary working capital, and gearing.[35] The gearing adjustment which abates the other operating adjustments by the proportion of debt financing, is a matter of some controversy in that it incorporates an element of the general purchasing power approach by recognizing that there is a gain through holding net monetary liabilities in a period of inflation. In continental Europe, there has been less enthusiasm to introduce inflation accounting despite recommendations on the subject, for example, in France and West Germany. In these countries, there have nevertheless been instances of periodic revaluations being required or permitted, and in France the most recent experience of this was in 1977 and 1978 when revaluations were required for all long-term or fixed assets. While the Netherlands is renowned for the development of replacement value accounting there is no compulsion to use the system nor even professional standards on the subject.

In the USA, regulation has developed only recently, despite a long history of enquiry into the subject, with a legal requirement imposed by the Securities and Exchange Commission (SEC) in 1976 to disclose replacement cost information relating to depreciation, cost of sales, fixed assets, and stocks. Subsequently, in 1979, the FASB issued Financial Accounting Standard No. 33 requiring supplementary disclosures on both a general purchasing power and a current cost basis.[36] Profit figures are required to be adjusted on both bases. In addition, the current cost of stocks and plant and equipment must be disclosed together with increases or decreases in current costs adjusted for general purchasing power changes, i.e. net of inflation. A further item of disclosure required is the purchasing power gain or loss on net monetary items. The noteworthy feature of this standard is its experimental nature in making available an array of information prepared using different inflation accounting systems.

In Australia and New Zealand, developments have been much more tentative than in the UK and USA. The accounting professions in both countries have issued recommendations which are based essentially on the current cost accounting system now required in the UK but with some local variations, especially as regards the treatment of monetary items. South Africa is apparently the only other country to have produced a guideline on the issue with recommendations similar to the UK system. Discussion is, of course, continuing in a number of other countries including Japan and Mexico, but there would appear to be little in the form of any regulation or recommendation as yet.

Taken overall, regulatory developments world-wide have been both few and relatively recent. The major alternative inflation accounting systems of general purchasing power accounting and current value accounting are both very much in evidence, though 'current cost accounting' appears to be the more popular system in a number of Anglo-Saxon countries. A period of further experimentation seems likely before the value of the various different alternatives can be assessed. In the meantime, MNCs will have the problem of coping with different requirements in different jurisdictions.

5.5.2 Reporting practices

The practice of reporting the impact of changing prices on profits and assets is not at all widespread apart from the USA, Canada, the Netherlands, Sweden, and the UK. The *Financial Times World Survey* (1980) revealed that 44 per cent of the 200 largest industrial corporations provide inflation accounting information either in the main accounts or, more commonly, in the form of supplementary data.[37] Of the 76 corporations providing disclosures, only three reported on a general purchasing power basis. The majority reported on a current cost or replacement cost basis. However, only three corporations provided such accounts as the main accounts, i.e. Philips and Heineken in the Netherlands and Ciba-Geigy in Switzerland. Of those providing supplementary data, 16 corporations provided current cost data incorporating a gearing or other monetary adjustment. Despite the low overall level of disclosure it is interesting to note that a number of MNCs, besides those already mentioned, voluntarily provided disclosures, including Sony (Japan), Electrolux (Sweden), and Nestlé (Switzerland). Of course, with FAS 33 in the USA and SSAP 16 in the UK, disclosure of supplementary inflation accounting information is now commonplace in respect to large corporations in these countries. Exhibits 5F and 5G provide examples from ITT (USA) and The Distillers Company (UK) respectively.

Exhibit 5F. ITT (USA)

Summary of Effects of Inflation (Unaudited)

Dollars in millions	Historic cost (as reported)	Constant dollar	Current cost
Results for 1980			
Sales and revenues	$23,819	$23,819	$23,819
Cost of sales and services	13,820	14,171	13,901
Depreciation	520	706	914
Other costs and expenses	8,297	8,446	8,395
Minority equity in income	47	23	16
US and foreign income taxes	331	331	331
Income*	$ 804	$ 142	$ 262
Reconciliation of Stockholders' Equity			
December 31, 1979			
Inventories	$ 3,647	$ 3,873	$ 3,709
Plant, property, and equipment, net	5,084	8,082	8,635
Other assets (liabilities) less minority	(3,096)	(3,348)	(3,168)
Stockholders' equity	5,635	8,607	9,176
Changes during 1980			
Income*	804	142	262
Gain on sale of Canadian timber facilities	90	90	90
Dividends declared	(359)	(359)	(359)
Other—including minority effects	104	110	66
Holding gains	—	1,553	948
Constant dollar adjustment	—	(1,553)	—
Purchasing power gain	—	327	—
Total changes	639	310	1,007
December 31, 1980			
Inventories	3,599	3,474	3,697
Plant, property, and equipment, net	5,215	7,905	9,105
Other assets (liabilities) less minority	(2,540)	(2,462)	(2,619)
Stockhoders' equity	$ 6,274	$ 8,917	$10,183

Summary of Effects of Inflation (Unaudited)—continued

Comparative Data Adjusted for Inflation (Average 1980 dollars)	1980	1979	1978	1977	1976
Consumer price index—average for year	246.8	217.5	195.4	181.5	170.5
Sales and revenues—					
As reported	$23,819	$22,056	$19,452	$16,759	$14,925
Constant dollars	23,819	25,027	24,569	22,802	21,604
Income*—					
As reported	804	703	—	—	—
Constant dollars	142	357	—	—	—
Current cost	262	443	—	—	—
Purchasing power gain on net Monetary items	327	374	—	—	—
Unrealized holding gain net of inflation	(492)	(762)	—	—	—
Earnings per common equivalent share*—					
As reported	5.50	4.95	—	—	—
Constant dollars	.96	2.46	—	—	—
Current cost	1.78	3.08	—	—	—
Stockholders' equity—current cost in constant dollars	9,675	9,860	—	—	—
Dividends declared per common share—					
As reported	2.45	2.25	2.05	1.82	1.64
Constant dollars	2.45	2.55	2.59	2.47	2.37
Market price per common share at year-end—					
As quoted	30.00	25.50	27.00	31.75	33.88
Constant dollars	28.65	27.37	32.84	42.11	47.97

* Exclusive of gain on sale of Canadian timber facilities in 1980 and the provision for close-down of Canadian pulp mill in 1979.
Source: ITT Annual Report, 1980.

Exhibit 5G. The Distillers Company (UK)

Group current cost accounts

Accounting policies

The current cost accounts presented on the following pages incorporate the effect of price changes on the operating assets of the business. The operating assets are included at their "value to the business", based generally on replacement cost, instead of the historical cost amounts. Subject to the special features described below, the accounting policies applied are the same as those in the historical cost accounts.

Fixed assets

Land & buildings are valued at open market value, where relevant, and otherwise at depreciated replacement cost. A valuation at September 1981 was prepared by James Barr & Son, Chartered Surveyors, for properties in Scotland and by Fuller Peiser, Chartered Surveyors, for properties elsewhere in the U.K. Updated values at the balance sheet date have been estimated in the light of advice from the valuers. Values for properties overseas are similarly based on professional valuations.

Plant & fittings are restated at depreciated replacement cost, estimated by using data compiled by expert technical staff and appropriate government indices.

Stocks

Stocks are valued at the lower of replacement cost and the estimated amount realisable. Replacement cost for major categories is specifically calculated and for other stocks is estimated using appropriate government indices. For Scotch whisky stocks a theoretical replacement cost is calculated, based on the current cost of carrying out the necessary sequence of production processes including the respective periods of maturation.

Associated company and other investments

The interest in United Glass p.l.c. is valued at the current cost accounting value of the underlying net assets. The share of the current cost loss for the year, incorporating the United Glass profit & loss account adjustments (including gearing), is brought into account.

Listed investments are valued at market value and unlisted investments at the directors' estimated value. Provision is made for the attributable deferred taxation.

Profit & loss account adjustments

The depreciation adjustment represents the amount by which annual depreciation calculated on the replacement cost of the fixed assets exceeds the depreciation charge in the historical cost accounts. Similarly the cost of sales adjustment represents the difference between the replacement cost of the stocks consumed in sales and the historical cost amounts.

The monetary working capital adjustment represents additional capital employed as a result of changes in price, as distinct from changes in volume, of the goods and services used by the business. The main adjustment is calculated by reference to the average level of trading debtors less creditors and movements in the UK general index of retail prices. An additional element relates to stocks of purchased seasonal produce and is calculated by reference to the average level of stocks carried and changes in relevant prices.

The gearing adjustment shows the effect of abating the other profit & loss account adjustments (including the associated company adjustments) in proportion to the extent that the operating assets are financed by borrowing. It is calculated using the ratio of net borrowing to net operating assets, measured over the year.

Current cost reserve

The revaluation surpluses on assets held at 31st March, being the difference between the current cost values attributable to the assets and the corresponding historical cost amounts, are reflected in the current cost reserve. These revaluation surpluses are unrealised.

Also included in the current cost reserve are revaluation surpluses which have been realised in the normal course of trading operations or on disposal of fixed assets or investments. The realised surpluses represent amounts retained as capital employed in order to maintain the operating capability of the business. The monetary working capital adjustment, which represents additional capital employed due to price changes, is similarly added to the current cost reserve.

Translation differences on exchange

All translation differences are taken directly to reserves. The differences other than those relating to long & medium term loans are treated as being equivalent to changes in capital employed as a consequence of price changes and are incorporated into the current cost reserve.

Corresponding amounts

In order to show the effect of general inflation and provide a more realistic basis for comparison, the figures originally reported for the previous year have been updated by a factor which compensates for the estimated change in the value of the £. (The updating factor applied to the 1981 figures is 1.104 based on the general index of retail prices which was 313.4 for March 1982 compared with 284.0 for March 1981.)

Group current cost accounts

year ended 31st March 1982

1981 Amounts as at March 1981 (note 4) £m	Profit & loss account	1982 £m	1981 Amounts updated for change in value of £ £m
1,041.3	**Turnover**	1,083.9	1,149.6
174.7	Trading profit per historical cost accounts	181.6	192.9
(20.3)	Depreciation adjustment	(22.2)	(22.4)
(55.5)	Cost of sales adjustment	(57.5)	(61.3)
(3.4)	Monetary working capital adjustment	(4.8)	(3.8)
95.5	**Current cost operating profit**	97.1	105.4
5.5	Income from investments	5.8	6.1
(7.6)	Share of loss of associated company (note 4)	(7.6)	(8.4)
93.4		95.3	103.1
(5.2)	Interest on net borrowing	(6.1)	(5.7)
88.2	**Current cost profit before taxation**	89.2	97.4
(53.5)	Taxation	(49.0)	(59.1)
0.1	Minority shareholders' interests	0.6	0.1
34.8	Current cost profit after taxation	40.8	38.4
5.8	Gearing adjustment	5.1	6.4
40.6	**Current cost profit attributable to shareholders***	45.9	44.8
(1.7)	Extraordinary items	(0.3)	(1.9)
(39.0)	Dividends	(42.7)	(43.1)
(0.1)	**Current cost surplus (deficit)**	2.9	(0.2)
11.18p	**Earnings per share***	12.64p	12.34p
10.75p	**Dividends per share**	11.75p	11.87p

1981 Amounts as at March 1981 £m	Balance sheet summary	1982 £m	1981 Amounts updated for change in value of £ £m
541.8	Fixed assets (note 3)	572.0	598.1
72.8	Associated company	74.3	80.4
64.3	Other investments	638	71.0
1,322.3	Stocks	1,431.5	1,459.8
109.7	Trading debtors less creditors	117.7	121.1
2,110.9	**Net operating assets**	2,259.3	2,330.4
(105.5)	Long & medium term loans	(105.0)	(116.4)
(14.8)	Bank loans & overdrafts	(11.8)	(16.4)
22.9	Liquid funds & short term deposits	45.6	25.3
(57.7)	Taxation & other non-trading liabilities	(48.4)	(63.7)
(155.1)	**Effective net borrowing**	(119.6)	(171.2)
1,955.8		2,139.7	2,159.2
181.6	Share capital	181.6	181.6
1,311.7	Current cost reserve (note 2)	1,497.4	1,311.7
—	Updating adjustment to shareholders' funds	—	200.4
433.3	Other reserves	428.4	433.3
1,926.6	**Shareholders' funds***	2,107.4	2,127.0
28.1	Proposed dividend	31.8	31.0
1.1	Minority interests	0.5	1.2
1,955.8	**Total shareholders' interests**	2,139.7	2,159.2
£5.30	**Shareholders' funds per share***	£5.80	£5.85

Notes to the current cost accounts

1. **Movements on reserves**	Current cost reserve £m	Other reserves £m	Total reserves £m
Reserves as at 31st March 1981	1,311.7	433.3	1,745.0
Updating adjustment to shareholders' funds	200.4	—	200.4
Reserves at 31st March 1981 updated	1,512.1	433.3	1,945.4
Surplus shown in profit & loss account		2.9	2.9
Less amount credited as gearing adjustment		(5.1)	(5.1)
Effective deficit from profit & loss account		(2.2)	(2.2)
Monetary working capital retention	4.8	—	4.8
Revaluation surpluses arising in year	176.3	—	176.3
Translation differences on exchange	4.6	(2.7)	1.9
	185.7	(4.9)	180.8
Less updating adjustment to shareholders' funds at 31st March 1981	(200.4)	—	(200.4)
Net movement after updating adjustment	(14.7)	(4.9)	(19.6)
Reserves at 31st March 1982	1,497.4	428.4	1,925.8

2. **Analysis of current cost reserve**

1981 £m		1982 £m
	Unrealised revaluation surpluses	
366.1	Fixed assets	374.8
34.0	Associated company	38.6
35.1	Other investments	24.8
560.0	Stocks	649.1
995.2		1,087.3
	Other items (from 1st April 1977)	
311.8	Revaluation surpluses realised	396.0
13.1	Monetary working capital retentions	17.9
(8.4)	Translation differences on exchange	(3.8)
1,311.7		1,497.4

3. Summary of fixed assets

1981 Current cost valuation £m		At 31st March 1982 Historical cost less depreciation £m	Unrealised revaluation surpluses £m	Current cost valuation £m
324.2	Land & buildings	96.4	244.6	341.0
217.6	Plant & fittings	100.8	130.2	231.0
541.8		197.2	374.8	572.0

4. Comparative figures for 1981

This year, in compliance with Statement of Standard Accounting Practice No 1 (Revised), the associated company's gearing adjustment is incorporated in the share of the loss brought into the Group profit & loss account. The 1981 figures in the profit & loss account are restated accordingly.

Source: The Distillers Company Annual Report, 1982.

5.5.3 Problems and prospects

Continuing inflation in many countries suggests that the need for and use of inflation accounting systems is likely to grow within the foreseeable future. However, a wide range of alternative systems are available, including those that can be classified as 'general purchasing power' systems, 'current value systems', or some combination of both. There is as yet no consensus on the most appropriate form of reporting and indeed there seems unlikely to be a universal answer to this question given the number of different perspectives possible. However, there is a trend towards the acceptance of some form of 'current cost accounting', a current value system based on the use of replacement values with the emphasis on maintaining physical capital, i.e. the productive capacity of the corporation. Despite this, there is considerable controversy over many aspects of 'current cost accounting', with special reference to the gearing adjustment and the treatment of gains and losses on monetary items. Other problems include the use of indices, especially the difficulties relating to foreign subsidiaries, and the verification of replacement costs for corporations in industries with rapid technological change. Accordingly, we are likely to see continued experimentation with various types of inflation accounting systems and a growing appreciation of the circumstances under which each alternative may or may not be feasible or useful in measuring profits and assets.

5.6 FOREIGN CURRENCY TRANSLATION

A unique problem of major importance for MNCs in the preparation of consolidated financial statements and segmental information is the translation of the financial statements of foreign subsidiary and associated corporations denominated in foreign currencies.[38] If consolidated financial statements are to be prepared denominated in the same currency, i.e. the currency of the headquarters of the MNC, then the translation of foreign currencies into the home currency is essential. Foreign currency translation is thus a process involving mathematical and accounting adjustments to the financial statements of foreign subsidiary and associated corporations. This should be distinguished from transactions which give rise to money in one currency being exchanged for money in another.

If MNC disclosures in the home currency are to be interpretable then foreign currency translation must be meaningfully carried out, as it is such an essential part of the system of information processing and communication about the MNC group as a whole. At the level of reports about the individual subsidiary corporation or sub-groups at country level, the problem is, of course, largely removed except to the extent that such corporations themselves have foreign assets and liabilities.

The importance of foreign currency translation and the problems surrounding it have been recognized only relatively recently with the growth of MNCs and the increasing volatility of exchange rates. The major problems are involved with how to account for exchange rate changes. Firstly, which rate should be used to translate the financial statements? Secondly, how should any gains and losses, or differences, arising out of the translation be treated? A related problem is whether or not, and if so how, to account for inflation before or after translation?

At present, there is a considerable variety of approaches in evidence and much controversy has been aroused. As regards the exchange rate to be used, the choice is essentially between the historic rate, i.e. the rate applicable when the translation was initially recorded in the accounts, and the current rate, i.e. the market rate applicable to the period for which the financial statements are prepared. A variety of methods have been developed which apply either the historic or current rate to some or all revenues, expenses, assets, and liabilities. The major alternatives are the 'temporal' method and the 'closing rate' method. The temporal method applies the current rate to all items measured in current money terms including long-term liabilities and the historic rate to all items measured in historic terms. The closing rate method, on the other hand, applies the current rate to all items. The effect of this is that all items are thereby exposed to the impact of changes in exchange rates, in contrast to the temporal method where this impact, so far as the financial statements are concerned, is a function of the measurement base used. The fact that items measured at historic cost are translated at historic exchange rates means that changes in exchange rates are effectively ignored by the accounting process. Apart from this, a major problem with the temporal method would seem to be the differential treatment of long-term assets, translated at historic rates, which are often matched by long-term liabilities, but translated at current rates, with apparently misleading effects. Other alternative methods of foreign currency translation include the monetary/non-monetary method, where only monetary items are translated using the current rate, and the current/non-current method, where only current items are translated at the current rate. Accordingly, both of these methods will have differential effects in terms of exchange gains/losses arising.

The controversy over the treatment of any gains and losses arising from exchange rate changes reported by the translation process stems from the question as to whether such gains/losses should be included in earnings/profits, or treated as adjustments only to shareholders' equity. This is complicated by the question of whether and how price changes should be accounted for. Given that there is a relationship between inflation in the home and host country and exchange rates prevailing between them, it would seem that inflation accounting is an integral part of an effective system of foreign currency translation. The use of historic rates may be just as misleading as the use of historic costs and is apparently perpetuated largely by an unwillingness to recognize the impact of price changes on the one hand and by adherence to the accounting conventions of consistency and prudence on the other.

5.6.1 Regulation

At the international level, there has been surprisingly little by way of developments relating to foreign currency translation. The UN (1977) proposals refer only to disclosure of the method of translation used. In contrast, the OECD (1976) guidelines, make no reference at all to this problem. The EEC, however, requires disclosure of the translation method used in both the *Fourth Directive* (1978) and the *Seventh Directive* (1983) on consolidated accounts. Moreover, the International Accounting Standards Committee has recently (July 1983) issued IAS 21 entitled 'Accounting for the effects of changes in Foreign Exchange Rates'. In this, the IASC recommends the use of the closing rate method except where the operations of the foreign subsidiary are an integral part of the operations of the parent, as in the case of a subsidiary operating primarily as a sales office, when the temporal method is used. Any translation gains/losses are not to be included in the profit and loss account but taken to shareholders' equity, except when using the temporal method, though gains and losses relating to long-term liabilities may be deferred rather than included in the calculation of earnings/profits.

At national level, many countries require the translation method used to be disclosed, e.g. Argentina, Australia, Canada, Japan, the Netherlands, the Philippines, South Africa, Sweden, the UK, and the

USA.[39] However, the method to be used is specified in very few countries. In the UK, where the closing rate method is widely used in practice, there is only now an accounting standard on the subject with the recent acceptance of SSAP 20, in April 1983, which formally adopted the closing rate method, though with exceptions similar to IAS 21. A major problem with the development of an international standard was that until recently the USA and UK practice of foreign currency translation were complete opposites. In the USA the temporal method was required by the FASB in FASB 8 (1975) until December 1981, when, following heavy criticism, FASB 52 was issued.[40] While this is very similar to the UK standard with its emphasis on the closing rate approach, there are some differences in detail especially in respect of disclosure where the US standard tends to be more comprehensive.

A major problem which has not yet been dealt with effectively at any level is that to adjust for exchange rate changes without accounting for inflation is never likely to offer more than a partial solution to the problem of providing meaningful consolidated and segmental information. While the use of historic exchange rates may find little justification, the use of current rates is little better without a similar updating of the underlying measurement system to account for changing prices. It may be hoped that experiments in the USA and UK with inflation accounting will lead eventually to the adoption of systems which may be properly and effectively used with current rate systems of foreign currency translation.

Irrespective of method, there is always the problem of how to treat the translation gain or loss arising as a result of exchange rate changes. By definition, only those items translated at current rates will be exposed to such gains/losses. The issue, however, concerns whether or not translation gains/losses should be included in earnings for the year, treated as extraordinary items to be disclosed 'below the line' in the income statement, or to be treated as a deferred item or adjustment to shareholders' equity in the balance sheet. As indicated earlier, in the UK and USA, all gains/losses arising under the closing rate method are to be treated as an adjustment to shareholders' equity and not to be included in the income statement. Gains or losses relating to intra-group transactions and balances of a trading nature are, on the other hand, to be included in earnings. The criterion used here would seem to be that of realization, i.e. if monetary conversion from one currency to another is uncertain and unlikely in the foreseeable future then a balance sheet treatment is appropriate. While this seems a realistic approach it requires considerable discretion in application.

5.6.2 Reporting practices

It is not surprising that the lack of regulation relating to foreign currency translation has given rise to the use of a considerable variety of methods in practice. The *Financial Times World Survey* (1980) of the 200 largest industrial corporations revealed that, of the 172 corporations providing consolidated financial statements, 37 per cent used the closing rate method, 20 per cent used the monetary/non-monetary or temporal methods (they are very similar), and 7 per cent used the current/non-current method. 12 per cent used a combination of methods, 1 per cent used historic rates only and the rest provided no information (these included five German corporations not providing world-wide consolidations).[41] An example from Royal Dutch/Shell of the application of the closing rate method *vis-à-vis* the temporal method is given in Exhibit 5H.

It is also apparent that the current rate method tends to be used most frequently in countries such as Australia, Denmark, France, Greece, Hong Kong, India, Japan, Kenya, the Netherlands, Singapore, Switzerland, and Uruguay as well as the UK and now the USA.[42] The temporal method, on the other hand, is used widely in countries such as Austria, Bermuda, Canada, Chile, Jamaica, Peru, and Venezuela. Other methods such as the monetary/non-monetary methods are widely used in the Bahamas, Guatemala, Korea, the Philippines, Sweden, and Taiwan whereas the current/non-current method is widely used in West Germany, New Zealand, Pakistan, and South Africa. This variety of translation methods is matched by a range of treatments of translation differences of gains and losses, e.g. all gains and losses to be included in earnings; all gains and losses to be included in shareholders' equity; or all losses to be recognized in earnings but gains to be deferred and included in balance sheet reserves.

5.6.3 Problems and prospects

Foreign currency translation poses many problems but is of fundamental importance in the context of consolidated and segmental information about MNC operations. Any flaws in the process of translation will have widespread repercussions in all aspects of information disclosure. Moreover, the usefulness of translation is dependent on the foreign subsidiary financial statements providing meaningful measurements in terms of accounting for changing prices under inflationary conditions.

Exhibit 5H. Royal Dutch/Shell Group of Companies

Foreign currency translation

Since 1975 the financial statements of the Royal Dutch/Shell Group of Companies have complied with the US Financial Accounting Standards Board standard on foreign currency translation (FAS 8). The basis of foreign currency translation and conversion was such that the various companies comprising the Group were treated as if all their transactions were conducted in sterling.

A new standard has recently been introduced, FAS 52, which recognizes the reality that Group companies operate in their own currencies. Consequently, the only translation differences which will influence net income of the Group are those which affect the local currency cash flows when these companies transact business in a currency other than their own. Upon consolidation, all assets and liabilities of non-sterling companies are translated to sterling at the rate of exchange applying on the date of the balance sheet, and any translation differences will be taken directly to a reserve account in the balance sheet. The income accounts of Group companies will be translated at average rates of exchange.

This current rate method of translation ensures that the sterling net income can be directly related to the underlying results of operating companies.

The charge to net income for the depreciation in sterling is different from the charge under FAS 8. This, together with the absence of translation gains and losses (both on monetary items and on stocks sold), which will be taken directly to reserves, forms the main differences, as far as net income is concerned, between the two bases.

The Group will adopt the new standard for reporting purposes from the first quarter of 1982. In the meantime, there is shown (left) a comparison of the existing approach with the results estimated on a current rate basis, which it is believed approximate those to be issued when FAS 52 is adopted by the Group.

| | 1981 | | | | | 1980 | | | | |
| | Quarters | | | | Total | Quarters | | | | Total |
	1st	2nd	3rd	4th	£ million	1st	2nd	3rd	4th	£ million
Reported net income (FAS 8 basis)	332	164	424	877	1,797	718	680	391	436	2,225
Reported net income less FAS 8 effects*	541	486	621	566	2,214	788	590	384	493	2,255
Estimated net income —current rate basis	550	460	520	460	1,990	840	580	420	520	2,360

* Net currency translation and conversion gains/losses on inventories sold and on monetary items.

Source: Royal Dutch/Shell Annual Report, 1981.

While there is a wide variety of methods practised world-wide, recent developments in the USA and UK herald a movement towards more up-to-date and useful information in the form of the closing rate method. This problem now seems to be receiving the attention it deserves though much experimentation and further research is warranted. However, in countries such as France, West Germany,

Sweden, Switzerland, and Japan, foreign currency translation remains a relatively neglected issue. At the international level, the IASC and international intergovernmental organizations such as the UN, OECD, and EEC can it seems only watch and wait upon developments by regulatory bodies at national level or by the MNCs themselves. In the meantime, there would appear to be strong arguments for requiring corporations to provide full disclosure of the methods used and the treatment of gains and losses arising from the translation of foreign currency financial statements.

5.7 NON-FINANCIAL (SOCIAL) REPORTING

The term 'non-financial reporting' is used here to refer to information disclosed in corporate reports which is additional to the conventional financial statements, viz. income statement, balance sheet, and funds statement. Additional financial information has already been discussed to some extent under the headings of segmental information, and transfer pricing and related party transactions. The focus here is on information, some of which may be financial in nature, which is likely to be of interest to user groups concerned with the social and economic impact of the MNC as well as its financial situation and performance. This type of reporting is often referred to as 'social reporting' with a number of user groups in mind, including governmental organizations, at national, regional, and international level; employees and trade unions; and other groups such as consumer organizations.[43] Under this broad banner, we can find both general-purpose reports and special reports for specific groups, e.g. 'employee reports' which are increasingly provided in many European countries. The term 'social reporting' is not at all well defined, however, and alternatives such as 'societal reporting' are sometimes used to distinguish reporting to society as a whole from reporting on social matters to employees of the corporation.

As our concern is to review all kinds of additional information which may be of interest to a wide range of user groups, we will use the term 'non-financial reporting' to include all areas of disclosure not covered by the financial statements. The emphasis of the discussion will be on the disclosure of information in general-purpose corporate reports and will include information relating to employment conditions and prospects, corporate organization, production, investment plans, value added reports, and statements about future prospects.

While this is an area of information disclosure which is of growing interest and concern it is not well developed in terms of identifying the information needs of the user groups involved, the means by which social costs and benefits will be measured and disclosed, and the criteria by which MNCs are to be held accountable for their 'social' and/or 'societal' performance.

5.7.1 Regulation

The UN (1977) proposals place special emphasis on 'the need to extend the scope of required disclosures beyond purely financial reporting' (p. 28). The issue of separate 'social' reports was favoured, but in view of the need for further work in this area it was recommended that for the time being non-financial information should be included as an integral part of the general-purpose corporate report. Areas identified for disclosure were labour and employment, production, investment programmes, organizational structure, and environmental measures. While the emphasis of the proposals is on non-financial information it was recognized that some financial information would also need to be given, e.g. employment costs, and the costs of environmental measures. It was also recognized that the aggregation of some kinds of non-financial information would not be useful and hence the disclosure requirements at group level were made less extensive than those at individual subsidiary level. Where a substantial amount of detailed information was to be disclosed it was considered that MNCs could issue supplements or special reports, e.g. employee reports, to be provided either on a confidential or publicly available basis as appropriate.

As regards the detailed items to be disclosed under each category, the UN proposals suggest that the MNC as a whole should provide the following information. Firstly, labour and employment information, including a description of labour relations policy and the number of employees both in total and segmented by geographical area and line of business. At the individual subsidiary level, the information would be more detailed, including, for example, number of women employees, labour turnover, accident rates, and employee costs (including social expenditures and costs of training). Secondly, production information, including the physical output by lines of business and a description of significant new products and processes. At the individual subsidiary level, this would be extended to include information about the source of raw materials and average annual capacity utilization. Thirdly, information about investment programmes, including descriptions of announced new capital expenditure, main projects including their impact on employment, and announced mergers and take-overs including their cost and impact on employment. Fourthly, information about organizational structure, including a description of the management structure, the names of directors, and the number of shareholders including the names of principal shareholders. Finally, a description of major environmental measures carried out would be disclosed, together with the costs involved.

This is a substantial list of requirements, but any suggestion that management should provide a general statement of future prospects is omitted.[44] Nor is there any mention of 'value added' statements which adopt a different perspective to income by disclosing the wealth created by all participants in the corporation, apart from suppliers, rather than emphasizing that proportion accruing to shareholders.[45] Such statements are increasingly disclosed in Europe, especially in the context of 'social' or 'employee' reports.

The UN recognized, however, that non-financial reporting was a relatively new area requiring further research and stated that their list represented but a first step towards the eventual development of 'comprehensive principles and standards for non-financial reporting'.

In contrast to the UN proposals, the OECD (1976) guidelines are very slender. The OECD recommends only that the average number of employees in each geographical area should be disclosed. The EEC *Fourth Directive* (1978) and *Seventh Directive* (1983) are only a little more substantial in scope. They require that the average number of employees, categorized by function, be disclosed together with employment costs, showing social security costs and pensions separately. As regards other areas covered by the UN, the EEC directives are flexible in that there are general requirements for the corporate report to 'include at least a fair review of the development of the company's business' and its 'likely future development'. However, no guidelines are given as to content and hence disclosure will be subject to managerial discretion.

In contrast, the proposed EEC directive on employee information and consultation arising out of the Vredeling proposals is considerably more extensive in scope.[46] This would require the regular provision of information, at subsidiary level, about the activities of the MNC group as a whole as well as the subsidiary. Such reports would include information relating to corporate organization structure; employment; the economic and financial situation; probable developments in production, sales, and employment; production and investment programmes; rationalization plans; and plans for new working methods or other methods that could have 'a substantial effect' on employee interests. While some of the financial information would seem to be covered already by the requirements of the *Fourth Directive* and *Seventh Directive*, the emphasis of the proposal is on providing employees with more up-to-date and future-orientated information of a social as well as financial nature. It is perhaps the emphasis on future-orientated information which has in particular generated the current considerable debate and controversy, despite the rather general nature of the proposals and the fact that many MNCs already provide some of this information, usually only qualitative in nature, in their annual reports. Apparently the major problems from the perspective of MNCs, as in other areas of information disclosure, include the costs of providing such reports and the competitive disadvantage that may arise if sensitive information were to become publicly available.

At the international professional level, the IASC has not yet considered questions relating to non-financial or social reporting. International trade union organizations (ITUCs), on the other hand, have indicated that MNCs should disclose information about the general economic development of the MNC; its factors of production; the volume of investment, past and future, and its effect on employment; wages and salary structures and the distribution of income to interest groups.[47] This latter item suggests the possibility of providing a value added statement though this is not explicitly mentioned. An interesting additional requirement in the context of information about financing is the provision of cash-flow statements, both past and future, on a receipts and payments basis. In support of this it is stated that 'in times of inflation, cash flow accounts have one particular advantage in that they are very up-to-date and thus largely free of distortions produced by inflation'.[48] The ITUCs place considerable emphasis on information about the development and strategy of the business. 'This should not only relate to the past but also to anticipated and planned developments and measures. The basic assumptions on which the future prospects are based must be stated and explained; necessary adjustments to former assumptions and expectations must be explained.'[49] Apart from the above, a considerable quantity of information is required on matters including: the effect of the order book on employment, training and promotion, accidents, plans to harmonize work, and 'an overall view of the relations of the undertaking with society should basically be aimed at in the form of a social balance sheet, though for this fixed forms and contents should be developed so that the corresponding reports cannot be misused for public relations or other purposes'.[50]

At national level, regulation governing non-financial reporting items is sparse compared to the UN and ITUCs, apart from France and the USA. In France, large corporations are required by a 1977 law to publish a social report (Bilan Social).[51] It is quite separate from the corporate annual report and therefore may be regarded as a special report. Detailed information must be disclosed about a wide range of matters including employment; wages, salaries, and social security payments; hygiene and safety conditions of work; training; and trade union activities. The emphasis of these requirements is on the impact of the corporation on employees. Information relating to employees is also required to be disclosed by some other countries including the USA, UK, Brazil, Japan, Malaysia, Norway, and Sweden, but the instances are few and the required disclosures relatively minimal. However, the USA, through the SEC, requires more than most with respect to the UN proposals at least at group level, though there are no requirements to provide a geographical analysis of employees nor descriptions of labour relations policy and management structure. In the EEC countries, the low overall level of disclosure seems likely to change following the enactment of the *Fourth Directive* and the *Seventh Directive*, but the loose framing of the requirements makes it difficult to offer any predictions of a precise nature.

5.7.2 Reporting practices

Despite the contrast between the list of proposals at international level, especially by the UN, and the paucity of regulation at national level, it is evident that there is a substantial amount of voluntary disclosure in practice, not least by MNCs. Naturally, there are considerable variations in the type and extent of disclosure across countries, but there does seem to be a growing trend especially by large corporations towards disclosing more non-financial information. This is evident especially in Europe, with particular reference to France, West Germany, the Netherlands, and Sweden where 'social reporting' has become established in practice.[52]

The *Financial Times World Survey* (1980) of the 200 largest industrial corporations provides further evidence. Disclosures were analysed under the headings of employment reports, value added statements, statements about future prospects and corporate objectives, operating and trading data in volume form, energy and environment statements, and analyses of shareholders and statements about share performance.[53]

As regards employment reports, 49 per cent of the corporations surveyed contained clearly defined sections covering information in this category. The most detailed information was given by corporations in France, West Germany, and Sweden with notable examples being Moët-Hennessy (France), GHH and Daimler Benz (West Germany), and Svenska Cellulose (Sweden). Disclosure in the UK and to a lesser extent the USA was by way of contrast, relatively limited taken overall, though Ford in the USA and Boots together with Marks and Spencer in the UK were noteworthy exceptions. A recent example of some interest is given by the BBA Group (UK) in Exhibit 5I. While many MNCs go beyond what is required in their own countries, very few match up fully to the UN proposals. For example, only 19 per cent of the corporations surveyed disclosed a geographical analysis of employees. However, a wide range of information was presented often going beyond existing regulation. Eighteen per cent of corporations disclosed their policies regarding trade union relations (notably USA corporations), 20 per cent disclosed their policies for consulting and communicating with employees (notably French and Dutch corporations), 23 per cent disclosed information about health and safety at work (notably French, West German, Australian, and USA corporations), 12.5 per cent disclosed their policies concerning redundancies, 16 per cent disclosed policies about employee welfare (notably French and West German corporations), 41.5 per cent disclosed training policies (notably French, West German, Australian and USA corporations), and 13 per cent disclosed policies about the employment of women and minority groups (notably USA corporations). As regards employment costs, only 46.5 per cent disclosed these costs for the group as a whole, with but a handful of corporations providing additional segmental information.

Value added statements are an innovation in corporate reporting which is very much European in origin—the purpose of the report being to show the results of operations attributable to all participants, apart from suppliers, and the distribution of wealth thus created to investors, employees, lenders, and governments.[54] While there are a number of problems in practice concerning measurement and presentation, e.g. whether or not depreciation should be deducted in the calculation of value added, it would seem to have some potential for development in the context of 'social' or 'employee' reporting. An example from Bowater (UK) is given in Exhibit 5J. Such a statement could be adapted to show value added on a country-by-country basis disclosing internal and external inputs and outputs.[55] This could be especially useful for governmental organizations. The *Financial Times World Survey* (1980) revealed that 17.5 per cent of corporations disclosed value added statements (notably West German and UK corporations), which is significant given that such a statement is not required by law or professional accounting standards anywhere in the world. A more recent survey of UK corporate reporting shows that as many as 35 per cent of the largest 100 corporations ace currently providing a value added statement.[56]

Exhibit 5I. BBA Group (UK)

Employment report

1 Numbers employed

The total number of employees at 31st December 1981 was 5,980 analysed as follows:

By divisions	Automotive		Industrial and others		Total	
	1981	1980	1981	1980	1981	1980
United Kingdom	1,920	1,806	1,327	1,704	3,247	3,510
Overseas	2,443	2,460	290	257	2,733	2,717
	4,363	4,266	1,617	1,961	5,980	6,227

	Men		Women		Total	
By age						
The age brackets of employees were:						
Under 20	187	146	39	58	226	204
20–29	1,110	1,043	297	345	1,407	1,388
30–39	1,244	1,344	307	326	1,551	1,670
40–49	1,142	1,193	318	332	1,460	1,525
50–59	890	940	249	270	1,139	1,210
60–65	173	206	8	8	181	214
Over 65	16	15	—	1	16	16
	4,762	4,887	1,218	1,340	5,980	6,227
Geographically						
United Kingdom	2,605	2,806	642	704	3,247	3,510
Overseas	2,157	2,081	576	636	2,733	2,717
	4,762	4,887	1,218	1,340	5,980	6,227

2 **Remuneration**	United Kingdom		Overseas		Total	
	£	£	£	£	£	£
Aggregate remuneration	18,778,000	21,562,000	22,061,000	20,490,000	40,839,000	42,052,000
Average remuneration	5,776	5,255	8,099	7,365	6,835	6,108

3 Sales per employee

Average sales per employee	17,000	16,000	28,000	25,000	22,000	20,000

4 Employee benefits

	£'000	£'000
Contributions to pension schemes	3,811	4,292
Medical and industrial health expenses	460	480
Canteen subsidies	331	396
Sports and welfare	83	81
	4,685	5,249

5 Pension Fund

The BBA Group Pension Fund in the United Kingdom has been increasing pensions annually at the discretion of the Trustees, in order to minimize the impact of inflation on pensioners. In 1981, following the latest actuarial report, it was possible to increase pensions in such a way that the loss of their purchasing power since 1963 was reduced to a maximum of 2% per annum (compound). Deferred pensioners also had their prospective entitlements increased.

It is only reasonable to allocate sufficient resources to combat inflation in this way since to do otherwise is to negate the purpose of having a pension fund. Because of prudent funding policies and a good investment return, we have been able to achieve our objectives with only a marginal increase in the level of contributions over the period concerned.

As a consequence of the reduction in earnings which some employees had suffered recently, their pension prospects had been reduced. To combat this, the formula for calculating the pension was changed so as to have regard to the real value of the purchasing power of their earnings in the last ten years of service.

In the last two years the number of employees has fallen; so also has the number of members of the pension fund. There are approximately 3,500 members and nearly 1,100 pensioners. Normal retirement age is 65 for men and 60 for women, and at that age a member receives a pension based upon service with the company and final earnings.

On death in service, a lump sum of twice the annual amount of earnings is paid and in addition a widow of a married member receives a pension equal to half his pension, based on full prospective service but current levels of pay. The fund guarantees to pay members' pensions for at least five years. Widows of pensioners also receive a pension at half rate.

The fund is valued at £35,000,000 of which approximately 40% is invested in property. The company's contribution rate is 14.75% of contributory earnings and the amount available for investment is about £3,500,000 per annum.

There are equivalent arrangements for retirement pensions in overseas companies, as permitted by legislation and following local custom.

6 Employment of disabled persons

We continue to pay attention to the employment of both registered disabled persons, as defined in the Disabled Persons (Employment) Act 1944, and to the non-registered disabled, and accept this area as a social responsibility.

Applications for employment, received from disabled persons, are given full and fair consideration and are assessed on the abilities, not the disabilities, of the applicants.

In the event of an employee becoming disabled during employment, every practical step is taken to ensure continuity of employment and, where necessary, training is given to meet changed circumstances.

Disabled employees are given the same opportunities regarding training, career development, and promotion, as those given to other employees.

Source: BBA Group Annual Report, 1981.

Exhibit 5J. Bowater (UK)

		1981 £ million	1980 £ million
Value added and wealth created	Sales	1,728	1,760
	Materials and services consumed	1,232	1,350
	Value added	496	410
	Amount required to fund replacement of fixed assets	67	59
	Wealth created by the Organization through the efforts of people and the use of assets and finance	429	351
	Distributed as follows Employees: wages, pensions, and other benefits	333	298
	Lenders: interest on loans and overdrafts net of gearing adjustment	17	11
	Shareholders: dividends to shareholders in the Corporation and in subsidiary companies	25	27
	Governments: taxes payable	50	43
		425	379
	Reinvested to finance expansion (excess of amount distributed over wealth created): Corporation shareholders' funds	1	(26)
	Minority shareholders' funds	3	(2)
		429	351

Source: Bowater Annual Report, 1981.

As regards information about future prospects, the *Financial Times World Survey* (1980) revealed that 37 per cent of corporations provided a section highlighting this and a further 21 per cent mentioned future prospects in passing. However, very few corporations provided any quantification as regards future sales (9 per cent) and earnings (5 per cent). Forecasts relating to capital expenditure, financing, job creation, and dividend policy were also rarely in evidence.

Information about operating and trading in volume form was also fairly widespread according to the *Financial Times World Survey* (1980), though disclosed by a minority of corporations. Volume data for sales and production were given by 32.5 and 38 per cent of corporations respectively. Additionally, market share information was disclosed by 19 per cent of corporations.

However, information about energy policy and matters relating to the environment was rarely provided. Notable exceptions as regards energy disclosures included Elf-Aquitaine in France, Proctor and Gamble in the USA, and Nippon Steel in Japan. As regards the environment, Bayer, BASF, and Hoechst in West Germany all provided substantial reports but the standard of reporting varied considerably across countries and industries. Taken overall, it would seem that very few MNCs are giving serious consideration to these issues in their corporate reports.

5.7.3 Problems and prospects

Despite growing pressure at the international level, especially by the UN, for more disclosure in the area of non-financial or 'social' reporting, the extent of regulation at national level is sparse with the notable exception of France, where 'social' reports are required by law. However, the extent of voluntary disclosure is significant and growing, especially in European countries such as West Germany, the Netherlands, and Sweden where additional special 'social' or 'employee' reports are often provided. In the UK there is also a significant move towards the disclosure of value added statements in corporate annual reports and the provision of special reports to employees. Not surprisingly, corporate reporting practices vary across countries and industries according to circumstances and social/societal pressures, e.g. the European concern with employee welfare and trade unions can be contrasted with the concern in the USA for consumers and minorities. Taken on a world-wide basis, of course, there is a relatively low overall level of disclosure by large corporations. Nevertheless many corporations, including MNCs, provide non-financial information without any compulsion to do so and this practice is growing.

Non-financial reporting is an area which warrants considerable study and further research as it is not well developed. Experiments with various forms of reporting, especially those being developed in Europe, seem likely to improve our knowledge of what could be useful and of the costs and benefits involved. More problematic is the development of generally accepted criteria, including appropriate measurement methods, by which MNCs and other corporations are to be held accountable for the social and economic impact of their operations.

5.8 CONCLUSIONS

From this brief review of major areas of interest and concern in the context of MNC information disclosure it is evident that while there is a demand for more information, especially at the international inter-governmental level of the UN, there are many problems to be resolved if an effective response is to be possible by MNCs on a world-wide basis.

Developments seem likely to be slow, given the conceptual and practical accounting difficulties yet to be overcome in areas of key concern, viz. consolidated financial statements, segmental information, transfer pricing and related party transactions, accounting for inflation, foreign currency translation, and non-financial (social) reporting. This is the case even in the USA which is the only country with a level of regulation, with the exception of non-financial reporting, which approaches the UN proposals. By comparison, regulation in the UK and Canada is only moderate, whereas other countries which are significant home bases for MNCs, such as West Germany, Japan, Switzerland, France, the Netherlands, Sweden, Belgium, and Italy, are relatively lacking in regulation. Thus experience of many aspects of disclosure is limited. However, many MNCs are disclosing information about their activities, albeit of varying quantity and quality, with no compulsion to do so. On the other hand, many presumably do not consider it in their interests, nor do they see it necessary, to disclose additional information. Hence they are unlikely to do so unless compelled by legal requirements or mandatory stock exchange rules/accounting standards.

The existing pattern and variety of regulation and reporting experience at national level is clearly a serious obstacle to any rapid development of information disclosure by MNCs without agreement and co-operation at the international inter-governmental level, e.g. by the UN, OECD, and EEC. Such initiatives would need to be supported by appropriate involvement at the professional level to facilitate the process of innovation and implementation in practice. The experience of the UN, OECD, and EEC to date suggests that MNC accounting disclosure standards may emerge only gradually. Indeed, there is perhaps already detectable a realization that demands for information may need to be tempered in the light of the many problems involved.

Possibly the most fundamental problem is the lack of well-developed systems for reporting the complexity of MNC operations. Furthermore, the costs and benefits of alternative forms of reporting have also to be adequately assessed. Irrespective of the will or requirement to disclose, ways and means to do so which are fully effective have yet to be devised, thus limiting the capacity for choice by all concerned with information disclosure by MNCs.

Overview

MNCs have become subject to pressure for more accountability and information disclosure as a consequence of their power to control and move resources internationally. It is this characteristic, combined with the attendant factors of size and complexity, relative to the domestic corporation, that distinguishes the MNC.

Whatever the merits of the claims made by the many participants in the process of setting international standards of accounting and reporting by MNCs, there is clearly a well-articulated demand for additional as well as more comparable information by a wide range of organizations and user groups. These groups include governments, with special reference to international inter-governmental organizations, trade unions and employees, investors and financial analysts, bankers and lenders, the general public, and accountants and auditors.

While there are some similarities in the problems associated with information disclosure by MNCs compared to domestic corporations, there is no doubt that issues relating to MNCs are more complex in terms of identifying the user groups and participants involved, in determining their information needs, in assessing the costs and benefits of information disclosure, and in considering the many factors involved in the standard-setting process.

Despite some elements of common interest it is evident that there are a number of significant differences between participants concerning the quantity of information to be disclosed, the basis upon which the information is to be measured, the degree of uniformity to be desired, the role of 'special' as opposed to 'general-purpose' reports and the extent to which information disclosure is to be mandatory. The problems of validating the demands of participants and resolving conflicts are also unsettled and warrant further investigation. At the same time, the perspective of management as information providers has to be considered, especially in respect to the costs involved, including competitive disadvantage, and apparent problems of implementation.

Major areas of concern in the context of accounting and information disclosure by MNCs in general-purpose corporate reports include: reporting on the world-wide operations of the group with particular reference to consolidated financial statements; funds statements; segmental information especially on a geographical or multi-dimensional basis; transfer pricing and related party transactions; reporting the effects of inflation; foreign currency translation; and non-financial or social reporting, including information about employment conditions and prospects, organizational matters, production, investment plans, and the environment.

Many important aspects of MNC accounting and information disclosure are not at all well developed, at both the conceptual and technical level, even in countries such as the USA and UK, where relatively extensive information disclosure is currently required and practised. Further research, innovation and experimentation is warranted in many areas which are currently matters of debate. In the meantime, the capacity for choice by accounting policy-makers is necessarily limited.

The development of information disclosure by MNCs in the context of regulation is essentially a political or social choice process and thus it seems likely that standards of information disclosure will be harmonized effectively only at the international inter-governmental level, e.g. the UN, OECD, and EEC. Accordingly, the accounting profession (and the IASC) is likely to have a supportive rather than a leading role to play. But it will be an essential role, nevertheless, if desired standards of MNC accounting and reporting are to be implemented satisfactorily in practice.

Notes and References

CHAPTER 1: INTRODUCTION

1. The terms 'multinational enterprises', 'multinational companies' and 'transnational corporations', are alternatives in use, the latter in particular by the UN. The term 'multinational corporation' (MNC), is used here and defined broadly to mean a corporation which owns and/or controls economic resources in two or more countries. This is considered to be a useful working definition though it is appreciated that there is an extensive literature concerned with this aspect of the subject and that more precise definitions may be necessary according to the circumstances.
2. See, for example: Hood, Neil and Young, Stephen. *The Economics of Multinational Enterprise* (Longman, 1979)
3. See, for example, Gray, S. J., Shaw, J. C., and McSweeney L. B. 'Accounting Standards and Multinational Corporations' *Journal of International Business Studies* (Spring/Summer 1981)
4. The principal statements are as follows: United Nations, *International Standards of Accounting and Reporting for Transnational Corporations* (New York: UN, 1977); Organization for Economic Co-operation and Development. *International Investment and Multinational Enterprises* (Paris: 1976, revised 1979); European Economic Community, *Fourth Council Directive for Co-ordination of National Legislation Regarding the Annual Accounts of Limited Liability Companies* (Brussels: 1978); *Seventh Council Directive on Consolidated Accounts* (Brussels: June 1983); *Proposal for a Directive on Procedures for Informing and Consulting the Employees of Undertakings with Complex Structures, in Particular Transnational Undertakings* (Brussels: October 1980, revised 1983)
5. See, for example: European Federation of Financial Analysts Societies. *Corporate Reporting in Europe* (Paris: 1970)
6. See, for example: International Confederation of Free Trade Unions, European Trade Union Confederation, World Confederation of Labour. *Trade Union Requirements for Accounting and Publication by Undertakings and Groups of Companies* (Brussels: 1977)
7. International Accounting Standards Committee. *Objectives and Procedures* (London: 1983)

8. See, for example: De Bruyne, D. 'Global Standards: A Tower of Babel' *Financial Executive* (February 1980)

CHAPTER 2: THE EVOLUTION OF ACCOUNTABILITY AND INFORMATION DISCLOSURE

1. Note that the term 'accountability' implies the rendering of an account, i.e. the disclosure of information, and the submission of that account to external verification, i.e. audit by or on behalf of those to whom the corporation and its management is accountable. See Bird, P. *Accountability: Standards for Financial Reporting* (Accountancy Age Books, 1973)
2. For reviews and analyses of the environmental factors involved, see: Mueller, Gerhard, G. *International Accounting* (New York: Macmillan, 1967); Zeff, S. A. *Forging Accounting Principles in Five Countries: A History and Analysis of Trends* (Champaign, Illinois: Stipes, 1972); Choi, F. D. S. and Mueller, Gerhard, G. *An Introduction to Multinational Accounting* (Prentice-Hall, 1978) ch. 2; Nobes, C. W. and Parker, R. H. (Editors) *Comparative International Accounting* (Philip Allan, 1981) ch. 7; Arpan, Jeffrey S. and Radebaugh, Lee H. *International Accounting and Multinational Enterprises* (Warren, Gorham, and Lamont, 1981) ch. 2
3. See Radebaugh, Lee H. 'Environmental Factors Influencing the Development of Accounting Objectives, Standards and Practices in Peru' *International Journal of Accounting* (Fall 1975)
4. See for example: Frank, W. G. 'An Empirical Analysis of International Accounting Principles' *Journal of Accounting Research* (Autumn 1979); Gray, S. J. 'The Impact of International Accounting Differences from a Security Analysis Perspective: Some European Evidence' *Journal of Accounting Research* (Spring 1980); Nair, R. D. and Frank, W. G. 'The Impact of Disclosure and Measurement Practices on International Accounting Classifications' *Accounting Review* (July 1980)
5 Nobes and Parker. *Op. cit.* (1981) p. 213
6. Chatfield, Michael. *A History of Accounting Thought* (Krieger, 1977); Lee, T. A. and Parker, R. H. (Editors) *The Evolution of Corporate Financial Reporting* (Nelson, 1979); Most, Kenneth S. *Accounting Theory* (Grid, 1982) ch. 3; Littleton, A. C. and Zimmerman, V. K. *Accounting Theory: Continuity and Change* (Prentice-Hall, 1962)
7. See, for example: Galbraith, John K. *The New Industrial State* (Boston: Houghton Mifflin, 1967); Larner, R. J. *Management Control and the Large Corporation* (University Press, Dunellin, 1970).
8. See for example: Berle, A. Jr. and Means, G. C. *The Modern Corporation and Private Property* (New York: Harcourt Brace and World, 1967; originally published in 1932 by Macmillan); Galbraith *Op. cit.*; Zeitlin, M. 'Corporate Ownership and the Capitalist Class', *American Journal of Sociology* (March 1979); Jensen, Michael C. and Meckling, William H. 'Theory of the Firm: Managerial Behaviour, Agency Costs, and Ownership Structure' *Journal of Financial Economics* (October 1976)
9. See, for example: Benston, George J. *Corporate Financial Disclosure in*

the U.K. and the U.S.A. (Saxon House and the Institute of Chartered Accountants in England and Wales, 1976). Beaver, William H. *Financial Reporting: An Accounting Revolution* (Prentice-Hall, 1981)

10. By public corporations is meant corporations which do not restrict the number of shareholders nor exclude the offer or transfer of shares or debentures to the public. The absence of these restrictions are prerequisites to being listed on a stock exchange. The description of a public corporation varies from country to country, for example, public limited company in the UK, Aktiengesellschaft in West Germany, Naamloze Vennootschap in the Netherlands, Société Anonyme in France

11. See; Choi, Frederick D. S. 'European Disclosure: The Competitive Disclosure Hypothesis' *Journal of International Business Studies* (Fall 1974); Barrett, M. Edgar. 'The Extent of Disclosure in Annual Reports of Large Companies in Seven Countries' *International Journal of Accounting* (Spring 1977); Gray, *Op. cit* (1980)

12. See, for example: Readman, Peter. *The European Money Puzzle* (London: Michael Joseph, 1973); Samuels, J. M., Groves, R. E. V., and Goddard, C. S. *Company Finance in Europe* (London: Institute of Chartered Accountants in England and Wales, 1975)

13. See: Enthoven, Adolf, J. H. *Accountancy and Economic Development Policy* (Amsterdam: North-Holland, 1973); Beeny, James H. *European Financial Reporting—France* (London: Institute of Chartered Accountants in England and Wales, 1976)

14. Benston, *Op. cit* (1976)

15. See for example: in the UK, the Accounting Standards (Steering) Committee. *The Corporate Report* (London: 1975); and, in France, Sudreau, P. *Rapport du Comité d'Étude Pour La Réforme de l'Entreprise* (Paris: La Documentation Française, 1975)

16. See, for example: Curzon, G. and Curzon, V. *The Multinational Enterprise in a Hostile World* (London: Macmillan, 1977)

17. See Ramm, T. 'Federal Republic of Germany' in *International Encyclopaedia for Labour Law and Industrial Relations* (The Netherlands: Kluwer Law, 1979)

18. Rostow, W. W. *The Stages of Economic Growth* (Cambridge, 1960)

19. See for example: United Nations Conference on Trade and Development. *Dominant Positions of Market Power of Transnational Corporations—Use of the Transfer Pricing Mechanism* (New York: UN, 1978); United Nations. *The Impact of Multinational Corporations and the Development Process and on International Relations* (New York: UN, 1974); UK Monopolies Commission, *Chlordiazepoxide and Diazepam* (London: HMSO, 1973); United States Senate. *The ITT Co. and Chile 1970–71*. Report to the Committee on Foreign Relations by the Subcommittee on Multinational Corporations of the United States Senate (Washington: US Government Printing Office, 1973)

20. Maisonrouge, J. (President of IBM Corporation). Address: 'How International Business can further World Understanding' (1971)

21. Organization for Economic Co-operation and Development. *Transfer Pricing and Multinational Enterprises*. Report of the OECD Committee on Fiscal Affairs (Paris: OECD, 1979); Arpan, and Radebaugh. *Op. cit* (1981) ch. 10

22. See: Hood, Neil and Young, Stephen *The Economics of Multinational Enterprise* (Longman, 1979) ch. 4
23. See: Coase, R. H. 'The Nature of the Firm' *Economica* (November 1937); Buckley, P. J. and Casson, M. *The Future of the Multinational Enterprise* (Macmillan, 1978)
24. Vernon, Raymond. *Storm over the Multinationals: The Real Issues* (London: Macmillan, 1978)
25. Robbins, S. M. and Stobaugh, R. B. *Money in the Multinational Enterprise* (London: Longman, 1974)
26. See, for example: Shulman, J. 'When the Price is Wrong—By Design' *Colombia Journal of World Business* (May–June, 1967); Plasschaert, S. *Transfer Pricing and Multinational Corporations* (Saxon House/ECSIM, 1979)
27. See: Plasschaert. *Op. cit.* (1979)
28. Organization for Economic Co-operation and Development. *Op. cit.* (1979)
29. *Ibid.*
30. For reviews of research findings, see: Plasschaert. *Op. cit.* (1979); Hood and Young. *Op. cit.* (1979) ch. 3
31. Maisonrouge. *Op. cit.* (1971)
32. See, for example: Robbins and Stobaugh. *Op. cit.* (1974)

CHAPTER 3: THE DEMAND FOR INFORMATION: PARTICIPANTS AND PRESSURES

1. See, for example: United Nations. *International Standards of Accounting and Reporting for Transnational Corporations* (New York: UN, 1977); Organization for Economic Co-operation and Development. *International Investment and Multinational Enterprises* (Paris: 1976, revised 1979); International Confederation of Free Trade Unions, European Trade Union Confederation, World Confederation of Labour. *Trade Union Requirements for Accounting and Publication by Groups of Companies* (Brussels: 1977); International Accounting Standards Committee. *Objectives and Procedures* (London, 1983)
2. Gold, M., Levie H., and Moore, R. *The Shop Steward's Guide to the Use of Company Information* (Nottingham: Spokesman, 1979); International Confederation of Free Trade Unions. *Trade Unions and the Transnationals. A Handbook for Negotiations* (Brussels: 1979)
3. Banks, R. F. and Stieber, J. (Editors) *Multinationals, Unions and Industrial Relations in the Industrialised World* (New York: Cornell University, 1977); International Confederation of Free Trade Unions. *Op. cit.* (1979)
4. See: Beaver, William H. *Financial Reporting: An Accounting Revolution* (Prentice-Hall, 1981)
5. See, for example: Mueller, Gerhard, G. *International Accounting* (New York: Macmillan, 1967); Benston, George J. *Corporate Financial Disclosure in the U.K. and U.S.A.* (Saxon House and the Institute of Chartered Accountants in England and Wales, 1976); Nobes, C. W. and Parker, R. H. (Editors) *Comparative International Accounting* (Philip Allan, 1981)

Part I; Arpan, Jeffrey S. and Radebaugh, Lee H. *International Accounting and Multinational Enterprises* (Warren, Gorham, and Lamont, 1981)

6. United Nations. *Op. cit.* (1977)
7. See: Seidl-Hohenveldern, I. 'The United Nations and Transnational Corporations' in Simmonds K. R. (Editor) *Legal Problems of Multinational Corporations* (London: The British Institute of International and Comparative Law, 1977)
8. United Nations *Op. cit.* (1977); United Nations. *Transnational Corporations in World Development: A Re-Examination* (New York; UN, 1978); Commission of the European Communities. *Bulletin of the European Communities* (Supplement 15/73, 1973)
9. United Nations. *International Standards of Accounting and Reporting—Technical Papers* (New York: UN, 1977)
10. Plasschaert, S. *Transer Pricing and Multinational Corporations* (Saxon House/ECSIM, 1978)
11. United Nations. *The Impact of Multinational Corporations on Development and on International Relations* (New York: UN, 1974)
12. United Nations. *International Standards of Accounting and Reporting for Transnational Corporations* (New York: UN, 1977)
13. United Nations. Economic and Social Council Resolution 1979/44. *Establishment of an Ad Hoc Intergovernmental Working Group of Experts on International Standards of Accounting and Reporting.* (New York: UN, 1979)
14. United Nations. *International Standards of Accounting and Reporting. Report of the Ad Hoc Intergovernmental Working Group of Experts on International Standards of Accounting and Reporting* (New York: UN, 1982)
15. *Ibid.* para. 38
16. Organization for Economic Co-operation and Development. *International Investment and Multinational Enterprises. Guidelines for Multinational Enterprises.* (Paris: 1976, revised 1979)
17. Organization for Economic Co-operation and Development. *International Investment and Multinational Enterprises. Review of the 1976 Declaration and Decisions* (Paris: 1979)
18. Organization for Economic Co-operation and Development. *Accounting Practices in OECD Member Countries* (Paris: 1980)
19. See, for example: Nobes, and Parker, *Op. cit.* (1981) ch. 12
20. See, for example: Gray, S. J. *Corporate Reporting and Investor Decisions in the EEC: The Comparability Problem* (International Centre for Research in Accounting, University of Lancaster, 1973)
21. European Economic Community. *Fourth Council Directive for Co-ordination of National Legislation Regarding the Annual Accounts of Limited Liability Companies·* (Brussels: 1978)
22. For a review of the impact of the *Fourth Directive* in the EEC countries, see: Ernst and Whinney. *The Fourth Directive* (London: Kluwer, 1979)
23. For an explanation and discussion of the meaning of 'a true and fair view' see Flint, David. *A True and Fair View in Company Accounts* (The Institute of Chartered Accountants of Scotland and Gee and Co., 1981)
24. European Economic Community. *Seventh Council Directive on Consolidated Accounts* (Brussels: June 1983)
25. Commission of the European Communities. *Proposal for a Directive on Procedures for Informing and Consulting the Employees of Undertakings*

with Complex Structures, in Particular Transnational Undertakings (Brussels: October 1980, revised 1983)

26. International Confederation of Free Trade Unions. *Op. cit.* (1979)
27. See: Blake, D. H. 'Corporate Structure and International Trade Unionism' *Columbia Journal of World Business* (March/April 1972); Wilms-Wright, C. *Transnational Corporations: A Strategy for Control* (London: Fabian Society, 1977)
28. See: Trade Union Research Unit, Ruskin College. *Acquisition and Use of Company Information by Trade Unions* (Oxford: 1977)
29. Wilms-Wright. *Op. cit*; (1977); Martens, B. 'The European Trade Union's Stand' in *Investment and Disinvestment Policies of Multinational Corporations in Europe* (Saxon House/ECSIM, 1979); Lea, D. 'International Companies and Trade Union Interests' in Dunning, J. H. (Editor) *The Multinational Enterprise* (London: Allen and Unwin, 1971)
30. See, for example: Martens. *Op. cit.* (1979)
31. See: Trade Union Research Unit, Ruskin College, Oxford. *Some Limitations of Company Accounts: A Discussion Paper* (Oxford: 1978)
32. See, for example: Transport and General Workers Union. *Ford: Wage Claim 1978* (London: 1978)
33. See: Gold, Levie, and Moore. *Op. cit.* (1979)
34. See International Confederation of Free Trade Unions, European Trade Union Conference, World Confederation of Labour. *Op. cit* (1977)
35. Aggarwal, R. and Baker, J. C. 'Using Foreign Subsidiary Accounting Data: A Dilemma for the Multinational Corporation' *Columbia Journal of World Business* (Fall 1975); Robbins, S. M. and Stobaugh, R. B. 'The Bent Measuring Stick for Foreign Subsidiaries' *Harvard Business Review* (September/October, 1973)
36. See: Vernon, Raymond. *Storm over the Multinationals: The Real Issues* (London: Macmillan Press, 1977)
37. See, for example Mason, Alister K. *Related Party Transactions* (Canadian Institute of Chartered Accountants, 1979)
38. *Ibid.*
39. See, for example, Plasschaert. *Op. cit* (1978); Arpan, and Radebaugh. *Op. cit.* (1981) ch. 10
40. Choi, Frederick, D. S. and Mueller, Gerhard G. *An Introduction to Multinational Accounting* (Prentice-Hall, 1978); Thomas, Arthur L. 'Transfer Prices of the Multinational Firm: When will they be Arbitrary' *Abacus* (June 1971)
41. See: Mason. *Op. cit*; (1979); American Institute of Certified Public Accountants. *Related Party Transactions. Statement on Auditing Standards No. 6.* (New York: 1975)
42. American Accounting Association. *Report of the Committee on International Accounting.* Supplement to *The Accounting Review* (1973)
43. Robbins and Stobaugh. *Op. cit.* (1973)
44. Mason. *Op. cit.* (1979)
45. See: American Accounting Association. *Op. cit.* (1973); Burns, J. M. *Accounting Standards and International Finance: With special Reference to Multinationals* (Washington DC: American Enterprise Institute for Public Policy Research, 1976); United Nations *Op. cit.* (1977)
46. See, for example, Beaver. *Op. cit.* (1981) ch. 1
47. See: European Federation of Financial Analysts Societies. *Corporate*

Reporting in Europe (Paris: 1970); International Accounting Standards Committee, *Op. cit.* (1983); United Nations *Op. cit.* (1977). Organization for Economic Co-operation and Development. *Accounting Practices in OECD Member Countries* (Paris: 1980)

48. European Economic Community. *Op. cit.* (1978)
49. See, for example, Foster, George. *Financial Statement Analysis* (Prentice-Hall, 1978)
50. European Federation of Financial Analysts Societies. *Op. cit.* (1970)
51. See, for example, Beaver. *Op. cit.* (1981); Foster. *Op. cit.* (1978); Keane, Simon N. *The Efficient Market Hypothesis* (Gee and Co. for the Institute of Chartered Accountants of Scotland, 1980)
52. See Emmanuel, C. R. and Gray, S. J. 'Segmental Disclosure by Multi-business Multinational Companies: A Proposal' *Accounting and Business Research* (Summer 1978)
53. Organization for Economic Co-operation and Development. *Op. cit.* (1980) Part I
54. See, for example, Gray, S. J. 'The Impact of International Accounting Differences from a Security Analysis Perspective: Some European Evidence' *Journal of Accounting Research* (Spring 1980)
55. See Choi, Frederick D. S. and Mueller, Gerhard G. *An Introduction to Multinational Accounting* (Prentice-Hall, 1978) ch. 4
56. See International Monetary Fund. *International Capital Markets, Developments and Prospects 1982* (July 1982)
57. See Choi, Frederick D. S. 'Financial Disclosure and Entry to the European Capital Market' *Journal of Accounting Research* (Autumn 1973)
58. See, for example, Ramanathan, K. V. 'Towards a Theory of Corporate Social Accounting' *The Accounting Review* (July 1976)
59. See Buckley, John W. and O'Sullivan, Peter R. 'International Economics and Multinational Accounting Firms' in John C. Burton (Editor) *The International World of Accounting* (1980 Proceedings of the Arthur Young Professors Roundtable, USA)
60. International Accounting Standards Committee. *Op. cit.* (1983)
61. See Mason, Alister, K. 'The Evolution of International Accounting Standards' in Choi, Frederick D. S. (Editor) *Multinational Accounting. A Research Framework for the Eighties* (UMI Research Press, 1981)
62. See, for example, Chetkovich, Michael N. 'The International Federation of Accountants: Its Organization and Goals' *International Journal of Accounting Education and Research* (Fall 1979)
63. See for example, Choi, F. D. S. and Mueller, G. G. *Op. cit.* (1978) ch. 5; Mueller, Gerhard G. 'The Race to Set International Standards for Financial Accounting and Reporting' *The Annals of the School of Business Administration, Kobe University* (No. 25, 1981)

CHAPTER 4: THE SUPPLY OF INFORMATION: MANAGERIAL PERSPECTIVES

1. See: Watson, W. H. Jr. 'Global Role for U.S. Stock Exchange *Columbia Journal of World Business* (Spring 1974); Arpan, Jeffrey, S. and Rade-

baugh, Lee H. *International Accounting and Multinational Enterprises* (Warren, Gorham, and Lamont, 1981) ch. 3

2. United Nations. *International Standards of Accounting and Reporting for Transnational Corporations.* (New York: UN, 1977); International Confederation of Free Trade Unions, European Trade Union Conference, World Confederation of Labour. *Trade Union Requirements for Accounting and Publication by Undertakings and Groups of Companies* (Brussels: 1977)

3. United Nations. *Op. cit.* (1977)

4. See, for example: Lee, T. A. and Tweedie, D. P. *The Private Shareholder and the Corporate Report* (London: Institute of Chartered Accountants in England and Wales, 1977); also *The Institutional Investor and Financial Information* (London: Institute of Chartered Accountants in England and Wales, 1981)

5. See, for example: Foster, George. *Financial Statement Analysis* (Prentice-Hall, 1978); Keane, Simon M. *The Efficient Market Hypothesis* (Gee and Co., for the Institute of Chartered Accountants of Scotland, 1980)

6. See: Peasnell, K. V. *Accounting Objectives: A Critique of the Trueblood Report* (Lancaster: International Centre for Research in Accounting, University of Lancaster, 1974); Argleys, F. 'Meeting the Needs of Users of Published Financial Statements' *The Accountant* (8 December 1977); Palmer, J. R. *The Use of Accounting Information in Labour Negotiations* (New York: National Association of Accountants, 1971); Trade Union Research Unit, Ruskin College. *Employee Consultants and Information Disclosure: Some Notes on the Swedish Experience* (Oxford, 1980)

7. See: Choi, Frederick, D. S. and Mueller, Gerhard G. *An Introduction to Multinational Accounting* (Prentice-Hall, 1978) ch. 4

8. Financial Accounting Standards Board. *Objectives of Financial Reporting by Business Enterprises.* Statement of Accounting Concepts No. 1 (FASB, 1978)

9. American Institute of Certified Public Accountants. *Report of the Accounting Objectives Study Group* (New York: AICPA, 1973)

10. See: De Bruyne, D 'Global Standards: A Tower of Babel?' *Financial Executive* (February 1980)

11. Organization for Economic Co-operation and Development. *International Investment and Multinational Enterprises* (Paris: 1976, revised 1979)

12. Accounting Standards (Steering) Committee. *The Corporate Report* (London: 1975)

13. See, for example, Watts, Ross L. 'Corporate Financial Statements: A Product of the Market and Political Processes' *Australian Journal of Management* (April 1977); Watts, Ross L. and Zimmerman, J. L. 'Towards a Positive Theory of the Determination of Accounting Standards' *The Accounting Review* (January 1978)

14. See United States—Business and Industry Advisory Committee. *A Discussion of Provision of Data on MNC Operations* (New York: BIAC 1974)

15. Confederation of British Industry. *Communications with People at Work* (London, 1977); Marsh, A. and Hussey, R. *Survey of Employee Reports* (London: Tolley, 1979); Moore, R. 'Information to Unions: Use or Abuse' *Personnel Management* (May 1980)

16. See: Fox, A. *Industrial Sociology and Industrial Relations.* Research Paper No. 3 Royal Commission on Trade Unions and Employers' Associations (London: HMSO, 1966)

17. Confederation of British Industry. *The Provision of Information by Multinational Enterprises in the U.K.* (London: 1975)
18. United States—Business and Industry Advisory Committee. *Op. cit.* (1974)
19. Vernon, Raymond. *Storm over the Multinationals: The Real Issues* (London: Macmillan Press, 1977)
20. See: Behrman, J. N. *Demand for Information from Multinational Enterprises* (New York: Fund for Multinational Management Education/Council of the Americas, 1976); International Chamber of Commerce. *ICC Comments on the Report of the UN Expert Group on Accounting Standards and Reporting* (Paris: 1978); Organization for Economic Co-operation and Development. *International Investment and Multinational Enterprises—Review of the 1976 Declaration and Decisions* (Paris: 1979)
21. Gold, H. P. 'Accounting Standards and Multinational Corporations' in Leach, R. and Stamp, E. (Editors) *British Accounting Standards: The First Ten Years* (Cambridge: Woodhead-Faulkner, 1981)
22. For example: United Nations *Op. cit.* (1977); Organization for Economic Co-operation and Development *Op. cit.* International Confederation of Free Trade Unions, European Trade Union Confederation, World Confederation of Labour *Op. cit.* (1977)
23. See, for example: International Chamber of Commerce. *Op. cit.* (1978); Organization for Economic Co-operation and Development *Op. cit.* (1979)
24. Gold, *Op. cit.* (1981); Organization for Economic Co-operation and Development *Op. cit.* (1979)
25. See Alhashim, D. D. and Robertson, J. W. (Editors) *Accounting for Multinational Enterprises* (Indianapolis: Bobbs-Merrill, 1978)
26. Schwamm, H. and Geemidis, D. *Codes of Conduct for Multinational Companies: Issues and Positions* (Brussels: ECSIM, 1977); Organization for Economic Co-operation and Development *Op. cit.* (1979)
27. See, for example, Edwards, J. R. 'The Accounting Profession and Disclosure in Published Reports 1925–1935' *Accounting and Business Research* (Autumn 1976)
28. International Chamber of Commerce *Op. cit* (1978); United Nations *Op. cit.* (1977)
29. See: Mautz, R. K. and May, W. G. *Financial Disclosure in a Competitive Economy* (New York: Research Foundation of the Financial Executives Institute, 1978)
30. See: Behrman, *Op. cit.* (1976)
31. See, for example: Trade Union Research Unit, Ruskin College. *Some Limitations of Company Accounts. A Discussion Paper* (Oxford, 1978)
32. W. F. Mueller, quoted in Mautz and May *Op. cit.* (1978) p. 57.
33. Commission on Industrial Relations. *Disclosure of Information* Report No. 31 (London: HMSO, 1972); Organization for Economic Co-operation and Development *Op. cit.* (1979)
34. See: Hood, N. and Young, S. *The Economics of Multinational Enterprise* (Longman, 1979)
35. See United Nations. *National Legislation and Regulations Relating to Transnational Corporations:* (New York: UN, 1978)
36. See International Chamber of Commerce. *Op. cit.* (1978)
37. See United Nations. *Transnational Corporations: Views and Proposals of NonGovernmental Interests on a Code of Conduct* (New York: UN, 1976)
38. *Report to the Cost Accounting Standards Board by a Special Group of*

Consultants to Consider Issues Relating to Comparing Costs and Benefits (New York: CASB, 1978)

CHAPTER 5: INFORMATION DISCLOSURE: REGULATION AND PRACTICE

1. See, for example, Gray, S. J. 'Segment Reporting and the EEC Multi-nationals' *Journal of Accounting Research* (Autumn 1978)
2. Fitzgerald, R. D., Stickler, A. D. and Watts, T. R. *International Survey of Accounting Principles and Reporting Practices* (Butterworths and Price Waterhouse International, 1979); Organization for Economic Co-operation and Development, *Accounting Practices in OECD Member Countries* (Paris: 1980); Lafferty, Michael and Cairns, David. *Financial\Times World Survey of Annual Reports, 1980* (London: Financial Times, 1980)
3. While the criteria used to evaluate reporting practices in each country were arbitrary and the sample sizes, upon which generalizations were based, very small, this study contains a wealth of interesting information about the reporting practices of a selection of the world's largest corporations.
4. United Nations. *International Standards of Accounting and Reporting for Transnational Corporations* (New York: UN, 1977)
5. Organization for Economic Co-operation and Development. *International Investment and Multinational Enterprises* (Paris: 1976, revised, 1979)
6. European Economic Community. *Seventh Council Directive on Consolidated Accounts* (Brussels: June 1983)
7. See, for example, Beeny, J. H. *European Financial Reporting: West Germany* (London: Institute of Chartered Accountants in England and Wales, 1975); Nobes, C. W. and Parker, R. H. (Editors) *Comparative International Accounting* (Philip Allan, 1981) ch. 9
8. Nobes and Parker *Op. cit.* (1981) ch. 9
9. See: Fitzgerald, Stickler, and Watts. *Op. cit.* (1979)
10. See: Arpan, Jeffrey S. and Radebaugh, Lee H. *International Accounting and Multinational Enterprises* (Warren, Gorham, and Lamont, 1981) p. 211
11. Lafferty and Cairns. *Op. cit.* (1980) ch. 6
12. See, for example: Fitzgerald, Stickler, and Watts. *Op. cit.* (1979); Organization for Economic Co-operation and Development. *Op. cit.* (1980)
13. See, for example, Nobes and Parker, *Op. cit.* (1981) ch. 9
14. Fitzgerald, Stickler and Watts. *Op. cit.* (1979)
15. Lafferty and Cairns. *Op. cit.* (1980) ch. 7
16. For a review of this topic, see Gray, S. J. 'Segmental or Disaggregated Financial Statements' in Lee, T. A. (Editor) *Developments in Financial Reporting* (Philip Allan, 1981) ch. 2
17. United Nations. *Op. cit.* (1977) p. 30
18. Organization for Economic Co-operation and Development. *Op. cit.* (1979) p. 18
19. Financial Accounting Standards Board (USA). Financial Accounting Standard No. 14 *Financial Reporting for Segments of a Business* (FASB, 1976);

Canadian Institute of Chartered Accountants. Section 1700. *Segmented Information* (CICA, 1979)

20. Fitzgerald, Stickler and Watts. *Op. cit.* (1979); Organization for Economic Co-operation and Development. *Op. cit.* (1980)
21. Lafferty and Cairns. *Op. cit.* (1980) ch. 8
22. Gray. *Op. cit.* (1978); Gray, S. J. and Radebaugh, Lee H. 'International Segment Reporting by Multinational Enterprises: A US–UK Comparative Study. 'Paper presented to the American Accounting Association, Annual Meeting, Chicago, August 1981
23. Gray and Radebaugh. *Op. cit.* (1981)
24. See, for example, Plasschaert, S. *Transfer Pricing and Multinational Corporations* (Saxon House/ECSIM, 1979)
25. United Nations. *Op. cit.* (1977), p. 40
26. Fitzgerald, Stickler, and Watts. *Op. cit.* (1979); Organization for Economic Co-operation and Development. *Op. cit.* (1980)
27. Fitzgerald, Stickler, and Watts. *Op. cit.* (1979); Organization for Economic Co-operation and Development. *Op. cit.* (1980)
28. Fitzgerald, Stickler, and Watts. *Op. cit.* (1979)
29. Lafferty and Cairns. *Op. cit.* (1980) ch. 6
30. Gray and Radebaugh. *Op. cit.* (1981)
31. See, for example: Gray, S. J. 'The Impact of International Accounting Differences from a Security Analysis Perspective: Some European Evidence' *Journal of Accounting Research* (Spring 1980); Nobes and Parker. *Op. cit.* (1981)
32. See, for example: Arpan and Radebaugh. *Op. cit.* (1981) ch. 8; Nobes and Parker. *Op. cit.* (1981) ch. 10.
33. United Nations. *Op. cit.* (1977) p. 35
34. See, for example, Kirkman, P. R. A. *Accounting Under Inflationary Conditions* (Allen and Unwin, second edition, 1978); Miller, Edward L. *Inflation Accounting* (Van Nostrand Reinhold Company, 1980)
35. For further detail see: *Statement of Standard Accounting Practice No. 16* (March, 1980). Also Westwick, C. A. 'The Lessons to be Learned from the Development of Inflation Accounting in the U.K.' *Accounting and Business Research* (Autumn 1980)
36. For further details see: Financial Accounting Standards Board. *Financial Accounting Standard No. 33* (FASB, 1979). Also Miller. *Op. cit.* (1980)
37. Lafferty and Cairns. *Op. cit.* (1980) ch. 9
38. Arpan and Radebaugh. *Op. cit.* (1981) ch. 5; Nobes and Parker. *Op. cit.* (1981) ch. 11
39. Fitzgerald, Stickler, and Watts. *Op. cit.* (1979)
40. Financial Accounting Standards Board. Statement of Financial Accounting Standards No. 52. *Foreign Currency Translation* (December 1981)
41. Lafferty and Cairns. *Op. cit.* (1980) ch. 19
42. Fitzgerald, Stickler, and Watts. *Op. cit.* (1979); Organization for Economic Co-operation and Development. *Op. cit.* (1980)
43. See, for example, Lee, T. A. (Editor) *Developments in Financial Reporting* (Philip Allan, 1981) chs. 8 and 10; Schreuder, Hein. 'Employees and the Corporate Social Report: The Dutch Case' *The Accounting Review* (April 1981); Schoenfeld, H. M. *The Status of Social Reporting in Selected Countries*. Contemporary Issues in International Accounting, Occasional Paper No. 1 (University of Illinois, 1978)

44. Information of a qualitative nature is disclosed by a majority of large European MNCs, see Gray, S. J. 'Managerial Forecasts and European Multinational Company Reporting' *Journal of International Business Studies* (Fall 1978)

45. See, for example: Gray, S. J. and Maunders, K. T. *Value Added Reporting: Uses and Measurement* (London: Association of Certified Accountants, 1980)

46. Commission of the European Communities. *Proposal for a Directive on Procedures for Informing and Consulting the Employees of Undertakings with Transnational Undertakings* (Brussels: 1980, revised 1983)

47. International Conference of Free Trade Unions, World Confederation of Labour, European Trade Union Confederation. *Trade Union Requirements for Accounting and Publication by Undertakings and Groups of Companies* (Brussels: 1977)

48. *Ibid.* p. 12

49. *Ibid.* p. 14

50. *Ibid.* p. 14

51. For a review, see Lee, T. A. (Editor) *Developments in Financial Reporting* (Philip Allan, 1981) ch. 10; also Arpan and Radebaugh. *Op. cit.* (1981) ch. 9

52. See, for example: Schreuder. *Op. cit.* (1981); Schoenfeld. *Op. cit.* (1978); Schreuder, Hein. 'Corporate Social Reporting in the Federal Republic of Germany: An Overview' *Accounting Organisations and Society* (Vol. 4, No. 1/2, 1979)

53. Lafferty and Cairns. *Op. cit.* (1980) chs. 24–29

54. See, for example: Gray and Maunders. *Op. cit.* (1980)

55. This has been suggested, for example, by Enthoven, Adolf J. H. 'Social and Political impact of Multinational Corporations on Third World Countries (and its accounting implications)'. Paper presented to the American Accounting Association, Annual Meeting, 1976

56. Gray and Maunders. *Op. cit.* (1980)

APPENDICES

Appendix I

The United Nations Proposals (1977): Extract from the Group of Experts Report on 'International Standards of Accounting and Reporting for Transnational Corporations' (UN, 1977, pp 53–79)

PART I. FINANCIAL INFORMATION

Introduction

The lists of minimum items which follow have been elaborated with a view to improving the disclosure of financial information in general purpose reports. Nevertheless, each list embodies certain major reporting standards and requirements to disclose transactions between group companies of an enterprise and between group companies and associated companies. Certain of these standards and disclosure requirements are described below.

Financial information, enterprise as a whole. The list of minimum items in part I, section A, includes, in addition to disclosure items, certain major reporting standards, for example:

(1)   Consolidation of group companies is expected, exceptions are to be justified and accounted for by the equity method.

(2)   Similarly, associated companies are to be accounted for by the equity method, exceptions are to be compensated for by disclosure in the foot-notes of the equity in net assets and net income for the period.

(3)   A statement of sources and uses of funds is required to accompany a balance-sheet and statement of profit and loss and be accorded the same status as those primary financial statements.

(4)   Disaggregation of certain consolidated financial information is required by geographical area. However, many transactions between members of the group are not eliminated for this purpose as they are in consolidated financial statements.

(5)   Disaggregation of certain consolidated financial information is required by line of business. However, many transactions between members of the group are not eliminated for this purpose as they are in consolidated financial statements.

139

(6)   Disclosure of the identity of members of a group of companies and associated companies and the basis of transactions between them is required.

Financial information, individual member company. The list of minimum items in part I, section B, also includes certain major reporting standards, for example:

(1)   Disclosure of items and descriptions of accounting policies related to transactions between group companies and between group companies and associated companies.

(2)   A statement of sources and uses of funds is required to accompany a balance-sheet and statement of profit and loss and be accorded the same status as those primary financial statements.

(3)   A description of principal activities and new investments in each foreign geographical area or country. Export sales are required to be disclosed separately.

(4)   Segmentation of sales is required by line of business.

Fundamental accounting assumptions

There are fundamental accounting assumptions that govern the preparation of financial statements—so fundamental that they are usually not stated. Some are:

(1)   Going concern

It is assumed that the enterprise will not of necessity be liquidated or materially curtail its operations. Otherwise net realizable value in the circumstances should be incorporated in the financial statements where losses from such actions are foreseeable.

(2)   Accrual

Revenues and costs are accrued as earned or incurred, rather than as money is received or paid, and entered into the statement of profit and loss in the period to which they relate.

(3)   Substance over form

Transactions and other events are accounted for in accordance with financial reality and not merely with their legal form.

(4)   Prudence

Uncertainty attaches to many balances carried forward in a statement of financial position. Prudence dictates the determination of conservative amounts of the net realizable value of assets. Prudence dictates the accrual of probable losses. Prudence does not, however, justify the creation of secret or hidden reserves.

Only departures from these fundamentals are disclosed.

Definition of certain financial statement items

The following definitions of certain captions commonly found in primary financial statements are described below for the benefit of readers who are not professional accountants.

Balance-sheet

Property, plant, and equipment

An accepted summary caption, considered equivalent to fixed assets, but more descriptive. Includes for example:

Land

Land and leasehold improvements

Buildings

Machinery and equipment (excludes small, easily lost tools having a relatively short life)

Furniture and office equipment

May also include special jigs and dies related to specific products and generally amortized over an estimated total units expected to be sold.
Also includes construction in process and assets not in use.[a]

Other (long-term) investments

An expenditure made to hold securities in another company which is neither a group company nor an associated company, yet it is the intention of management to hold such securities for a considerable time.

Indicate market value

Quoted market prices are used where available. Where market quotations are not available, the board of directors is expected to determine a net realizable value. If cost exceeds market or net realizable value, cost should be written down if a permanent impairment in the investment has occurred.

Other long-term receivables

Where these did not arise from usual trade terms, the nature of the transaction giving rise to the balance should be described. For example, 'Receivable from sale of plant due in 5 equal annual instalments—interest at 8 per cent.'

Purchased goodwill

Generally, the excess of the expenditure for a consolidated company over the fair value of identifiable assets at the date of acquisition.

Patents, trade marks, and similar intangibles

Expenditures made to acquire or develop them. Not a valuation, unless identified as such in those jurisdictions that permit it.

---

[a] Where these items are material or large in relation to the most recent five years, they are disclosed separately.

Deferred charges (describe)

Excludes prepaid expenses reported under current assets. Used as 'other' long-term assets and hence an appropriate descriptive caption should be used in place of deferred charges if a material balance is carried. Generally, expenditures not recognized as a cost of operations in the period in which incurred but carried forward to be written off over a period of years. Not an asset as the word is commonly used.

Cash

Cash on hand and cash in banks, including time deposits due within a short period.

Marketable securities

Excludes securities held for non-working capital purposes (see other long-term investments). Includes only negotiable stocks and bonds. Presumes sales would not adversely influence the quoted market prices.

Net realizable values

Application of a net realizable value test to the amounts recorded by conventions varies according to the type of asset. Ordinarily, it is an amount not in excess of estimated sales price less cost to complete, if necessary, and cost to sell.

Receivables—directors and officers
Payables—directors and officers

Balances that might otherwise be considered immaterial should be reported because of the nature of this account. Balances resulting from ordinary recurring transactions are not required to be separately reported if clearly immaterial.

Prepaid expenses

This nondescript title usually suffices in the current asset category because of the immateriality of balances for items such as prepaid insurance and rent. If material, appropriate descriptions should be used. It is presumed that the items will be charged to expense in the next business cycle, usually on a time-expired basis not exceeding one year.

Other liabilities and provisions—deferred taxes

These are not liabilities at the balance-sheet date but the result of provisions out of income usually for having entered items as a deduction for tax purposes before the items are reported as costs or expenses for financial statement purposes.

Other liabilities and provisions—deferred income

An appropriate descriptive caption should be used in place of deferred income. Generally, amounts received or receivables, but relating to products or services yet to be furnished. Requires accruals for expenditures yet to be incurred in order to earn the income and hence explanatory material in the foot-notes to describe the accounting principles applied.

Shareholders' equity—reserves

Unless otherwise stated, it is presumed that the balance has been created out of transfers from retained earnings and that there have been no charges except to return amounts no longer required to unrestricted retained earnings. Any other changes during a period should be described to permit a reader to adjust the profit and loss statement if his standard is an all-inclusive income statement.

Profit and Loss statement

Sales

Revenue arising from sales of products, merchandise, and services in exchange for cash or a promise to pay cash, generally at determinable fixed future dates. Other revenue, such as investment income or royalties, should be separately disclosed.

Depreciation

Depreciation for the period is an amount derived from an allocation of the cost of the asset (or other basis described), less salvage value if any, over its estimated useful life in a systematic and rational manner. It may or may not coincide with 'deductions' allowed for income tax purposes. If depletion of the cost of an acquired natural resource is involved, the depletion for the period is usually a proration of the cost (or other basis described) of the total resources on the unit-of-production method and the account title is *Depreciation and depletion* or if applicable *Depreciation, depletion, and amortization* (of assets limited in life by exhaustion of connected resources, such as oil in the ground).

Unusual charges and credits

This caption should not be used alone. If used, it is a marginal caption with no amount of money. Used to head descriptive captions thereunder, such as 'Loss from earthquake'. Usually a subtotal precedes this caption, such as income before unusual charges.

SECTION A. ENTERPRISE AS A WHOLE

List of minimum items for general purpose reporting in financial statements of a transnational corporation

1. Main items in financial statements

Balance-sheet

Long-term assets

Property, plant, and equipment
  Gross
  Accumulated depreciation

Other long-term assets
  Investments
    Group companies not consolidated
    Associated companies
    Other investments and indicate market value

Long-term receivables
  Group companies not consolidated
  Associated companies
  Other long-term receivables

Purchased goodwill

Patents, trade marks and similar intangibles

Deferred charges (Describe)

Current assets

Cash

Marketable securities and indicate market value

Receivables
  Accounts and notes—Trade[a]
  Directors and officers of the group
  Other

Inventories—not in excess of net realizable value

Prepaid expenses

---

[a] Disclose separately, if material, amounts receivable from and payable to group companies not consolidated and associated companies.

Total assets

Long-term liabilities

Loans and debentures[a]

Current liabilities

Loans and overdrafts

Current portions of long-term liabilities and provisions

Payables
  Accounts and notes—Trade[a]
  Directors and officers of the group
  Taxes on income
  Dividends payable
  Other accounts payable and accrued expenses

Other liabilities and provisions

Deferred taxes

Deferred income

Provision for pensions

Other provisions (describe), such as:
  Warranties
  Estimated losses on firm sales or purchase contracts

Minority interests

  in group companies consolidated

Shareholders' equity

Capital shares
  Describe each class
  Movements during the period

Other equity accounts
  Capital paid-in excess of par
  Revaluation surplus
  Reserves
  Retained earnings
  Movements during the period (describe)

Total shareholders' equity

  Comment—Much of the foregoing information may be disclosed in the foot-
notes.

Balance-sheet foot-notes

(Disclose amounts unless a description only is called for)

Where property, plant, and equipment is material in relation to total assets, disclose an appropriate breakdown

Where inventories are a material item of working capital, disclose a breakdown appropriate to activities, such as: raw material, work in process, finished goods, spare parts and supplies

Indicate assets restricted or pledged and liabilities secured

As to loans and debentures, summarize the total by currencies, interest rates, and maturities

Description of pension plans and service and severance benefits and arrangements for funding. Indicate the amount of rights earned but not provided for. Disclose amounts receivable from or payable to pension funds of the company

Lease and other long-term commitments quantified (describe)

Contingent assets and liabilities (indicate nature and quantify if possible)

Contracts for future capital expenditures quantified (omit amounts which can be financed with current working capital)

Material events that have occurred after the balance-sheet date (quantify if possible)

Comment—Foot-note information may be disclosed in the face of the balance-sheet.

Profit and Loss statement

Sales
    Report sales net of sales or similar taxes or disclose the amount of such taxes separately if included

Gross profit[a]

Interest and investment income

Equity in income (profit and loss) of associated companies

Depreciation

Amortization of intangibles[b]

---

[a] The gross profit should be presented so as to show sales for the period and:
    (1) Cost of sales, or
    (2) The production for the period and costs related thereto subdivided as to their nature.
[b] May be combined with depreciation if adequately described and related to producing facilities.

Interest expense

Taxes on income

Unusual charges and credits (describe)

Minority interest in income of group companies consolidated

Net income

Profit and loss statement foot-notes

(Disclose amounts)

Transactions with group companies not consolidated should be disclosed either on the face of the profit and loss statement in separate lines adjacent to similar revenue or expense items resulting from transactions with parties outside the group, or parenthetically, or in foot-notes appropriately referenced.

Depending on the relative significance of such transactions, disclosure of the total revenue and a description of the principal items therein, and the total purchases and a description of the principal items therein, may suffice.

Depending on the relative significance of transactions with associated companies, similar disclosures should be made but separately.

Wages and salaries, including fringe and other benefits (voluntary and obligatory) or disclose such benefits separately

Pension, service, and severance benefits (not to be included in wages and salaries)

Research and development (total of amount amortized and amount expensed directly during the period)

Leasing expense for the period

Foreign exchange gain or loss

Comment—Foot-note information may be disclosed in the face of the profit and loss statement.

Statement of sources and uses of funds
(Not applicable to banks)

The statement may account for either the change between periods in working capital, or cash and temporary cash investments provided the change in each working capital item is shown.

The statement may begin with net income (before unusual items), or omit non-cash items by beginning with revenue.

As a subtotal the statement should show the funds provided from or used in operations and disclose unusual items separately.

The statement should disclose all financing and investing activities.

This statement is required whenever a balance-sheet and statement of profit and loss are presented.

Statement of sources and uses of funds

The following is an example of items and is not all inclusive.

Net income

Minority interest in net income of group companies consolidated

Provision for depreciation

Change in balance of deferred income taxes

Change in balance of estimated warranty expenses beyond one year

Amortization of goodwill and organization or start-up expenses deferred

Exchange gains and losses on long-term debt

Undistributed earnings of associated companies

Working capital provided by operations (a subtotal)

Proceeds from sale of property, plant, and equipment

Proceeds from sale of other long-term assets

Proceeds from sale of a company or a group of assets

Outlays for purchase of property, plant, and equipment

Outlays for purchase of other long-term assets

Outlays for purchase of a company or a group of assets

Dividends in cash and dividends in other assets, including dividends by group companies consolidated to minority interests

Issue, redemption and repayment of long-term debt, reclassification of short-term portion of long-term debt, and conversion of long-term debt to common or ordinary shares

Issue of shares for cash or other assets and redemption or purchase of shares for cash or other assets

Conversion of preferred shares to common or ordinary shares

Notes. The amount of funds provided by grants from Governments as a subsidy should be disclosed separately.

When a company or a group of assets is purchased or sold, a foot-note should disclose the amounts of the principal assets and liabilities involved in the lump sum reported in the statement or a foot-note ιo the balance-sheet should include such disclosures.

2. Disclosure of accounting policies

The notes to the financial statements should disclose all significant accounting policies which have been used, including over-all evaluation policies (e.g., historical cost, application of a general purchasing power index, replacement value or any other basis).

Description of consolidation policy for:
    Inclusion and exclusion of group companies in consolidation
    Carrying associated companies
    Elimination of intra-group profits
    Translating accounts in a foreign currency

Description of the basis of accounting for:
    Transactions between group companies and
    Transactions between group companies and associated companies

Criteria for the selection of geographical areas or countries reported separately

Criteria for segmentation by lines of business reported separately

3. Information concerning members of a group and associated companies

Disclosure of identity of parent company if its name is not included in the name of the group

List of other individual companies within the group
    Where voluminous, list principal companies and indicate where complete list is publicly available

    Also indicate:
        Percentage owned
        Geographical area or country of operations

    Justify exclusion of any such company from consolidation

Account for an excluded group company by the equity method or carry at cost or less with disclosure of the equity in net assets and net income in the foot-notes

List of associated companies
    Where voluminous, list principal companies and indicate where complete list is publicly available

    Also indicate:
        Percentage owned
        Geographical area or country of operations

Account for such companies by the equity method or justify carrying them at cost or less with disclosure of the equity in net assets and net income in the foot-notes.

4. Segmentation by geographical area

Preference is expressed for segmenting assets according to the location of the assets and not necessarily the location of the records, and attributing revenue to the geographical area of the last significant value added by operations.

Segment and disclose geographically

Sales to unaffiliated customers

Transfers to other geographical areas (eliminated in consolidation)

Operating results, such as profit before general corporate expenses, interest expense, taxes on income, and unusual items

Does not prohibit segmenting net income as well

To the extent identifiable with a geographical area, disclose

Total assets or net assets or total assets and total liabilities, and at least:
Property, plant, and equipment, gross
Accumulated depreciation
Other long-term assets

New investment in property, plant and equipment

Describe principal activities in each geographical area or country

Disclose the basis of accounting for transfers between areas or countries

Disclose exposure to exceptional risks of operating in other countries

Note. Amounts disclosed should aggregate to the total of the item shown in the consolidated financial statements or reconciling amounts should be given.

5. Segmentation by line of business

Segment and disclose by line of business

Sales to unaffiliated customers

Transfers to other lines of business (eliminated in consolidation)

Operating results, such as profit before general corporate expenses, interest expense, taxes on income, and unusual items

Does not prohibit segmenting net income as well

To the extent identifiable with a line of business, disclose

Total assets or net assets or total assets and total liabilities, and at least:
Property, plant, and equipment, gross
Accumulated depreciation
Other long-term assets

New investment in property, plant, and equipment

Describe the principal products and services in each line of business

Disclose the basis of accounting for transfers between lines of business

Note. Amounts disclosed should aggregate to the total of the item shown in the consolidated financial statements or reconciling amounts should be given.

SECTION B. INDIVIDUAL MEMBER COMPANY

List of minimum items for general purpose reporting in financial statements of an individual member company (including the parent company) of a group of companies comprising a transnational corporation

It is not intended that the parent company should issue financial statements of each individual member company in its language and currency. The list which follows is intended for application by the individual member company in the issuance of its own general purpose annual report.

An individual company may be a transnational corporation (see definitions), in which case the standards in this list are applicable to it.

1. Main items in financial statements

Balance-sheet

Long-term assets

Property, plant, and equipment
    Gross
    Accumulated depreciation

Other long-term assets
    Investments
        Group companies
        Associated companies
        Other investments and indicate market value

    Long-term receivables
        Group companies
        Associated companies
        Other long-term receivables

Patents, trade marks, and similar intangibles

Deferred charges (describe)

Current assets

Cash

Marketable securities and indicate market value

Receivables
  Accounts and notes—Trade
  Directors and officers of the group
  Intercompany
  Other

Inventories—
  not in excess of net realizable value

Prepaid expenses

Total assets

Long-term liabilities

Loans and debentures (other than intercompany)

Intercompany loans

Current liabilities

Loans and overdrafts

Current portions of long-term liabilities and provisions

Payables
  Accounts and notes—Trade
  Directors and officers of the group
  Intercompany
  Taxes on income
  Dividends payable
  Other accounts payable and accrued expenses

Other liabilities and provisions

Deferred taxes

Deferred income

Provision for pensions

Other provisions (describe), such as:
  Warranties
  Estimated losses on firm
    sales or
    purchase contracts

Shareholders' equity

Capital shares
  Describe each class
  Movements during the period

Other equity accounts
  Capital paid-in in excess of par
  Revaluation surplus
  Reserves
  Retained earnings
  Movements during the period
    (describe)

Total shareholders' equity

Comment—Much of the foregoing information may be disclosed in the foot-notes.

Balance-sheet foot-notes

(Disclose amounts unless a description only is called for)

Where property, plant, and equipment is material in relation to total assets, disclose an appropriate breakdown

Where inventories are a material item of working capital, disclose a breakdown appropriate to activities, such as: raw material, work in process, finished goods, spare parts and supplies

Indicate assets restricted or pledged and liabilities secured

Indicate by currency accounts receivable or payable in a foreign currency unless hedged

As to loans and debentures, summarize the total by currencies, interest rates, and maturities

Description of pension plans and service and severance benefits and arrangements for funding. Indicate the amount of rights earned but not provided for. Disclose amounts receivable from or payable to pension funds of the company

Lease and other long-term commitments quantified (describe)

Contingent assets and liabilities (indicate nature and quantify if possible)

Contracts for future capital expenditure quantified
  (omit amounts which can be financed with current working capital)

Material events that have occurred after the balance-sheet date (quantify if possible)

Comment—Foot-note information may be disclosed in the face of the balance-sheet.

Profit and loss statement

Sales
  Report sales net of sales or similar taxes or disclose the amount of such taxes separately if included. Disclose the amount of export sales separately

Gross profit[a]

Interest and investment income

Equity in income (profit and loss) of associated companies

Depreciation

Amortization of intangibles[b]

Interest expense

Taxes on income

Unusual charges and credits (describe)

Net income

Profit and loss statement foot-notes

(Disclose amounts)

Transactions with group companies should be disclosed either on the face of the profit and loss statement in separate lines adjacent to similar revenue or expense items resulting from transactions with parties outside the group, or parenthetically, or in foot-notes appropriately referenced.

Depending on the relative significance of such transactions, give a description of the transactions (summarized when appropriate) for the period reported on, including amounts, if any, and such other information as deemed necessary to an understanding of the effects on the financial statements.

Depending on the relative significance of transactions with its associated companies, an individual company should make similar disclosures separately.

Wages and salaries, including fringe and other benefits (voluntary and obligatory) or disclose such benefits separately

Pension, service, and severance benefits (not to be included in wages and
salaries)

Research and development (total of amount amortized and amount expensed
directly during the period)

Leasing expense for the period

Foreign exchange gain or loss

Comment—Foot-note information may be disclosed in the face of the profit
and loss statement.

---

[a] The gross profit should be presented so as to show sales for the period and:
    (1)   Cost of sales, or
    (2)   the production for the period and costs related thereto subdivided as to their
        nature.
  [b] May be combined with Depreciation if adequately described and related to producing
facilities.

Statement of sources and uses of funds

(Not applicable to banks)

The statement may account for either the change between periods in working capital, or cash and temporary cash investments provided the change in each working capital item is shown.

The statement may begin with net income (before unusual items) or omit non-cash items by beginning with revenue.

As a subtotal the statement should show the funds provided from or used in operations and disclose unusual items separately.

The statement should disclose all financing and investing activities.

This statement is required whenever a balance-sheet and statement of profit and loss are presented.

Statement of sources and uses of funds

The following is an example of items and is not all inclusive.

Net income

Provision for depreciation

Change in balance of deferred income taxes

Change in balance of estimated warranty expenses beyond one year

Amortization of goodwill and organization or start-up expenses deferred

Exchange gains and losses on long-term debt

Undistributed earnings of associated companies

Working capital provided by operations (a subtotal)

Proceeds from sale of property, plant, and equipment

Proceeds from sale of other long-term assets

Proceeds from sale of a company or a group of assets

Outlays for purchase of property, plant and equipment

Outlays for purchase of other long-term assets

Outlays for purchase of a company or a group of assets

Dividends in cash and dividends in other assets

Issue, redemption and repayment of long-term debt, reclassification of short-term portion of long-term debt, and conversion of long-term debt to common or ordinary shares

Issue of shares for cash or other assets and redemption or purchase of shares for cash or other assets

Conversion of preferred shares to common or ordinary shares

Notes. The amount of funds provided by grants from Governments as a subsidy should be disclosed separately.

When a company or a group of assets is purchased or sold, a foot-note should disclose the amounts of the principal assets and liabilities involved in the lump sum reported in the statement or a foot-note to the balance-sheet should include such disclosures.

2. Disclosure of accounting policies

The notes to the financial statements should disclose all significant accounting policies which have been used, including over-all valuation policies (e.g., historical cost, application of a general purchasing power index, replacement value, or any other basis).

Description of policy for:
Carrying associated companies
Elimination of profits on sales to associated companies
Translating accounts of associated companies in a foreign currency

Description of the basis of accounting for:
Transactions with other members of the group

Transactions with associated companies

3. Financial information on members of a group of companies

Disclosure of identity of immediate and ultimate parent company

A parent company lists controlled companies

List of associated companies
Where voluminous, list principal companies and indicate where complete list is publicly available
Indicate the geographical area or country of operations
Account for such companies by the equity method or justifying carrying them at cost or less with disclosure of the equity in net assets and net income in the foot-notes

Disclosure of the amount of guarantees on behalf of other members of the group

4. Disclosure of foreign assets

Describe principal activities by foreign geographical area or country

New investment in property, plant and equipment by foreign geographical area or country

Disclose exposure to exceptional risks of operating in other countries

5. Segmentation by line of business

If an individual member company is in a single line of business, it should identify the broad industry in which it operates and describe the principal products or services. A company operating in more than one industry should make the disclosures listed below.

Criteria for segmentation by lines of business reported separately

Describe the principal products and services in each line of business

Sales by line of business, with intersegment sales disclosed separately

New investment in property, plant and equipment by line of business

Disclose the basis of accounting for transfers between lines of business

Note. Amounts disclosed should aggregate to the total of the item shown in the financial statements or reconciling amounts should be given.

PART II. NON-FINANCIAL INFORMATION

Introduction

The lists of minimum items which follow have been promulgated with a view to improving disclosure of non-financial information in general purpose reports. Although financial statements of enterprises and companies have been made public in one form or another for a great number of years, the need for more information on non-financial aspects of the activities of transnational corporations has been recognized more recently. No broad guidelines, principles and standards for reporting have as yet been elaborated at the international level.

On the other hand, non-financial reporting by transnational corporations has become a necessity in view of the increasing interest of investors, labour, Governments, and other interested parties in monitoring the economic and social impact of the activities of these corporations and their subsidiaries. Non-financial items in the lists of minimum items should therefore be included in general purpose reports, even if this does not correspond as yet to the established principles and standards of reporting. At this time, such information is not generally 'covered' by the opinion of the independent auditor. Future work in this area will eventually lead to the development of comprehensive principles and standards for non-financial reporting. The lists which follow represent a first step in this direction.

Some non-financial information that is relevant at the national level loses significance when combined at the enterprise level with similar information but from different environments. Consequently, some items required at the national level are not included in the list for the enterprise as a whole.

SECTION A. ENTERPRISE AS A WHOLE

List of minimum items for general purpose reporting of a transnational corporation

1. Labour and employment

   (a) Description of general corporate labour relations policy if any, such as trade union recognition, complaints and dispute settlement mechanism and procedure
   (b) Number of employees as at year end
      (i)   Total
      (ii) breakdown by geographical area
      (iii) Breakdown by line of business, if feasible

2. Production

   (a) Physical output by principal lines of business in accordance with normal industrial practice
   (b) Description of significant new products and processes

3. Investment programme

   (a) Description of announced new capital expenditure
   (b) Description of main projects, including their cost, estimated additions to capacity, estimated direct effect on employment in the enterprise
   (c) Description of announced mergers and takeovers, including their cost and estimated direct effect on employment

4. Organizational structure

   (a) Description of management structure, e.g. degree of centralization for decision-making
   (b) Names of members of the board of directors and, where applicable, the supervisory board of the parent company and a description of their affiliations with companies outside the group[a]
   (c) Number of owners or shareholders and, where known, the names of the principal owners or shareholders

5. Environmental measures

   Description of types of major or special environmental measures carried out, together with cost data, where available

---

[a] Reference may be made to the report of the ultimate parent.

SECTION B. INDIVIDUAL MEMBER COMPANY

List of minimum items for general purpose reporting of an individual member company (including the parent company) of a group of companies comprising a transnational corporation

1. Labour and employment

   (a) Description of labour relations policy
       (i) Trade union recognition[b]
       (ii) Complaints and dispute settlement mechanism and procedure[b]
   (b) Number of employees as at year end and annual average
   (c) Number employed by function (professional, production, etc.)
   (d) number of women employees by function
   (e) Number of national employees by function
   (f) Average hours worked per week
   (g) Labour turnover, annual rate
   (h) Absenteeism—working hours lost (number and as percentage of total working hours per year)
   (i) Accident rates (describe basis)
   (j) Description of health and safety standards
   (k) Employee costs
       (i) Total wages, salaries, and other payments to employees (before tax)
       (ii) Social expenditures paid to institutions and Government for benefit of workers (excluding pension schemes reported in the profit and loss statement)
       (iii) Summary description and cost of training programmes

2. Production

   (a) Description of practices regarding acquisition of raw materials and components (indicate percentage acquired from intercompany foreign sources and percentage from all foreign sources)
   (b) Indicate average annual capacity utilization in accordance with normal industrial practice
   (c) Physical output by principal lines of business in accordance with normal industrial practice
   (d) Description of significant new products and processes

3. Investment programme

   (a) Description of announced new capital expenditure
   (b) Description of main projects, including their cost, estimated additions to capacity, estimated direct effect on employment
   (c) Description of announced mergers and takeovers, including their cost and estimated direct effect on employment

---

[b] For reporting of these items, reference may be made to the application of national laws, agreements with trade unions, or publicly available written company policies.

4. Organizational structure

(a) Names of members of board of directors and, where applicable, the supervisory board and a description of their affiliations with companies outside the group

(b) Number of owners or shareholders and, where known, the names of the principal owners or shareholders

5. Environmental measures

Description of types of major or special environmental measures carried out, together with cost data, where available

Appendix II

The OECD Guidelines for Multinational Enterprises (1976, revised 1979)

DECLARATION
ON INTERNATIONAL INVESTMENT
AND MULTINATIONAL ENTERPRISES
(21st June 1976)

THE GOVERNMENTS OF OECD
MEMBER COUNTRIES

CONSIDERING

- that international investment has assumed increased importance in the world economy and has considerably contributed to the development of their countries;

- that multinational enterprises play an important role in this investment process;

- that co-operation by Member countries can improve the foreign investment climate, encourage the positive contribution which multinational enterprises can make to economic and social progress, and minimise and resolve difficulties which may arise from their various operations.

- that, while continuing endeavours within the OECD may lead to further international arrangements and agreements in this field, it seems appropriate at this stage to intensify their co-operation and consultation on issues relating to international investment and multinational enterprises through interrelated instruments each of which deals with a different aspect of the matter and together constitute a framework within which the OECD will consider these issues:

DECLARE:

Guidelines for Multinational Enterprises	I.	that they jointly recommend to multinational enterprises operating in their territories the observance of the Guidelines as set forth in the Annex hereto having regard to the considerations and understandings which introduce the Guidelines and are an integral part of them;

National Treatment II.

1. that Member countries should, consistent with their needs to maintain public order, to protect their essential security interests and to fulfil commitments relating to international peace and security, accord to enterprises operating in their territories and owned or controlled directly or indirectly by nationals of another Member country (hereinafter referred to as 'Foreign-Controlled Enterprises') treatment under their laws, regulations, and administrative practices, consistent with international law and no less favourable than that accorded in like situations to domestic enterprises (hereinafter referred to as 'National Treatment');

2. that Member countries will consider applying 'National Treatment' in respect of countries other than Member countries;

3. that Member countries will endeavour to ensure that their territorial subdivisions apply 'National Treatment';

4. that this Declaration does not deal with the right of Member countries to regulate the entry of foreign investment or the conditions of establishment of foreign enterprises;

International Investment Incentives and Disincentives III.

1. that they recognise the need to strengthen their co-operation in the field of international direct investment.

2. that they thus recognise the need to give due weight to the interests of Member countries affected by specific laws, regulations, and administrative practices in this field (hereinafter called 'measures') providing official incentives and disincentives to international direct investment;

3. that Member countries will endeavour to make such measures as transparent as possible, so that their importance and purpose can be ascertained and that information on them can be readily available;

Consultation Procedures	IV.	that they are prepared to consult one another on the above matters in conformity with the Decisions of the Council relating to Inter-Governmental Consultation procedures on the Guidelines for Multinational Enterprises, on National Treatment and on International Investment Incentives and Disincentives;
Review	V.	that they will review the above matters within three years* with a view to improving the effectiveness of international economic co-operation among Member countries on issues relating to international investment and multinational enterprises.

Annex to the Declaration of 21st June, 1976 by Governments of OECD Member Countries on International Investment and Multinational Enterprises

GUIDELINES FOR MULTINATIONAL ENTERPRISES

1.   Multinational enterprises now play an important part in the economies of Member countries and in international economic relations, which is of increasing interest to governments. Through international direct investment, such enterprises can bring substantial benefits to home and host countries by contributing to the efficient utilization of capital, technology and human resources between countries and can thus fulfil an important role in the promotion of ecnomic and social welfare. But the advances made by multinational enterprises in organizing their operations beyond the national framework may lead to abuse of concentrations of economic power and to conflicts with national policy objectives. In addition, the complexity of these multinational enterprises and the difficulty of clearly perceiving their diverse structures, operations, and policies sometimes give rise to concern.

2.   The common aim of the Member countries is to encourage the positive contributions which multinational enterprises can make to economic and social progress and to minimize and resolve the difficulties to which their various operations may give rise. In view of the transnational structure of such enterprises, this aim will be furthered by co-operation among the OECD countries where the headquarters of most of the multinational enterprises are established and which are the location of a substantial part of their operations. The guidelines set out hereafter are designed to assist in the achievement of this common aim and to contribute to improving the foreign investment climate.

---

* NOTE: The Turkish Government did not participate in the Declaration and abstained from the Decisions.

3.   Since the operations of multinational enterprises extend throughout the world, including countries that are not Members of the Organisation, international co-operation in this field should extend to all States. Member countries will give their full support to efforts undertaken in co-operation with non-member countries, and in particular with developing countries, with a view to improving the welfare and living standards of all people both by encouraging the positive contributions which multinational enterprises can make and by minimizing and resolving the problems which may arise in connection with their activities.

4.   Within the Organization, the programme of co-operation to attain these ends will be a continuing, pragmatic and balanced one. It comes within the general aims of the Convention on the Organization for Economic Co-operation and Development (OECD) and makes full use of the various specialised bodies of the Organisation, whose terms of reference already cover many aspects of the role of multinational enterprises, notably in matters of international trade and payments, competition, taxation, manpower, industrial development, science and technology. In these bodies, work is being carried out on the identification of issues, the improvement of relevant qualitative and statistical information and the elaboration of proposals for action designed to strengthen inter-governmental co-operation. In some of these areas procedures already exist through which issues related to the operations of multinational enterprises can be taken up. This work could result in the conclusion of further and complementary agreements and arrangements between governments.

5.   The initial phase of the co-operation programme is composed of a Declaration and three Decisions promulgated simultaneously as they are complementary and inter-connected, in respect of guidelines for multinational enterprises national treatment for foreign-controlled enterprises and international investment incentives and disincentives.

6.   The guidelines set out below are recommendations jointly addressed by Member countries to multinational enterprises operating in their territories. These guidelines, which take into account the problems whikh can arise because of the international structure of these enterprises, lay down standards for the activities of these enterprises in the different Member countries. Observance of the guidelines is voluntary and not legally enforceable. However, they should help to ensure that the operations of these enterprises are in harmony with national policies of the countries where they operate and to strengthen the basis of mutual confidence between enterprises and States.

7.   Every State has the right to prescribe the conditions under which multinational enterprises operate within its national jurisdiction, subject to international law and to the international agreements to which it has subscribed. The entities of a multinational enterprise located in various countries are subject to the laws of these countries.

8.   A precise legal definition of multinational enterprises is not required for the purposes of the guidelines. These usually comprise companies or other entities whose ownership is private, state or mixed, established in different countries and so linked that one or more of them may be able to exercise a significant influence over the activities of others and, in particular, to share knowledge and resources with the others. The degree of autonomy of each entity in relation to the others varies widely from one multinational enterprise

to another, depending on the nature of the links between such entities and the fields of activity concerned. For these reasons, the guidelines are addressed to the various entities within the multinational enterprise (parent companies and/ or local entities) according to the actual distribution of responsibilities among them on the understanding that they will co-operate and provide assistance to one another as necessary to facilitate observance of the guidelines. The word 'enterprise' as used in these guidelines refers to these various entities in accordance with their responsibilities.

9.   The guidelines are not aimed at introducing differences of treatment between multinational and domestic enterprises; wherever relevant they reflect good practice for all. Accordingly, multinational and domestic enterprises are subject to the same expectations in respect of their conduct wherever the guidelines are relevant to both.

10.   The use of appropriate international dispute settlement mechanisms, including arbitration, should be encouraged as a means of facilitating the resolution of problems arising between enterprises and Member countries.

11.   Member countries have agreed to establish appropriate review and consultation procedures concerning issues arising in respect of the guidelines. When multinational enterprises are made subject to conflicting requirements by Member countries, the governments concerned will co-operate in good faith with a view to resolving such problems either within the Committee on International Investment and Multinational Enterprises established by the OECD Council on 21st January, 1975, or through other mutually acceptable arrangements.

Having regard to the foregoing considerations, the Member countries set forth the following guidelines for multinational enterprises with the understanding that Member countries will fulfil their responsibilities to treat enterprises equitably and in accordance with international law and international agreements, as well as contractual obligations to which they have subscribed.

GENERAL POLICIES

Enterprises should
1.   take fully into account established general policy objectives of the Member countries in which they operate;

2.   in particular, give due consideration to those countries' aims and priorities, with regard to economic and social progress, including industrial and regional development, the protection of the environment, the creation of employment opportunities, the promotion of innovation and the transfer of technology;

3.   while observing their legal obligations concerning information, supply their entities with supplementary information the latter may need in order to meet requests by the authorities of the countries in which those entities are located for information relevant to the activities of

those entities, taking into account legitimate requirements of business confidentiality;

4. favour close co-operation with the local community and business interests;

5. allow their component entities freedom to develop their activities and to exploit their competitive advantage in domestic and foreign markets, consistent with the need for specialisation and sound commercial practice;

6. when filling responsible posts in each country of operation, take due account of individual qualifications without discrimination as to nationality, subject to particular national requirements in this respect;

7. not render—and they should not be solicited or expected to render—any bribe or other improper benefit, direct or indirect, to any public servant or holder of public office;

8. unless legally permissible, not make contributions to candidates for public office or to political parties or other political organisations;

9. abstain from any improper involvement in local political activities.

DISCLOSURE OF INFORMATION

Enterprises should, having due regard to their nature and relative size in the economic context of their operations and to requirements of business confidentiality and to cost, publish in a form suited to improve public understanding a sufficient body of factual information on the structure, activities and policies of the enterprise as a whole, as a supplement, in so far as necessary for this purpose, to information to be disclosed under the national law of the individual countries in which they operate. To this end, they should publish within reasonable time limits, on a regular basis, but at least annually, financial statements and other pertinent information relating to the enterprise as a whole, comprising in particular:

i) the structure of the enterprise, showing the name and location of the parent company, its main affiliates, its percentage ownership, direct and indirect, in these affiliates, including shareholdings between them;

ii) the geographical areas* where operations are carried out and the principal activities carried on therein by the parent company and the main affiliates;

---

* For the purposes of the guideline on disclosure of information the term 'geographical area' means groups of countries or individual countries as each enterprise determines is appropriate in its particular circumstances. While no single method of grouping is appropriate for all enterprises or for all purposes, the factors to be considered by an enterprise would include the significance of operations carried out in individual countries or areas as well as the effects on its competitiveness, geographic proximity, economic affinity, similarities in business environments and the nature, scale and degree of interrelationship of the enterprises' operations in the various countries.

iii) the operating results and sales by geographical area and the sales in the major lines of business for the enterprise as a whole;

iv) significant new capital investment by geographical area and, as far as practicable, by major lines of business for the enterprise as a whole;

v) a statement of the sources and use of funds by the enterprise as a whole;

vi) the average number of employees in each geographical area;

vii) research and development expenditure for the enterprise as a whole;

viii) the policies followed in respect of intra-group pricing;

ix) the accounting policies, including those on consolidation, observed in compiling the published information.

COMPETITION

Enterprises should, while conforming to official competition rules and established policies of the countries in which they operate,

1. refrain from actions which would adversely affect competition in the relevant market by abusing a dominant position of market power, by means of, for example,

a) anti-competitive acquisitions,
b) predatory behaviour toward competitors,
c) unreasonable refusal to deal,
d) anti-competitive abuse of industrial property rights,
e) discriminatory (i.e. unreasonably differentiated) pricing and using such pricing transactions between affiliated enterprises as a means of affecting adversely competition outside these enterprises;

2. allow purchasers, distributors and licensees freedom to resell, export, purchase and develop their operations consistent with law, trade conditions, the need for specialisation and sound commercial practice;

3. refrain from participating in or otherwise purposely strengthening the restrictive effects of international or domestic cartels or restrictive agreements which adversely affect or eliminate competition and which are not generally or specifically accepted under applicable national or international legislation.

4. be ready to consult and co-operate, including the provision of information, with competent authorities of countries whose interests are directly affected in regard to competition issues or investigations. Provision of information should be in accordance with safeguards normally applicable in this field.

FINANCING

Enterprises should, in managing the financial and commercial operations of their activities, and especially their liquid foreign assets and liabilities, take into consideration the established objectives of the countries in which they operate regarding balance of payments and credit policies.

TAXATION

Enterprises should

1. upon request of the taxation authorities of the countries in which they operate, provide, in accordance with the safeguards and relevant procedures of the national laws of these countries, the information necessary to determine correctly the taxes to be assessed in connection with their operations, including relevant information concerning their operations in other countries;

2. refrain from making use of the particular facilities available to them, such as transfer pricing which does not conform to an arm's length standard, for modifying in ways contrary to national laws the tax base on which members of the group are assessed.

EMPLOYMENT AND INDUSTRIAL RELATIONS

Enterprises should, within the framework of law, regulations and prevailing labour relations and employment practices, in each of the countries in which they operate,

1. respect the right of their employees, to be represented by trade unions and other bona fide organisations of employees, and engage in constructive negotiations, either individually or through employers' associations, with such employee organisations with a view to reaching agreements on employment conditions, which should include provisions for dealing with disputes arising over the interpretation of such agreements, and for ensuring mutually respected rights and responsibilities;

2. a) provide such facilities to representatives of the employees as may be necessary to assist in the development of effective collective agreements,

   b) provide to representatives of employees information which is needed for meaningful negotiations on conditions of employment;

3. provide to representatives of employees where this accords with local law and practice, information which enables them to obtain a true and fair view of the performance of the entity or, where appropriate, the enterprise as a whole;

4. observe standards of employment and industrial relations not less favourable than those observed by comparable employers in the host country;

5. in their operations, to the greatest extent practicable, utilise, train and prepare for upgrading members of the local labour force in co-operation

with representatives of their employees and, where appropriate, the relevant governmental authorities;

6. in considering changes in their operations which would have major effects upon the livelihood of their employees, in particular in the case of the closure of an entity envoling collective lay-offs or dismissals, provide reasonable notice of such changes to representatives of their employees, and where appropriate to the relevant governmental authorities, and cooperate with the employee representatives and appropriate governmental authorities so as to mitigate to the maximum extent practicable adverse effects;

7. implement their employment policies including hiring, discharge, pay, promotion and training without discrimination unless selectivity in respect of employee characteristics is in furtherance of established governmental policies which specifically promote greater equality of employment opportunity;

8. in the context of bona fide negotiations* with representatives of employees on conditions of employment, or while employees are exercising a right to organise, not threaten to utilise a capacity to transfer the whole or part of an operating unit from the country concerned nor transfer employees from the enterprises' component entities in other countries in order to influence unfairly those negotiations or to hinder the exercise of a right to organise;

9. enable authorised representatives of their employees to conduct negotiations on collective bargaining or labour management relations issues with representatives of management who are authorised to take decisions on the matters under negotiation.

SCIENCE AND TECHNOLOGY

Enterprises should
1. endeavour to ensure that their activities fit satisfactorily into the scientific and technological policies and plans of the countries in which they operate, and contribute to the development of national scientific and technological capacities, including as far as appropriate the establishment and improvement in host countries of their capacity to innovate;

2. to the fullest extent practicable, adopt in the course of their business activities practices which permit the rapid diffusion of technologies with due regard to the protection of industrial and intellectual property rights;

---

* Bona fide negotiations may include labour disputes as part of the process of negotiation. Whether or not labour disputes are so included will be determined by the law and prevailing employment practices of particular countries.

3. when granting licences for the use of industrial property rights or when otherwise transferring technology do so on reasonable terms and conditions.

REVISED DECISION OF THE COUNCIL ON INTER-GOVERNMENTAL CONSULTATION PROCEDURES ON THE GUIDELINES FOR MULTINATIONAL ENTERPRISES

THE COUNCIL,

Having regard to the Convention on the Organisation for Economic Cooperation and Development of 14th December, 1960 and, in particular, to Articles 2 *d*), 3 and 5 *a*) thereof;

Having regard to the Resolution of the Council of 22nd December, 1976 on the Terms of References of the Committee on International Investment and Multinational Enterprises and, in particular to paragraph 2 thereof [C (76) 209 (Final)];

Taking note of the Declaration by the Governments of OECD Member countries of 21st June, 1976 in which they jointly recommend to multinational enterprises the observance of guidelines for multinational enterprises;

Having regard to the Decision of the Council of 21st June, 1976 on Inter-Governmental Consultation Procedures on the Guidelines for Multinational Enterprises [C (76) 117];

Recognising the desirability of setting forth procedures by which consultations may take place on matters related to these guidelines;

Considering the Report on the Review of the 1976 Declaration and Decisions on International Investment and Multinational Enterprises [C (79) 102 (Final)];

On the proposal of the Committee on International Investment and Multinational Enterprises;

DECIDES:

1.   The Committee on International Investment and Multinational Enterprises (hereinafter called 'the Committee') shall periodically or at the request of a Member country hold an exchange of views on matters related to the Guidelines and the experience gained in their application. The Committee shall be responsible for clarification of the Guidelines. Clarification will be provided as required. The Committee shall periodically report to the Council on these matters.

2.   The Committee shall periodically invite the Business and Industry Advisory Committee to OECD (BIAC) and the Trade Union Advisory Committee to OECD (TUAC) to express their views on matters related to the

Guidelines. In addition, exchanges of views with the advisory bodies on these matters may be held upon request by the latter. The Committee shall take account of such views in its reports to the Council.

If it so wishes, an individual enterprise will be given the opportunity to express its views either orally or in writing on issues concerning the Guidelines involving its interests.

The Committee shall not reach conclusions on the conduct of individual enterprises.

Member countries may request that consultations be held in the Committee on any problem arising from the fact that multinational enterprises are made subject to conflicting requirements. Governments concerned will co-operate in good faith with a view to resolving such problems, either within the Committee or through other mutually acceptable arrangements.

This Decision shall be reviewed at the latest in five years. The Committee shall make proposals for this purpose as appropriate.

This Decision replaces Decision [C (76) 117].

REVISED DECISION OF THE COUNCIL ON NATIONAL TREATMENT

THE COUNCIL,

Having regard to the Convention on the Organisation for Economic Co-operation and Development of 14th December, 1960 and, in particular, to Articles 2 *c*), 2 *d*), 3 and 5 *a*) thereof;

Having regard to the Resolution of the Council of 22nd December, 1976 on the Terms of Reference of the Committee on International Investment and Multinational Enterprises and, in particular, to paragraph 2 thereof [C (76) 209 (Final)];

Taking note of the Declaration by the Governments of OECD Member countries of 21st June, 1976 on National Treatment;

Having regard to the Decision of the Council of 21st June, 1976 on National Treatment [C (76) 118];

Considering that it is appropriate to establish within the Organisation suitable procedures for reviewing laws, regulations and administrative practices (hereinafter referred to as 'measures') which depart from 'National Treatment';

Considering the Report on the Review of the 1976 Declaration and Decisions on International Investment and Multinational Enterprises [C (79) 102 (Final)];

On the proposal of the Committee on International Investment and Multinational Enterprises;

DECIDES:

1.   Measures taken by a Member country constituting exceptions to 'National Treatment' (including measures restricting new investment by 'Foreign-Controlled Enterprises' already established in their territory) in effect on 21st June, 1976 shall be notified to the Organisation within 60 days after that date.

2.   Measures taken by a Member country constituting new exceptions to 'National Treatment' (including measures restricting new investment by 'Foreign-Controlled Enterprises' already established in their territory) taken after 21st June 1976 shall be notified to the Organisation within 30 days of their introduction together with the specific reasons therefor and the proposed duration thereof.

Measures introduced by a territorial subdivision of a Member country, pursuant to its independent powers, which constitute exceptions to 'National Treatment', shall be notified to the Organisation by the Member country concerned, insofar as it has knowledge thereof, within 30 days of the responsible officials of the Member country obtaining such knowledge.

The Committee on International Investment and Multinational Enterprises (hereinafter called 'the Committee') shall periodically review the application of 'National Treatment' (including exceptions thereto) with a view to extending such application of 'National Treatment'. The Committee shall make proposals as and when necessary in this connection.

The Committee may periodically invite the Business and Industry Advisory Committee to OECD (BIAC) and the Trade Union Advisory Committee to OECD (TUAC) to express their views on matters related to National Treatment and shall take account of such views in its periodic reports to the Council.

The Committee shall act as a forum for consultations, at the request of a Member country, in respect of any matter related to this instrument and its implementation, including exceptions to 'National Treatment' and their application.

Member countries shall provide to the Committee, upon its request, all relevant information, concerning measures pertaining to the application of 'National Treatment' and exceptions thereto.

This Decision shall be reviewed at the latest in five years. The Committee shall make proposals for this purpose as appropriate.

This Decision shall replace Decision [C (76) 118].

REVISED DECISION OF THE COUNCIL ON INTERNATIONAL INVESTMENT INCENTIVES AND DISINCENTIVES

THE COUNCIL,

Having regard to the Convention on the Organisation for Economic Co-operation and Development of 14th December, 1960 and, in particular, Articles 2 c), 2 d), 2 e), 3 and 5 a) thereof;

Having regard to the Resolution of the Council of 22nd December, 1976 on the Terms of Reference of the Committee on International Investment and Multinational Enterprises and, in particular, paragraph 2 thereof [C (76) 209 (Final)];

Taking note of the Declaration by the Governments of OECD Member countries of 21st June, 1976 on International Investment Incentives and Disincentives;

Having regard to the Decision of the Council of 21st June, 1976 on International Investment Incentives and Disincentives [C (76) 119];

Considering the Report on the Review of the 1976 Declaration and Decisions on International Investment and Multinational Enterprises [C (79) 102 (Final)];

On the proposal of the Committee on International Investment and Multinational Enterprises;

DECIDES:

1.   Consultations will take place in the framework of the Committee on International Investment and Multinational Enterprises at the request of a Member country which considers that its interests may be adversely affected by the impact on its flow of international direct investments of measures taken by another Member country specifically designed to provide incentives or disincentives for international direct investment. Having full regard to the national economic objectives of the measures and without prejudice to policies designed to redress regional imbalances, the purpose of the consultations will be to examine the possibility of reducing such effects to a minimum.

2.   Member countries shall supply, under the consultation procedures, all permissible information relating to any measures being the subject of the consultation.

The Committee may periodically invite the Business and Industry Advisory Committee to OECD (BIAC) and the Trade Union Advisory Committee to OECD (TUAC) to express their views on matters relating to international investment incentives and disincentives and shall take account of these views in its periodic reports to the Council.

The Decision shall be reviewed at the latest in five years. The Committee on International Investment and Multinational Enterprises shall make proposals for this purpose as appropriate.

This Decision shall replace Decision [C (76) 119].

Appendix III

The EEC Seventh Directive on Consolidated Accounts (1983) (Official Journal, 18 July 1983, No. L193)

SEVENTH COUNCIL DIRECTIVE

of 13 June 1983

based on the Article 54 (3) (g) of the Treaty on consolidated accounts

(83/349/EEC)

THE COUNCIL OF THE EUROPEAN COMMUNITIES,

Having regard to the Treaty establishing the European Economic Community, and in particular Article 54 (3) (g) thereof,

Having regard to the proposal from the Commission (¹),

Having regard to the opinion of the European Parliament (²),

Having regard to the opinion of the Economic and Social Committee (³),

Whereas on 25 July 1978 the Council adopted Directive 78/660/EEC (⁴) on the coordination of national legislation governing the annual accounts of certain types of companies; whereas many companies are members of bodies of undertakings; whereas consolidated accounts must be drawn up so that financial information concerning such bodies of undertakings may be conveyed to members and third parties; whereas national legislation governing consolidated accounts must therefore be coordinated in order to achieve the objectives of comparability and equivalence in the information which companies must publish within the Community;

Whereas, in the determination of the conditions for consolidation, account must be taken not only of cases in

(¹) OJ No C 121, 2. 6. 1976, p. 2.
(²) OJ No C 163, 10.7. 1978, p. 60.
(³) OJ No C 75, 26. 3. 1977, p. 5.

(⁴) OJ No L 222, 14.8.1978, p. 11.

which the power of control is based on a majority of voting rights but also of those in which it is based on agreements, where these are permitted; whereas, furthermore, Member States in which the possibility occurs must be permitted to cover cases in which in certain circumstances control has been effectively exercised on the basis of a minority holding; whereas the Member States must be permitted to cover the case of bodies of undertakings in which the undertakings exist on an equal footing with each other;

Whereas the aim of coordinating the legislation governing consolidated accounts is to protect the interests subsisting in companies with share capital; whereas such protection implies the principle of the preparation of consolidated accounts where such a company is a member of a body of undertakings, and that such accounts must be drawn up at least where such a company is a parent undertaking; whereas, furthermore, the cause of full information also requires that a subsidiary undertaking which is itself a parent undertaking draw up consolidated accounts; whereas, nevertheless, such a parent undertaking may, and, in certain circumstances, must be exempted from the obligation to draw up such consolidated accounts provided that its members and third parties are sufficiently protected;

Whereas, for bodies of undertakings not exceeding a certain size, exemption from the obligation to prepare consolidated accounts may be justified; whereas, accordingly, maximum limits must be set for such exemptions; whereas it follows therefrom that the Member States may either provide that it is sufficient to exceed the limit of one only of the three criteria for the exemption not to

apply or adopt limits lower than those prescribed in the Directive;

Whereas consolidated accounts must give a true and fair view of the assets and liabilities, the financial position and the profit and loss of all the undertakings consolidated taken as a whole; whereas, therefore, consolidation should in principle include all of those undertakings; whereas such consolidation requires the full incorporation of the assets and liabilities and of the income and expenditure of those undertakings and the separate disclosure of the interests of persons outwith such bodies; whereas, however, the necessary corrections must be made to eliminate the effects of the financial relations between the undertakings consolidated;

Whereas a number of principles relating to the preparation of consolidated accounts and valuation in the context of such accounts must be laid down in order to ensure that items are disclosed consistently, and may readily be compared not only as regards the methods used in their valuation but also as regards the periods covered by the accounts;

Whereas participating interests in the capital of undertakings over which undertakings included in a consolidation exercise significant influence must be included in consolidated accounts by means of the equity method;

Whereas the notes on consolidated accounts must give details of the undertakings to be consolidated;

Whereas certain derogations originally provided for on a transitional basis in Directive 78/660/EEC may be continued subject to review at a later date,

HAS ADOPTED THIS DIRECTIVE:

SECTION 1

Conditions for the preparation of consolidated accounts

Article 1

1. Member State shall require any undertaking governed by its national law to draw up consolidated accounts and a consolidated annual report if that undertaking (a parent undertaking):

(a) has a majority of the shareholders' or members' voting rights in another undertaking (a subsidiary undertaking); or

(b) has the right to appoint or remove a majority of the members of the administrative, management or supervisory body of another undertaking (a subsidiary undertaking) and is at the same time a shareholder in or member of that undertaking; or

(c) has the right to exercise a dominant influence over an undertaking (a subsidiary undertaking) of which it is a shareholder or member, pursuant to a contract entered into with that undertaking or to a provision in its memorandum or articles of association, where the law governing that subsidiary undertaking permits its being subject to such contracts or

provisions. A Member State need not prescribe that a parent undertaking must be a shareholder in or member of its subsidiary undertaking. Those Member States the laws of which do not provide for such contracts or clauses shall not be required to apply this provision; or

(d) is a shareholder in or member of an undertaking, and:

(aa) a majority of the members of the administrative, management or supervisory bodies of that undertaking (a subsidiary undertaking) who have held office during the financial year, during the preceding financial year and up to the time when the consolidated accounts are drawn up, have been appointed solely as a result of the exercise of its voting rights; or

(bb) controls alone, pursuant to an agreement with other shareholders in or members of that undertaking (a subsidiary undertaking), a majority of shareholders' or members' voting rights in that undertaking. The Member States may introduce more detailed provisions concerning the form and contents of such agreements.

The Member States shall prescribe at least the arrangements referred to in (bb) above.

They may make the application of (aa) above dependent upon the holding's representing 20% or more of the shareholders' or members' voting rights.

However, (aa) above shall not apply where another undertaking has the rights referred to in subparagraphs (a), (b) or (c) above with regard to that subsidiary undertaking.

2. Apart from the cases mentioned in paragraph 1 above and pending subsequent coordination, the Member States may require any undertaking governed by their national law to draw up consolidated accounts and a consolidated annual report if that undertaking (a parent undertaking) holds a participating interest as defined in Article 17 of Directive 78/660/EEC in another undertaking (a subsidiary undertaking), and:

(a) it actually exercises a dominant influence over it; or

(b) it and the subsidiary undertaking are managed on a unified basis by the parent undertaking.

(a) attaching to shares held on behalf of a person who is neither the parent undertaking nor a subsidiary thereof; or

(b) attaching to shares held by way of security, provided that the rights in question are exercised in accordance with the instructions received, or held in connection with the granting of loans as part of normal business activities, provided that the voting rights are exercised in the interests of the person providing the security.

3. For the purposes of Article 1 (1) (a) and (d), the total of the shareholders' or members' voting rights in the subsidiary undertaking must be reduced by the voting rights attaching to the shares held by that undertaking itself by a subsidiary undertaking of that undertaking or by a person acting in his own name but on behalf of those undertakings.

Article 2

1. For the purposes of Article 1 (1) (a), (b) and (d), the voting rights and the rights of appointment and removal of any other subsidiary undertaking as well as those of any person acting in his own name but on behalf of the parent undertaking or of another subsidiary undertaking must be added to those of the parent undertaking.

2. For the purpose of Article 1 (1) (a), (b) and (d), the rights mentioned in paragraph 1 above must be reduced by the rights:

Article 3

1. Without prejudice to Articles 13, 14 and 15, a parent undertaking and all of its subsidiary undertakings shall be undertakings to be consolidated regardless of where the registered offices of such subsidiary undertakings are situated.

2. For the purposes of paragraph 1 above, any subsidiary undertaking of a subsidiary undertaking shall be considered a subsidiary undertaking of the parent undertaking which is the parent of the undertakings to be consolidated.

Article 4

1. For the purposes of this Directive, a parent undertaking and all of its subsidiary undertakings shall be undertakings to be consolidated where either the parent undertaking or one or more subsidiary undertakings is established as one of the following types of company:

(a) *in Germany:*

die Aktiengesellschaft, die Kommanditgesellschaft auf Aktien, die Gesellschaft mit beschränkter Haftung;

(b) *in Belgium:*

la société anonyme/de naamloze vennootschap – la société en commandite par actions / de commanditaire vennootschap op aandelen – la société de personnes à responsabilité limitée / de personenvennootschap met beperkte aansprakelijkheid;

(c) *in Denmark:*

aktieselskaber, kommanditaktieselskaber, anpartsselskaber;

(d) *in France:*

la société anonyme, la société en commandite par actions, la société à responsabilité limitée;

(e) *in Greece:*

η ανώνυμη εταιρία, η εταιρία περιορισμένης ευθύνης, η ετερόρρυθμη κατά μετοχές εταιρίας

(f) *in Ireland:*

public companies limited by shares or by guarantee, private companies limited by shares or by guarantee;

(g) *in Italy:*

la società per azioni, la società in accomandita per azioni, la società a responsabilità limitata;

(h) *in Luxembourg:*

la société anonyme, la société en commandite par actions, la société à responsabilité limitée;

(i) *in the Netherlands:*

de naamloze vennootschap, de besloten vennootschap met beperkte aansprakelijkheid;

(j) *in the United Kingdom:*

public companies limited by shares or by guarantee, private companies limited by shares or by guarantee.

2. A Member State may, however, grant exemption from the obligation imposed in Article 1 (1) where the parent undertaking is not established as one of the types of company listed in paragraph 1 above.

Article 5

1. A Member State may grant exemption from the obligation imposed in article 1 (1) where the parent undertaking is a financial holding company as defined in Article 5 (3) of Directive 78/660/EEC, and:

(a) it has not intervened during the financial year, directly or indirectly, in the management of a subsidiary undertaking;

(b) it has not exercised the voting rights attaching to its participating interest in respect of the appointment of a member of a subsidiary undertaking's administrative, management or supervisory bodies during the financial year or the five preceding financial years or, where the exercise of voting rights was necessary for the operation of the administrative, management or supervisory bodies of the subsidiary undertaking, no shareholder in or member of the parent undertaking with majority voting rights or member of the administrative, management or supervisory bodies of that undertaking or of a member thereof with majority voting rights is a member of the administrative, management or supervisory bodies of the subsidiary undertaking and the members of those bodies so appointed have fulfilled their functions without any interference or influence on the part of the parent undertaking or of any of its subsidiary undertakings;

(c) it has made loans only to undertakings in which it holds participating interests. Where such loans have been made to other parties, they must have been repaid by the end of the previous financial year: and

(d) the exception is granted by an administrative authority after fulfilment of the above conditions has been checked.

2. (a) Where a financial holding company has been exempted, Article 43 (2) of Directive 78/660/EEC shall not apply to its annual accounts with respect to any majority holdings in subsidiary undertakings as from the date provided for in Article 49 (2).

(b) The disclosures in respect of such majority holdings provided for in point 2 of Article 43 (1) of Directive 78/660/EEC may be omitted when their nature is such that they would be seriously prejudicial to the company, to its shareholders or members or to one of its subsidiaries. A Member State may make such omissions subject to prior administrative or judicial authorization. Any such omission must be disclosed in the notes on the accounts.

Article 6

1.   Without prejudice to Articles 4 (2) and 5, a Member State may provide for an exemption from the obligation imposed in Article 1 (1) if as at the balance sheet date of a parent undertaking the undertakings to be consolidated do not together, on the basis of their latest annual accounts, exceed the limits of two of the three criteria laid down in Article 27 of Directive 78/660/EEC.

2.   A Member State may require or permit that the set-off referred to in Article 19 (1) and the elimination referred to in Article 26 (1) (a) and (b) be not effected when the aforementioned limits are calculated. In that case, the limits for the balance sheet total and net turnover criteria shall be increased by 20%.

3.   Article 12 of Directive 78/660/EEC shall apply to the above criteria.

4.   This Article shall not apply where one of the undertakings to be consolidated is a company the securi-

ties of which have been admitted to official listing on a stock exchange established in a Member State.

5. For 10 years after the date referred to in Article 49 (2), the Member States may multiply the criteria expressed in ECU by up to 2,5 and may increase the average number of persons employed during the financial year to a maximum of 500.

Article 7

1. Notwithstanding Articles 4 (2), 5 and 6, a Member State shall exempt from the obligation imposed in Article 1 (1) any parent undertaking governed by its national law which is also a subsidiary undertaking if its own parent undertaking is governed by the law of a Member State in the following two cases:

(a) where that parent undertaking holds all of the shares in the exempted undertaking. The shares in that undertaking held by members of its administrative, management or supervisory bodies pursuant to an obligation in law or in the memorandum or articles of association shall be ignored for this purpose; or

(b) where that parent undertaking holds 90% or more of the shares in the exempted undertaking and the remaining shareholders in or members of that undertaking have approved the exemption.

In so far as the laws of a Member State prescribe consolidation in this case at the time of the adoption of this Directive, that Member State need not apply this

provision for 10 years after the date referred to in Article 49 (2).

2. Exemption shall be conditional upon compliance with all of the following conditions:

(a) the exempted undertaking and, without prejudice to Articles 13, 14 and 15, all of its subsidiary undertakings must be consolidated in the accounts of a larger body of undertakings, the parent undertaking of which is governed by the law of a Member State;

(b) (aa) the consolidated accounts referred to in (a) above and the consolidated annual report of the larger body of undertakings must be drawn up by the parent undertaking of that body and audited, according to the law of the Member State by which the parent undertaking of that larger body of undertakings is governed, in accordance with this Directive;

(bb) the consolidated accounts referred to in (a) above and the consolidated annual report referred to in (aa) above, the report by the person responsible for auditing those accounts and, where appropriate, the appendix referred to in Article 9 must be published for the exempted undertaking in the manner prescribed by the law of the Member State governing that undertaking in accordance with Article 38. That Member State may require that those documents be published in its official language and that the translation be certified;

(c) the notes on the annual accounts of the exempted undertaking must disclose:

(aa) the name and registered office of the parent undertaking that draws up the consolidated accounts referred to in (a) above; and

(bb) the exemption from the obligation to draw up consolidated accounts and a consolidated annual report.

3. A Member State need not, however, apply this Article to companies the securities of which have been admitted to official listing on a stock exchange established in a Member State.

Article 8

1. In cases not covered by Article 7 (1), a Member State may, without prejudice to Articles 4 (2), 5 and 6, exempt from the obligation imposed in Article 1 (1) any parent undertaking governed by its national law which is also a subsidiary undertaking, the parent undertaking of which is governed by the law of a Member State, provided that all the conditions set out in Article 7 (2) are fulfilled and that the shareholders in or members of the exempted undertaking who own a minimum proportion of the subscribed capital of that undertaking have not requested the preparation of consolidated accounts at least six months before the end of the financial year. The Member States may fix that proportion at not more than 10% for public limited liability companies and for limited partnerships with share capital, and at not more than 20% for undertakings of other types.

2. A Member State may not make it a condition for this exemption that the parent undertaking which prepared the consolidated accounts described in Article 7 (2) (a) must also be governed by its national law.

3. A Member State may not make exemption subject to conditions concerning the preparation and auditing of the consolidated accounts referred to in Article 7 (2) (a).

Article 9

1. A Member State may make the exemptions provided for in Articles 7 and 8 dependent upon the disclosure of additional information, in accordance with this Directive, in the consolidated accounts referred to in Article 7 (2) (a), or in an appendix thereto, if that information is required of undertakings governed by the national law of that Member State which are obliged to prepare consolidated accounts and are in the same circumstances.

2. A Member State may also make exemption dependent upon the disclosure, in the notes on the consolidated accounts referred to in Article 7 (2) (a), or in the annual accounts of the exempted undertaking, of all or some of the following information regarding the body of undertakings, the parent undertaking of which it is exempting from the obligations to draw up consolidated accounts:

— the amount of the fixed assets,

— the net turnover,

— the profit or loss for the financial year and the amount of the capital and reserves,

— the average number of persons employed during the financial year.

Article 10

Articles 7 to 9 shall not affect any Member State's legislation on the drawing up of consolidated accounts or consolidated annual reports in so far as those documents are required:

— for the information of employees or their representatives, or

— by an administrative or judicial authority for its own purposes.

drawn up in accordance with this Directive;

(c) the consolidated accounts referred to in (a) above must have been audited by one or more persons authorized to audit accounts under the national law governing the undertaking which drew them up.

2.   Articles 7 (2) (b) (bb) and (c) and 8 to 10 shall apply.

3.   A Member State may provide for exemptions under this Article only if it provides for the same exemptions under Articles 7 to 10.

Article 11

1.   Without prejudice to Articles 4 (2), 5 and 6, a Member State may exempt from the obligation imposed in Article 1 (1) any parent undertaking governed by its national law which is also a subsidiary undertaking of a parent undertaking not governed by the law of a Member State, if all of the following conditions are fulfilled:

(a) the exempted undertaking and, without prejudice to Articles 13, 14 and 15, all of its subsidiary undertakings must be consolidated in the accounts of a larger body of undertakings;

(b) the   consolidated   accounts referred to in (a) above and, where appropriate, the consolidated annual report must be drawn up in accordance with this Directive or in a manner equivalent to consolidated accounts and consolidated   annual   reports

Article 12

1.   Without prejudice to Articles 1 to 10, a Member State may require any undertaking governed by its national law to draw up consolidated accounts and a consolidated annual report if:

(a) that undertaking and one or more other undertakings with which it is not connected, as described in Article 1 (1) or (2), are managed on a unified basis pursuant to a contract concluded with that undertaking or provisions in the memorandum or articles of association of those undertakings; or

(b) the administrative, management or supervisory bodies of that undertaking and of one or more other undertakings with which it is not connected, as described in Article 1 (1) or (2), consist for the major part of the same persons in office during the financial year and until the consolidated accounts are drawn up.

2. Where paragraph 1 above is applied, undertakings related as defined in that paragraph together with all of their subsidiary undertakings shall be undertakings to be consolidated, as defined in this Directive, where one or more of those undertakings is established as one of the types of company listed in Article 4.

3. Articles 3, 4 (2), 5, 6, 13 to 28, 29 (1), (3), (4) and (5), 30 to 38, and 39 (2) shall apply to the consolidated accounts and the consolidated annual report covered by this Article, references to parent undertakings being understood to refer to all the undertakings specified in paragraph 1 above. Without prejudice to Article 19 (2), however, the items 'capital', 'share premium account', 'revaluation reserve', 'reserves', 'profit or loss brought forward', and 'profit or loss for the financial year' to be included in the consolidated accounts shall be the aggregate amounts attributable to each of the undertakings specified in paragraph 1.

Article 13

1. An undertaking need not be included in consolidated accounts where it is not material for the purposes of Article 16 (3).

2. Where two or more undertakings satisfy the requirements of paragraph 1 above, they must nevertheless be included in consolidated accounts if, as a whole, they are material for the purposes of Article 16 (3).

3. In addition, an undertaking need not be included in consolidated accounts where:

(a) severe long-term restrictions substantially hinder:

    (aa) the parent undertaking in the exercise of its rights over the assets or management of that undertaking; or

    (bb) the exercise of unified management of that undertaking where it is in one of the relationships defined in Article 12 (1); or

(b) the information necessary for the preparation of consolidated accounts in accordance with this Directive cannot be obtained without disproportionate expense or undue delay; or

(c) the shares of that undertaking are held exclusively with a view to their subsequent resale.

Article 14

1. Where the activities of one or more undertakings to be consolidated are so different that their inclusion in the consolidated accounts would be incompatible with the obligation imposed in Article 16 (3), such undertakings must, without prejudice to Article 33 of this Directive, be excluded from the consolidation.

2. Paragraph 1 above shall not be applicable merely by virtue of the fact that the undertakings to be consolidated are partly industrial, partly commercial, and partly provide services, or because such undertakings

carry on industrial or commercial activities involving different products or provide different services.

3. Any application of paragraph 1 above and the reasons therefor must be disclosed in the notes on the accounts. Where the annual or consolidated accounts of the undertakings thus excluded from the consolidation are not published in the same Member State in accordance with Directive 68/151/EEC (¹), they must be attached to the consolidated accounts or made available to the public. In the latter case it must be possible to obtain a copy of such documents upon request. The price of such a copy must not exceed its administrative cost.

Article 15

1. A Member State may, for the purposes of Article 16 (3), permit the omission from consolidated accounts of any parent undertaking not carrying on any industrial or commercial activity which holds shares in a subsidiary undertaking on the basis of a joint arrangement with one or more undertakings not included in the consolidated accounts.

2. The annual accounts of the parent undertaking shall be attached to the consolidated accounts.

3. Where use is made of this derogation, either Article 59 of Directive 78/660/EEC shall apply to the parent undertaking's annual accounts or the information which would have resulted from its application must be given in the notes on those accounts.

(¹) OJ No L 65, 14. 3. 1968, p. 8.

SECTION 2

The preparation of consolidated accounts

Article 16

1. Consolidated accounts shall comprise the consolidated balance sheet, the consolidated profit-and-loss account and the notes on the accounts. These documents shall constitute a composite whole.

2. Consolidated accounts shall be drawn up clearly and in accordance with this Directive.

3. Consolidated accounts shall give a true and fair view of the assets, liabilities, financial position and profit or loss of the undertakings included therein taken as a whole.

4. Where the application of the provisions of this Directive would not be sufficient to give a true and fair view within the meaning of paragraph 3 above, additional information must be given.

5. Where, in exceptional cases, the application of a provision of Articles 17 to 35 and 39 is incompatible with the obligation imposed in paragraph 3 above, that provision must be departed from in order to give a true and fair view within the meaning of paragraph 3. Any such departure must be disclosed in the notes on the accounts together with an explanation of the reasons for it and a statement of its effect on the assets, liabilities, financial position and profit or loss.

The Member States may define the exceptional cases in question and lay down the relevant special rules.

6. A Member State may require or permit the disclosure in the consolidated accounts of other information as well as that which must be disclosed in accordance with this Directive.

Article 17

1. Articles 3 to 10, 13 to 26, and 28 to 30 of Directive 78/660/EEC shall apply in respect of the layout of consolidated accounts, without prejudice to the provisions of this Directive and taking account of the essential adjustments resulting from the particular characteristics of consolidated accounts as compared with annual accounts.

2. Where there are special circumstances which would entail undue expense a Member State may permit stocks to be combined in the consolidated accounts.

Article 18

The assets and liabilities of undertakings included in a consolidation shall be incorporated in full in the consolidated balance sheet.

Article 19

1. The book values of shares in the capital of undertakings included in a consolidation shall be set off against

the proportion which they represent of the capital and reserves of those undertakings:

(a) That set-off shall be effected on the basis of book values as at the date as at which such undertakings are included in the consolidations for the first time. Differences arising from such set-offs shall as far as possible be entered directly against those items in the consolidated balance sheet which have values above or below their book values.

(b) A Member State may require or permit set-offs on the basis of the values of identifiable assets and liabilities as at the date of acquisition of the shares or, in the event of acquisition in two or more stages, as at the date on which the undertaking became a subsidiary.

(c) Any difference remaining after the application of (a) or resulting from the application of (b) shall be shown as a separate item in the consolidated balance sheet with an appropriate heading. That item, the methods used and any significant changes in relation to the preceding financial year must be explained in the notes on the accounts. Where the offsetting of positive and negative differences is authorized by a Member State, a breakdown of such differences must also be given in the notes on the accounts.

2. However, paragraph 1 above shall not apply to shares in the capital of the parent undertaking held either by that undertaking itself or by another undertaking included in the consolidation. In the consolidated accounts such shares shall be treated

as own shares in accordance with Directive 78/660/EEC.

the names and registered offices of the undertakings concerned shall be disclosed in the notes on the accounts.

Article 20

1. A Member State may require or permit the book values of shares held in the capital of an undertaking included in the consolidation to be set off against the corresponding percentage of capital only, provided that:

(a) the shares held represent at least 90% of the nominal value or, in the absence of a nominal value, of the accounting par value of the shares of that undertaking other than shares of the kind described in Article 29 (2) (a) of Directive 77/91/EEC(¹);

(b) the proportion referred to in (a) above has been attained pursuant to an arrangement providing for the issue of shares by an undertaking included in the consolidation; and

(c) the arrangement referred to in (b) above did not include a cash payment exceeding 10% of the nominal value or, in the absence of a nominal value, of the accounting par value of the shares issued.

2. Any difference arising under paragraph 1 above shall be added to or deducted from consolidated reserves as appropriate.

3. The application of the method described in paragraph 1 above, the resulting movement in reserves and

_____

(¹) OJ No L 26, 31. 1. 1977, p. 1.

Article 21

The amount attributable to shares in subsidiary undertakings included in the consolidation held by persons other than the undertakings included in the consolidation shall be shown in the consolidated balance sheet as a separate item with an appropriate heading.

Article 22

The income and expenditure of undertakings included in a consolidation shall be incorporated in full in the consolidated profit-and-loss account.

Article 23

The amount of any profit or loss attributable to shares in subsidiary undertakings included in the consolidation held by persons other than the undertakings included in the consolidation shall be shown in the consolidated profit-and-loss account as a separate item with an appropriate heading.

Article 24

Consolidated accounts shall be drawn up in accordance with the principles enunciated in Articles 25 to 28.

Article 25

1.   The methods of consolidation must be applied consistently from one financial year to another.

2.   Derogations from the provision of paragraph 1 above shall be permitted in exceptional cases. Any such derogations must be disclosed in the notes on the accounts and the reasons for them given together with an assessment of their effect on the assets, liabilities, financial position and profit or loss of the undertakings included in the consolidation taken as a whole.

Article 26

1.   Consolidated accounts shall show the assets, liabilities, financial positions and profits or losses of the undertakings included in a consolidation as if the latter were a single undertaking. In particular:

(a) debts and claims between the undertakings included in a consolidation shall be eliminated from the consolidated accounts;

(b) income and expenditure relating to transactions between the undertakings included in a consolidation shall be eliminated from the consolidated accounts;

(c) where profits and losses resulting from transactions between the undertakings included in a consolidation are included in the book values of assets, they shall be eliminated from the consolidated accounts. Pending subsequent coordination, however, a Member State may allow the eliminations mentioned above to be effected in proportion to the percentage of the capital held by the parent undertaking in each of the subsidiary undertakings included in the consolidation.

2.   A Member State may permit derogations from the provisions of paragraph 1 (c) above where a transaction has been concluded according to normal market conditions and where the elimination of the profit or loss would entail undue expense. Any such derogations must be disclosed and where the effect on the assets, liabilities, financial position and profit or loss of the undertakings, included in the consolidation, taken as a whole, is material, that fact must be disclosed in the notes on the consolidated accounts.

3.   Derogations from the provisions of paragraph 1 (a), (b) or (c) above shall be permitted where the amounts concerned are not material for the purposes of Article 16 (3).

Article 27

1.   Consolidated accounts must be drawn up as at the same date as the annual accounts of the parent undertaking.

2.   A   Member   State   may,

however, require or permit consolidated accounts to be drawn up as at another date in order to take account of the balance sheet dates of the largest number or the most important of the undertakings included in the consolidation. Where use is made of this derogation that fact shall be disclosed in the notes on the consolidated accounts together with the reasons therefor. In addition, account must be taken or disclosure made of important events concerning the assets and liabilities, the financial position or the profit or loss of an undertaking included in a consolidation which have occurred between that undertaking's balance sheet date and the consolidated balance sheet date.

3. Where an undertaking's balance sheet date precedes the consolidated balance sheet date by more than three months, that undertaking shall be consolidated on the basis of interim accounts drawn up as at the consolidated balance sheet date.

Article 28

If the composition of the undertakings included in a consolidation has changed significantly in the course of a financial year, the consolidated accounts must include information which makes the comparison of successive sets of consolidated accounts meaningful. Where such a change is a major one, a Member State may require or permit this obligation to be fulfilled by the preparation of an adjusted opening balance sheet and an adjusted profit-and-loss account.

Article 29

1. Assets and liabilities to be included in consolidated accounts shall be valued according to uniform methods and in accordance with Articles 31 to 42 and 60 of Directive 78/660/EEC.

2. (a) An undertaking which draws up consolidated accounts must apply the same methods of valuation as in its annual accounts. However, a Member State may require or permit the use in consolidated accounts of other methods of valuation in accordance with the above mentioned Articles of Directive 78/660/EEC.

(b) Where use is made of this derogation that fact shall be disclosed in the notes on the consolidated accounts and the reasons therefor given.

3. Where assets and liabilities to be included in consolidated accounts have been valued by undertakings included in the consolidation by methods differing from those used for the consolidation, they must be revalued in accordance with the methods used for the consolidation, unless the results of such revaluation are not material for the purposes of Article 16 (3). Departures from this principle shall be permitted in exceptional cases. Any such departures shall be disclosed in the notes on the consolidated accounts and the reasons for them given.

4. Account shall be taken in the consolidated balance sheet and in the consolidated profit-and-loss account of any difference arising on consolida-

tion between the tax chargeable for the financial year and for preceding financial years and the amount of tax paid or payable in respect of those years, provided that it is probable that an actual charge to tax will arise within the foreseeable future for one of the undertakings included in the consolidation.

5.   Where assets to be included in consolidated accounts have been the subject of exceptional value adjustments solely for tax purposes, they shall be incorporated in the consolidated accounts only after those adjustments have been eliminated. A Member State may, however, require or permit that such assets be incorporated in the consolidated accounts without the elimination of the adjustments, provided that their amounts, together with the reasons for them, are disclosed in the notes on the consolidated accounts.

Article 30

1.   A separate item as defined in Article 19 (1) (c) which corresponds to a positive consolidation difference shall be dealt with in accordance with the rules laid down in Directive 78/660/EEC for the item 'goodwill'.

2.   A Member State may permit a positive consolidation difference to be immediately and clearly deducted from reserves.

Article 31

An amount shown as a separate item, as defined in Article 19 (1) (c), which corresponds to a negative consolidation difference may be transferred to the consolidated profit-and-loss account only:

(a) where that difference corresponds to the expectation at the date of acquisition of unfavourable future results in that undertaking, or to the expectation of costs which that undertaking would incur, in so far as such an expectation materializes; or

(b) in so far as such a difference corresponds to a realized gain.

Article 32

1.   Where an undertaking included in a consolidation manages another undertaking jointly with one or more undertakings not included in that consolidation, a Member State may require or permit the inclusion of that other undertaking in the consolidated accounts in proportion to the rights in its capital held by the undertaking included in the consolidation.

2.   Articles 13 to 31 shall apply *mutatis mutandis* to the proportional consolidation referred to in paragraph 1 above.

3.   Where this Article is applied, Article 33 shall not apply if the undertaking proportionally consolidated is an associated undertaking as defined in Article 33.

Article 33

1. Where an undertaking included in a consolidation exercises a significant influence over the operating and financial policy of an undertaking not included in the consolidation (an associated undertaking) in which it holds a participating interest, as defined in Article 17 of Directive 78/660/EEC, that participating interest shall be shown in that consolidated balance sheet as a separate item with an appropriate heading. An undertaking shall be presumed to exercise a significant influence over another undertaking where it has 20% or more of the shareholders' or members' voting rights in that undertaking. Article 2 shall apply.

2. When this Article is applied for the first time to a participating interest covered by paragraph 1 above, that participating interest shall be shown in the consolidated balance sheet either:

(a) at its book value calculated in accordance with the valuation rules laid down in Directive 78/660/EEC. The difference between that value and the amount corresponding to the proportion of capital and reserves represented by that participating interest shall be disclosed separately in the consolidated balance sheet or in the notes on the accounts. That difference shall be calculated as at the date as at which that method is used for the first time; or

(b) at an amount corresponding to the proportion of the associated undertaking's capital and reserves represented by that participating interest. The difference between that amount and the book value calculated in accordance with the valuation rules laid down in Directive 78/660/EEC shall be disclosed separately in the consolidated balance sheet or in the notes on the accounts. That difference shall be calculated as at the date as at which that method is used for the first time.

(c) A Member State may prescribe the application of one or other of (a) and (b) above. The consolidated balance sheet or the notes on the accounts must indicate whether (a) or (b) has been used.

(d) In addition, for the purposes of (a) and (b) above, a Member State may require or permit the calculation of the difference as at the date of acquisition of the shares or, where they were acquired in two or more stages, as at the date on which the undertaking became an associated undertaking.

3. Where an associated undertaking's assets or liabilities have been valued by methods other than those used for consolidation in accordance with Article 29 (2), they may, for the purpose of calculating the difference referred to in paragraph 2 (a) or (b) above, be revalued by the methods used for consolidation. Where such revaluation has not been carried out that fact must be disclosed in the notes on the accounts. A Member State may require such revaluation.

4. The book value referred to in paragraph 2 (a) above, or the amount corresponding to the proportion of the associated undertaking's capital and reserves referred to in paragraph 2 (b) above, shall be increased or reduced by the amount of any variation which has taken place during the financial year in the proportion of the associ-

ated undertaking's capital and reserves represented by that participating interest; it shall be reduced by the amount of the dividends relating to that participating interest.

5. In so far as the positive difference referred to in paragraph 2 (a) or (b) above cannot be related to any category of assets or liabilities it shall be dealt with in accordance with Articles 30 and 39 (3).

6. The proportion of the profit or loss of the associated undertakings attributable to such participating interests shall be shown in the consolidated profit-and-loss account as a separate item under an appropriate heading.

7. The eliminations referred to in Article 26 (1) (c) shall be effected in so far as the facts are known or can be ascertained. Article 26 (2) and (3) shall apply.

8. Where an associated undertaking draws up consolidated accounts, the foregoing provisions shall apply to the capital and reserves shown in such consolidated accounts.

9. This Article need not be applied where the participating interest in the capital of the associated undertaking is not material for the purposes of Article 16 (3).

Article 34

In addition to the information required under other provisions of this Directive, the notes on the accounts must set out information in respect of the following matters at least:

1. The valuation methods applied to the various items in the consolidated accounts, and the methods employed in calculating the value adjustments. For items included in the consolidated accounts which are or were originally expressed in foreign currency the bases of conversion used to express them in the currency in which the consolidated accounts are drawn up must be disclosed.

2. (a) The names and registered offices of the undertakings included in the consolidation; the proportion of the capital held in undertakings included in the consolidation, other than the parent undertaking, by the undertakings included in the consolidation or by persons acting in their own names but on behalf of those undertakings; which of the conditions referred to in Articles 1 and 12 (1) following application of Article 2 has formed the basis on which the consolidation has been carried out. The latter disclosure may, however, be omitted where consolidation has been carried out on the basis of Article 1 (1) (a) and where the proportion of the capital and the proportion of the voting rights held are the same.

   (b) The same information must be given in respect of undertakings excluded from a consolidation pursuant to Articles 13 and 14 and, without prejudice to Article 14 (3), an explanation must be given for the exclusion of the undertakings referred to in Article 13.

3. (a) The names and registered offices of undertakings associated with an undertaking included in the consolidation as described in Article 33 (1) and the proportion of their capital held by undertakings included in the consolidation or by persons acting in their own names but on behalf of those undertakings.

(b) The same information must be given in respect of the associated undertakings referred to in Article 33 (9), together with the reasons for applying that provision.

4. The names and registered offices of undertakings proportionally consolidated pursuant to Article 32, the factors on which joint management is based, and the proportion of their capital held by the undertakings included in the consolidation or by persons acting in their own names but on behalf of those undertakings.

5. The name and registered office of each of the undertakings, other than those referred to in paragraphs 2, 3 and 4 above, in which undertakings included in the consolidation and those excluded pursuant to Article 14, either themselves or through persons acting in their own names but on behalf of those undertakings, hold at least a percentage of the capital which the Member States cannot fix at more than 20%, showing the proportion of the capital held, the amount of the capital and

reserves, and the profit or loss for the latest financial year of the undertaking concerned for which accounts have been adopted. This information may be omitted where, for the purposes of Article 16 (3), it is of negligible importance only. The information concerning capital and reserves and the profit or loss may also be omitted where the undertaking concerned does not publish its balance sheet and where less than 50% of its capital is held (directly or indirectly) by the abovementioned undertakings.

6. The total amount shown as owed in the consolidated balance sheet and becoming due and payable after more than five years, as well as the total amount shown as owed in the consolidated balance sheet and covered by valuable security furnished by undertakings included in the consolidation, with an indication of the nature and form of the security.

7. The total amount of any financial commitments that are not included in the consolidated balance sheet, in so far as this information is of assistance in assessing the financial position of the undertakings included in the sconsolidation taken as a whole. Any commitements concerning pensions and affiliated undertakings which are not included in the consolidation must be disclosed separately.

8. The consolidated net turnover as defined in Article 28 of Directive 78/660/EEC, broken down by categories of activity and into geographical markets in so far as, taking account of the manner in

which the sale of products and the provision of services falling within the ordinary activities of the undertakings included in the consolidation taken as a whole are organized, these categories and markets differ substantially from one another.

9. (a) The average number of persons employed during the financial year by undertakings included in the consolidation broken down by categories and, if they are not disclosed separately in the consolidated profit-and-loss account, the staff costs relating to the financial year.

   (b) The average number of persons employed during the financial year by undertakings to which Article 32 has been applied shall be disclosed separately.

10. The extent to which the calculation of the consolidated profit or loss for the financial year has been affected by a valuation of the items which, by way of derogation from the principles enunciated in Articles 31 and 34 to 42 of Directive 78/660/EEC and in Article 29 (5) of this Directive, was made in the financial year in question or in an earlier financial year with a view to obtaining tax relief. Where the influence of such a valuation on the future tax charges of the undertakings included in the consolidation taken as a whole is material, details must be disclosed.

11. The difference between the tax charged to the consolidated profit-and-loss account for the financial year and to those for earlier financial years and the amount of tax payable in respect of those years, provided that this difference is material for the purposes of future taxation. This amount may also be disclosed in the balance sheet as a cumulative amount under a separate item with an appropriate heading.

12. The amount of the emoluments granted in respect of the financial year to the members of the administrative, managerial and supervisory bodies of the parent undertaking by reason of their responsibilities in the parent undertaking and its subsidiary undertakings, and any commitments arising or entered into under the same conditions in respect of retirement pensions for former members of those bodies, with an indication of the total for each category. A Member State may require that emoluments granted by reason of responsibilities assumed in undertakings linked as described in Article 32 or 33 shall also be included with the information specified in the first sentence.

13. The amount of advances and credits granted to the members of the administrative, managerial and supervisory bodies of the parent undertaking by that undertaking or by one of its subsidiary undertakings, with indications of the interest rates, main conditions and any amounts repaid, as well as commitments entered into on their behalf by way of guarantee of any kind with an indication of the total for each category. A Member State may require that advances and credits granted by undertakings linked as described in Article 32 or 33 shall also be

included with the information specified in the first sentence.

Article 35

1.   A Member State may allow the disclosures prescribed in Article 34 (2), (3), (4) and (5):

(a) to take the form of a statement deposited in accordance with Article (1) and (2) of Directive 68/151/EEC; this must be disclosed in the notes on the accounts;

(b) to be omitted when their nature is such that they would be seriously prejudicial to any of the undertakings affected by these provisions. A Member State may make such omissions subject to prior administrative or judicial authorization. Any such omission must be disclosed in the notes on the accounts.

2.   Paragraph 1 (b) shall also apply to the information prescribed in Article 34 (8).

SECTION 3

The consolidated annual report

Article 36

1.   The consolidated annual report must include at least a fair review of the development of business and the position of the undertakings included in the consolidation taken as a whole.

2.   In respect of those undertakings, the report shall also give an indication of:

(a) any important events that have occurred since the end of the financial year;

(b) the likely future development of those undertakings taken as a whole;

(c) the activities of those undertakings taken as a whole in the field of research and development;

(d) the number and nominal value or, in the absence of a nominal value, the accounting par value of all of the parent undertaking's shares held by that undertaking itself, by subsidiary undertakings of that undertaking or by a person acting in his own name but on behalf of those undertakings. A Member State may require or permit the disclosure of these particulars in the notes on the accounts.

SECTION 4

The auditing of consolidated accounts

Article 37

1.   An undertaking which draws up consolidated accounts must have them audited by one or more persons authorized to audit accounts under the laws of the Member State which govern that undertaking.

2.   The person or persons responsible for auditing the consolidated

accounts must also verify that the consolidated annual report is consistent with the consolidated accounts for the same financial year.

SECTION 5

The publication of consolidated accounts

Article 38

1.   Consolidated accounts, duly approved, and the consolidated annual report, together with the opinion submitted by the person responsible for auditing the consolidated accounts, shall be published for the undertaking which drew up the consolidated accounts as laid down by the laws of the Member State which govern it in accordance with Article 3 of Directive 68/151/EEC.

2.   The second paragraph of Article 47 (1) of Directive 78/660/EEC shall apply with respect to the consolidated annual report.

3.   The following shall be substituted for the second subparagraph of Article 47 (1) of Directive 78/660/EEC: 'It must be possible to obtain a copy of all or part of any such report upon request: 'The price of such a copy must not exceed its administrative cost'.

4.   However, where the undertaking which drew up the consolidated accounts is not established as one of the types of company listed in Article 4 and is not required by its national

law to publish the documents referred to in paragraph 1 in the same manner as prescribed in Article 3 of Directive 68/151/EEC, it must at least make them available to the public at its head office. It must be possible to obtain a copy of such documents upon request. The price of such a copy must not exceed its administrative cost.

5.   Articles 48 and 49 of Directive 78/660/EEC shall apply.

6.   The Member States shall provide for appropriate sanctions for failure to comply with the publication obligations imposed in this Article.

SECTION 6

Transitional and final provisions

Article 39

1.   When, for the first time, consolidated accounts are drawn up in accordance with this Directive for a body of undertakings which was already connected, as described in Article 1 (1), before application of the provisions referred to in Article 49 (1), a Member State may require or permit that, for the purposes of Article 19 (1), account be taken of the book value of a holding and the proportion of the capital and reserves that it represents as at a date before or the same as that of the first consolidation.

2.   Paragraph 1 above shall apply *mutatis mutandis* to the valuation for the purposes of Article 33 (2) of a holding, or of the proportion of capital

and reserves that it represents in the capital of an undertaking associated with an undertaking included in the consolidation, and to the proportional consolidation referred to in Article 32.

3. Where the separate item defined in Article 19 (1) corresponds to a positive consolidation difference which arose before the date of the first consolidated accounts drawn up in accordance with this Directive, a Member State may:

(a) for the purposes of Article 30 (1), permit the calculation of the limited period of more than five years provided for in Article 37 (2) of Directive 78/660/EEC as from the date of the first consolidated accounts drawn up in accordance with this Directive; and

(b) for the purposes of Article 30 (2), permit the deduction to be made from reserves as at the date of the first consolidated accounts drawn up in accordance with this Directive.

Article 40

1. Until expiry of the deadline imposed for the application in national law of the Directives supplementing Directive 78/660/EEC as regards the harmonization of the rules governing the annual accounts of banks and other financial institutions and insurance undertakings, a Member State may derogate from the provisions of this Directive concerning the layout of consolidated accounts, the methods of valuing the items included in those accounts and the information to be given in the notes on the accounts:

(a) with regard to any undertaking to be consolidated which is a bank, another financial institution or an insurance undertaking;

(b) where the undertakings to be consolidated comprise principally banks, financial institutions or insurance undertakings.

They may also derogate from Article 6, but only in so far as the limits and criteria to be applied to the above undertakings are concerned.

2. In so far as a Member State has not required all undertakings which are banks, other financial institutions or insurance undertakings to draw up consolidated accounts before implementation of the provisions referred to in Article 49 (1), it may, until its national law implements one of the Directives mentioned in paragraph 1 above, but not in respect of financial years ending after 1993:

(a) suspend the application of the obligation imposed in Article 1 (1) with respect to any of the above undertakings which is a parent undertaking. That fact must be disclosed in the annual accounts of the parent undertaking and the information prescribed in point 2 of Article 43 (1) of Directive 78/660/EEC must be given for all subsidiary undertakings;

(b) where consolidated accounts are drawn up and without prejudice to Article 33, permit the omission from the consolidation of any of the above undertakings which is a subsidiary undertaking. The information prescribed in Article 34 (2) must be given in the notes on the accounts in respect of any such subsidiary undertaking.

3.   In the cases referred to in paragraph 2 (b) above, the annual or consolidated accounts of the subsidiary undertaking must, in so far as their publication is compulsory, be attached to the consolidated accounts or, in the absence of consolidated accounts, to the annual accounts of the parent undertaking or be made available to the public. In the latter case it must be possible to obtain a copy of such documents upon request. The price of such a copy must not exceed its administrative cost.

4.   Articles 2 and 3 (2) shall apply.

5.   When a Member State applies Article 4 (2), it may exclude from the applications of paragraph 1 above affiliated undertakings which are parent undertakings and which by virtue of their legal form are not required by that Member State to draw up consolidated accounts in accordance with the provisions of this Directive, as well as parent undertakings with a similar legal form.

Article 41

1.   Undertakings which are connected as described in Article 1 (1) (a), (b) and (d) (bb), and those other undertakings which are similarly connected with one of the aforementioned undertakings, shall be affiliated undertakings for the purposes of this Directive and of Directive 78/660/EEC.

2.   Where a Member State prescribes the preparation of consolidated accounts pursuant to Article 1 (1) (c), (d) (aa) or (2) or Article 12 (1), the undertakings which are connected as described in those Articles and those other undertakings which are connected similarly, or are connected as described in paragraph 1 above to one of the aforementioned undertakings, shall be affiliated undertakings as defined in paragraph 1.

3.   Even where a Member State does not prescribe the preparation of consolidated accounts pursuant to Article 1 (1) (c), (d) (aa) or (2) or Article 12 (1), it may apply paragraph 2 of this Article.

Article 42

The following shall be substituted for Article 56 of Directive 78/660/EEC:

'*Article 56*

1.   The obligation to show in annual accounts the items prescribed by Articles 9, 10 and 23 to 26 which relate to affiliated undertakings, as defined by Article 41 of Directive 83/349/EEC, and the obligation to provide information concerning these undertakings in accordance with Articles 13 (2), and 14 and point 7 of Article 43 (1) shall enter into force on the date fixed in Article 49 (2) of that Directive.

2.   The notes on the accounts must also disclose:

(a) the name and registered office of the undertaking which draws up the consolidated accounts of the largest body of undertakings of which the company forms part as a subsidiary undertaking;

(b) the name and registered office of the undertaking which draws up the consolidated accounts of the smallest body of undertakings of which the company forms part as a subsidiary undertaking and which is also included in the body of undertakings referred to in (a) above;

(c) the place where copies of the consolidated accounts referred to in (a) and (b) above may be obtained provided that they are available.'

Article 43

The following shall be substituted for Article 57 of Directive 78/660/EEC:

'*Article 57*

Notwithstanding the provisions of Directives 68/151/EEC and 77/91/EEC, a Member State need not apply the provisions of this Directive concerning the content, auditing and publication of annual accounts to companies governed by their national laws which are subsidiary undertakings, as defined in Directive 83/349/EEC, where the following conditions are fulfilled:

(a) the parent undertaking must be subject to the laws of a Member State;

(b) all shareholders or members of the subsidiary undertaking must have declared their agreement to the exemption from such obligation; this declaration must be made in respect of every financial year;

(c) the parent undertaking must have declared that it guarantees that commitments entered into by the subsidiary undertaking;

(d) the declarations referred to in (b) and (c) must be published by the subsidiary undertaking

as laid down by the laws of the Member State in accordance with Article 3 of Directive 68/151/EEC;

(e) the subsidiary undertaking must be included in the consolidated accounts drawn up by the parent undertaking in accordance with Directive 83/349/EEC;

(f) the above exemption must be disclosed in the notes on the consolidated accounts drawn up by the parent undertaking;

(g) the consolidated accounts referred to in (e), the consolidated annual report, and the report by the person responsible for auditing those accounts must be published for the subsidiary undertaking as laid down by the laws of the Member State in accordance with Article 3 of Directive 68/151/EEC.'

Article 44

The following shall be substituted for Article 58 of Directive 78/660/EEC:

'*Article 58*

A Member State need not apply the provisions of this Directive concerning the auditing and publication of the profit-and-loss account to companies governed by their national laws which are parent undertakings for the purposes of Directive 83/349/EEC where the following conditions are fulfilled:

(a) the parent undertaking must draw up consolidated accounts in accordance with Directive 83/349/EEC and be included in the consolidated accounts;

(b) the above exemption must be disclosed in the notes on the annual accounts of the parent undertaking;

(c) the above exemption must be disclosed in the notes on the consolidated accounts drawn up by the parent undertaking;

(d) the profit or loss of the parent company, determined in accordance with this Directive, must be shown in the balance sheet of the parent company.'

Article 45

The following shall be substituted for Article 59 of Directive 78/660/EEC:

'*Article 59*

1.   A Member State may require or permit that participating interests, as defined in Article 17, in the capital of undertakings over the operating and financial policies of which significant influence is exercised, be shown in the balance sheet in accordance with paragraphs 2 to 9 below, as sub-items of the items "shares in affiliated undertakings" or "participating interests", as the case may be. An undertaking shall be presumed to exercise a significant influence over another undertaking where it has 20% or more of the shareholders' or members' voting rights in that undertaking. Article 2 of Directive 83/349/EEC shall apply.

2.   When this Article is first applied to a participating interest covered by paragraph 1, it shall be shown in the balance sheet either:

(a) at its book value calculated in accordance with Articles 31 to 42. The difference between that value and the amount corresponding to the proportion of capital and reserves represented by the participating interest shall be disclosed separately in the balance sheet or in the notes on the accounts. That difference shall be calculated as at the date as at which the method is applied for the first time; or

(b) at the amount corresponding to the proportion of the capital and reserves represented by the participating interest. The difference between that amount and the book value calculated in accordance with Articles 31 to 42 shall be disclosed separately in the balance sheet or in the notes on the accounts. That difference shall be calculated as at the date as at which the method is applied for the first time.

(c) A Member State may prescribe the application of one or other of the above paragraphs. The balance sheet or the notes on the accounts must indicate whether (a) or (b) above has been used.

(d) In addition, when applying (a) and (b) above, a Member State may require or permit calculation of the difference as at the date of acquisition of the participating interest referred to in paragraph 1 or, where the acquisition took place in two or more stages, as at the date as at which the holding became a participating interest within the meaning of paragraph 1 above.

3.   Where the assets or liabilities of an undertaking in which a participating interest within the meaning of paragraph 1 above is held have been valued by methods other than

those used by the company drawing up the annual accounts, they may, for the purpose of calculating the difference referred to in paragraph 2 (a) or (b) above, be revalued by the methods used by the company drawing up the annual accounts. Disclosure must be made in the notes on the accounts where such revaluation has not been carried out. A Member State may require such revaluation.

4. The book value referred to in paragraph 2 (a) above, or the amount corresponding to the proportion of capital and reserves referred to in paragraph 2 (b) above, shall be increased or reduced by the amount of the variation which has taken place during the financial year in the proportion of capital and reserves represented by that participating interest; it shall be reduced by the amount of the dividends relating to the participating interest.

5. In so far as a positive difference covered by paragraph 2 (a) or (b) above cannot be related to any category of asset or liability, it shall be dealt with in accordance with the rules applicable to the item "goodwill".

6. (a) The proportion of the profit or loss attributable to participating interests within the meaning of paragraph 1 above shall be shown in the profit-and-loss account as a separate item with an appropriate heading.

   (b) Where that amount exceeds the amount of dividends already received the payment of which can be claimed, the amount of the difference must be placed in

a reserve which cannot be distributed to shareholders.

(c) A Member State may require or permit that the proportion of the profit or loss attributable to the participating interests referred to in paragraph 1 above be shown in the profit-and-loss account only to the extent of the amount corresponding to dividends already received or the payment of which can be claimed.

7. The eliminations referred to in Article 26 (1) (c) of Directive 83/349/EEC shall be effected in so far as the facts are known or can be ascertained. Article 26 (2) and (3) of that Directive shall apply.

8. Where an undertaking in which a participating interest within the meaning of paragraph 1 above is held draws up consolidated accounts, the foregoing paragraphs shall apply to the capital and reserves shown in such consolidated accounts.

9. This Article need not be applied where a participating interest as defined in paragraph 1 is not material for the purposes of Article 2 (3).'

Article 46

The following shall be substituted for Article 61 of Directive 78/660/EEC:

'*Article 61*

A Member State need not apply the provisions of point 2 of Article 43 (1) of this Directive concerning the amount of capital and reserves and profits and losses of the undertakings concerned to companies governed by their national laws which are parent undertakings for the purposes of Directive 83/349/EEC:

(a) where the undertakings concerned are included in consolidated accounts drawn up by that parent undertaking, or in the consolidated accounts of a larger body of undertakings as referred to in Article 7 (2) of Directive 83/349/EEC; or

(b) where the holdings in the undertakings concerned have been dealt with by the parent undertaking in its annual accounts in accordance with Article 59, or in the consolidated accounts drawn up by that parent undertaking in accordance with Article 33 of Directive 83/349/EEC.

Article 47

The Contact Committee set up pursuant to Article 52 of Directive 78/660/EEC shall also:

(a) facilitate, without prejudice to Articles 169 and 170 of the Treaty, harmonized application of this Directive through regular meetings dealing, in particular, with practical problems arising in connection with its application;

(b) advise the Commission, if necessary, on additions or amendments to this Directive.

Article 48

This Directive shall not affect laws in the Member States requiring that consolidated accounts in which undertakings not falling within their jurisdiction are included be filed in a register in which branches of such undertakings are listed.

Article 49

1. The Member States shall bring into force the laws, regulations and administrative provisions necessary for them to comply with this Directive before 1 January 1988. They shall forthwith inform the Commission thereof.

2. A Member State may provide that the provisions referred to in paragraph 1 above shall first apply to consolidated accounts for financial years beginning on 1 January 1990 or during the calendar year 1990.

3. The Member States shall ensure that they communicate to the Commission the texts of the main provisions of national law which they adopt in the field covered by this Directive.

Article 50

1. Five years after the date referred to in Article 49 (2), the Council, acting on a proposal from the

Commission, shall examine and if need be revise Articles 1 (1) (d) (second subparagraph), 4 (2), 5, 6, 7 (1), 12, 43 and 44 in the light of the experience acquired in applying this Directive, the aims of this Directive and the economic and monetary situation at the time.

2.   Paragraph 1 above shall not affect Article 53 (2) of Directive 78/660/EEC.

Article 51

This Directive is addressed to the Member States.

Done at Luxembourg, 13 June 1983.

For the Council

The President

H. TIETMEYER

Appendix IV

The Proposed EEC Directive on Employee Information and Consultation (1980, revised 1983): The Vredeling Proposals (Official Journal 1983, No. C217/3)

Commission of the European Communities

COM(83) 292 final
Brussels, 8 July 1983

Amended Proposal for a
COUNCIL DIRECTIVE
on procedures for informing and consulting employees

(presented by the Commission to the Council under Article 149, paragraph 2 of the EEC Treaty)

EXPLANATORY MEMORANDUM

The present proposal for a Directive, based on Article 100 of the EEC Treaty, concerns procedures for informing and consulting employees of large-scale undertakings in the Community who work in subsidiaries controlled by parent undertakings whether located in the Community or outside it. It applies equally to employees in, for example, branches or offices geographically separated from the undertaking of which they are a part.

A first proposal was submitted to the Council on 24 October 1980.(¹)

The Economic and Social Committee(²) approved the proposal by 79 votes to 61 with 11 abstentions, subject to the structure of the Directive being simplified.

The European Parliament(³) approved the Commission initiative by 161 votes to 61 with 84 abstentions, subject to a certain number of amendments.(⁴)

The amended proposal has been drafted in the light of these opinions and in accordance with the Commission's position as stated to the European Parliament on 17 November 1982.(⁵) Account has also been taken of the consultations with the interested parties which have taken place since the beginning of 1983.

1. Structure of the Directive

In accordance with the wishes of the Economic and Social Committee,(⁶) the structure of the Directive has been simplified by merging sections 2 and 3.

2. Preamble

The preamble has been developed in order to define more precisely the objective in view, the scope of this proposal in relation to other Commission proposals in the information field, and the content of this proposal.

A new recital has also been added as a consequence of the Commission's decision to comply with the European Parliament's wishes by dropping the provision which would have given employees the right to apply directly to the management of the parent undertaking (so-called 'by-pass' system). This recital specifies that the managements of subsidiaries should receive all appropriate information from the parent company and should have the necessary powers to conduct consultations with their employees in good faith. Such powers are particularly important when it is necessary to negotiate social and financial measures in favour of employees.

(¹) OJ No C 297, 15.11.1980, p. 3.
(²) OJ No C 77, 29.03.1982, p. 6
(³) OJ No C 13, 17.01.1983, p. 25.
(⁴) OJ No C 292, 8.11.1982, p. 33.
(⁵) COM (82) 758 final, 17.11.1982.
(⁶) OJ No C 77, 29.03.1982, point 19.

3. Comments on the Articles of the Directive

Article 1 (formerly Article 2)

Article 1(a) defines the concepts of 'parent undertaking' and 'subsidiary' by reference to the criteria adopted by the Council in the 7th Directive on company law.

As far as parent undertakings established within the Community are concerned, the question of whether an undertaking subject to the legislation of a particular Member State constitutes a parent undertaking will be a matter to be determined by that Member State by reference, in the legislation brought into force under this Directive, to the criteria provided for on a compulsory or optional basis in the 7th Directive. The term subsidiary will therefore apply to any undertaking in respect of which another undertaking established within the Community is deemed, under the legislation to which the latter is subject, to be a parent undertaking. In this case, the information and consultation requirements provided for in this Directive will be enforceable vis-à-vis both the parent undertaking and all its subsidiaries in the Community.

The second subparagraph of Article 1(a) deals with the relationship between a subsidiary located in the Community and a parent undertaking located outside the Community, stipulating that this is to be determined according to the Law of the Member State to which the subsidiary is subject.

A definition of *establishment* has been introduced in response to the numerous queries on this point which arose in the course of the consultations held by the Commission's departments. The definition of *employees' representatives* is taken from the Directive on the safeguarding of employees' rights in the event of transfers. The Commission has not followed the opinion of the European Parliament on this point; the latter was in favour, in particular, of the compulsory introduction in all Member States of a system of direct elections by secret ballot. The Commission has already informed the European Parliament that it approves the principle of direct elections, but that existing differences in industrial relations' systems in the various Member States cannot be ignored. The Commission would like each Member State to be able to introduce the direct election system, but the purpose of this Directive is limited to procedures for informing and consulting employees; it is not designed to change existing industrial relations' systems in the Community. The Commission has also notified the European Parliament that it cannot agree to excluding all persons carrying out managerial duties from representing employees but that—as in the Directive on employees' rights([1])—members of administrative, managing or supervisory bodies of companies will not constitute employee representatives for the purpose of this Directive.

([1]) Directive 77/187/EEC of 14.2.1977; OJ No L 61, 5.3.1977, p. 26.

Article 2 (formerly Articles 1, 4 and 10)

This Article brings about the fusing of the former Sections II and III as requested by the Economic and Social Committee. The European Parliament's position with regard to undertakings with political or religious 'tendencies', the press, etc. has been taken into account in Article 8 (final provisions, paragraph 2). The first indent (former Articles 1, 4 and 10) and the second indent (former Articles 1 and 9) of Article 2 (1) are worded to take account of the European Parliament's view that a threshold of 1000 employees should be introduced for the undertaking as a whole. Paragraph 2 (former Article 8) introduces a provision desired by the European Parliament: each subsidiary concerned in the Community will be held responsible in the event of a parent undertaking established outside the Community failing to fulfil its information and consultation obligations.

Article 3 (formerly Article 5)

This Article has been amended in line with the wishes of the European Parliament. The information which was to be provided every six months is now to be given annually. The information must be 'general' and 'intelligible' so as to give a clear picture of the activities of the undertaking as a whole. The treatment of information deemed to be secret is dealt with in Article 7, but Article 3(4) clearly indicates that secret information within the meaning of Article 7 need not be communicated. Points (f), (g) and (h) of Article 3(2) have been deleted and point (e) does not refer to 'programmes' but only to investment 'prospects'. Employees' representatives may request oral explanations and obtain answers, if necessary on a confidential basis (see paragraph 4). Lastly, and again in line with the opinion of the European Parliament, employees' representatives will be able to apply 'in writing' to the management of the parent undertaking if the management of the subsidiary has not communicated the relevant information within 30 days (paragraph 5).

In line with the Commission's statement to the European Parliament, the amended proposal provides for the communication not only of 'general' information but also of 'specific' information on a particular sector of production or geographical area in which the subsidiary is active (see Article 3(1)). As the Commission has already pointed out to the European Parliament, the information supplied should not be the same as that published pursuant to the 7th Directive which, although indeed available to the public, is in a form that is relatively inaccessible to employees. The latter should receive a clearer presentation better suited to their requirements, although based largely on the information to be published under the 7th Directive.

In addition to information on past events, it is necessary to provide data on the probable development of production, sales and employment, and future investment prospects.

In this context—and in line with the intentions announced to the European Parliament—Article 3(3) provides that, where the information referred to in paragraph 2 is brought up-to-date or published more frequently by virtue of other directives (e.g. the 7th, or 5th Directive) or national legislation, the management of the parent undertaking must also forward the updated information to the management of its subsidiaries and establishments in the Community, with a view to its communication (with the exception of information deemed secret within the meaning of Article 7(1) to the employees' representatives.

Article 3(6) deals with the problem of information rights for employees in sub-groups.

Article 4 (formerly Article 6)

This provision now reflects the amendments requested by the European Parliament. It specifies that the consultation procedure does not concern all employees in the Community but only those directly affected by a decision, indicates that a list of decisions is given purely by way of example (first sentence, paragraph 2) and requires prior consultation only if the decisions in question are liable to have serious consequences for the interests of employees. At the request of the Parliament, measures on health protection and occupational safety have been added to the list. In line with its stated intentions, the Commission has also expanded the list to include major modifications in working practices or production methods resulting from the introduction of new technologies. The Commission has, however, felt unable to accept the deletion of point (d) or the establishment of long-term cooperation with other undertakings or the cessation of such cooperation since the new provisions concerning secrecy (Article 7(1)) will enable managements to withhold information where its disclosure would be liable to lead to the failure of the undertaking's plans or substantially damage its interests.

In accordance with the request of the European Parliament, the system permitting a direct approach to the parent undertaking (paragraphs 4 and 5 of the original proposal) has been removed. Instead, paragraphs 3 to 5 of the revised text impose an obligation on the management of the subsidiary which it will not be able to ignore without incurring penalties (Article 4(8)).

The commission indicated in its statement to the European Parliament that consultation must take place before the final decision was taken but that the intention was not to impose a right of codetermination. In this context, Article 4(5) provides that the decision may be implemented as soon as the opinion of the employees' representatives is received. Failing this, management will be entitled to implement the decision following the expiry of the period accorded for the submission of an opinion (at least 30 days from the day on which the information was communicated).

There is, however, also provision for the employees' representatives to appeal to a tribunal or other competent authority for measures to be taken within a maximum period of 30 days to compel the management of the undertaking to fulfil its obligations. The purpose of this time limit is to ensure that implementation of the decision is not delayed unreasonably.

The fact that information is withheld on the grounds of secrecy does not release management from the obligation to consult the representatives of its employees on the measures planned in their respect (Article 5 (6)).

Article 5 (formerly Article 7)

Paragraph 2 has been amended, in the light of the Opinion of the European Parliament, to enable employees' representatives to decide whether they wish their right to be consulted to be transferred to a body representing employees at a higher level.

With a view to greater flexibility, paragraphs 4 and 5 have been taken from the Council Directive on procedures for informing and consulting employees in the event of transfers of undertakings.(¹)

Paragraph 4 replaces the original threshold of 100 employees per subsidiary with a more flexible base line. This has been made necessary by the introduction of a threshold of 1000 employees per group, since the application of two rigid thresholds jointly would have produced results other than those intended. The threshold produced by the new provision will vary from country to country. Individual Member States will have the option of limiting the information and consultation procedures provided for in the Directive to undertakings or establishments which, in terms of number of employees, fulfil the conditions for the creation of a collegiate body representing the workforce (Wirtschaftsausschuss, works council, conseil d'entreprise, comité d'entreprise, etc.) which can receive the information to be communicated under Article 3 and conduct the consultations referred to in Article 4.

Paragraph 5 permits Member States which so wish to preserve the existing systems for informing and consulting employees directly which are in operation in many undertakings, without prejudice to the employees' right to demand the application of the Directive in its entirety.

Article 6 (formerly Article 9)

This Article has been simplified at the request of the Economic and Social Committee and following consultation with the parties concerned.

Article 7 (formerly Article 15)

In accordance with the opinion of the European Parliament, the management of subsidiaries or establishments need not divulge to employees' representatives confidential information the disclosure of which would lead to the failure of the undertakings' plans or substantially damage its interests.

'Interests of the undertaking' means not only the interests of the subsidiary but also those of the parent undertaking. In particular, the interests of an undertaking might be damaged where the legislation of the state (within or outside the community) to which it was subject prohibited the communication to third parties of certain secret information. The violation of such a rule would

---

(¹) Directive 77/187/EEC, 14.2.1977 (Article 6(4), (5)).

be damaging to the interests of the undertaking (parent or subsidiary) within the meaning of Article 7.

The secrecy requirement concerns both regular information (new Article 3) and information communicated in the course of the consultation procedure (new Article 4), which is frequently the most 'sensitive' (merger or takeover projects, etc.).

The Commission has already informed the European Parliament about its position on this matter and its preference for a formula other than 'company secret', 'business secret' or 'industrial' or 'trade' secret, all of which are difficult to define and might not cover all the types of information whose premature disclosure would seriously affect the undertaking. The wording adopted is based on a provision in the Council Directive on information to be published on a regular basis by companies on the official stock-exchange listing.(¹) The Directive in no sense prejudices the parent undertaking's right to withhold from a subsidiary information which is secret within the meaning of Article 7. It does not attempt to regulate relations between management at the two levels (parent undertaking and subsidiary), but only relations between management and employees.

It would be unjust if the legitimate desire to safeguard the interests of undertakings were to deprive workers of the right to be informed and consulted with regard to measures directly affecting their employment or working conditions.

With this in mind, Article 4(6) provides that the employees' representatives must be informed and consulted at least 30 days before any decision on such matters is put into effect.

This formula is based on a similar provision in Directive 77/187/EEC (Article 6(1)).

Parliament is also aware of the Commission's view that management cannot be the sole judge of the secret or confidential nature of information without any possibility of appeal to a tribunal. The wording employed in this provision is taken from the Commission's original proposal.

Article 8

The Commission intends that Member States should be able to protect the freedoms of charitable, political or public information bodies (freedom of the press). Article 8(2) is designed to achieve this purpose. Special provisions are, however, only authorised to the extent necessary to ensure that the undertakings in question may exercise the freedoms to which they are entitled under national law.

(¹) Directive 82/121/EEC – 15.2.1982; OJ No L 48 – 20.2.1982 (Article 9 (4)).

ORIGINAL TEXT   *AMENDED TEXT*

THE COUNCIL OF THE
EUROPEAN COMMUNITIES,
Having regard to the Treaty
establishing the European Economic
Community, and in particular Article
100 thereof,
Having regard to the proposal from
the Commission,
Having regard to the opinion of the
European Parliament,
Whereas the Council adopted on 21
January 1974 a Resolution
concerning a social action
programme([1]);
Whereas in a common market where
national economies are closely
interlinked it is essential, if economic
activities are to develop in a
harmonious fashion, that
undertakings should be subject to the
same obligations in relation to
Community employees affected by
their decisions, whether they are
employed in the Member State to
whose legislation the undertaking is
subject or in another Member State;
Whereas the procedures for
informing and consulting employees
as embodied in legislation or
practised in the Member States are
often inconsistent with the complex
structure of the entity which takes
the decisions affecting them; whereas
this may lead to unequal treatment
of employees affected by the
decisions of one and the same
undertaking; whereas this may stem
from the fact that the information
and consultation procedures do not
apply beyond national boundaries;
Whereas this situation has a direct   No change
effect on the operation of the
common market and consequently
needs to be remedied by
approximating the relevant laws
while maintaining progress as

([1]) OJ No C13, 12.2.1974, p. 1.

ORIGINAL TEXT

AMENDED TEXT

required under Article 117 of the
Treaty;
Whereas this Directive forms part of
a series of directives and proposals
for directives in the field of company
and labour law.

Whereas Council Directive 75/129/
EEC of 17 February 1975 on the
approximation of the laws of the
Member States relating to collective
redundancies(1) and Council
Directive 77/187/EEC of 14 February
1977 on the safeguarding of
employees' rights in the event of
transfers of undertakings, businesses
or parts of businesses(2) incorporate
compulsory procedures for informing
and consulting the representatives of
the employees affected by the
operations in question and Council
Directive . . . of . . . . on the
structure of public limited companies
and the powers and obligations of
their organs(3) makes provision for
worker participation;
Whereas these information and
consultation requirements do not
aim to cover all situations likely to
affect the employees' interests and,
in particular, do not extend
specifically to decisions taken at
parent company level rather than
independently by the employing
subsidiary;
Whereas the concepts of 'parent
undertaking' and 'subsidiary' should
be defined using the same criteria as
those adopted in Council Directive
83/ . . .(1) on consolidated accounts;
whereas it should thus be the
responsibility of the Member State to
whose legislation a parent
undertaking is subject to ensure that
the latter fulfils its obligations under
the present Directive vis-àa-vis all its
subsidiaries within the Community;

(1) OJ L 48 of 22.2.1975, p. 29.
(2) OJ L 61 of 5.3.1977, p. 16.
(3) Amended proposal, OJ No C.
(4) OJ No L.

ORIGINAL TEXT   *AMENDED TEXT*

the present Directive vis-à-vis all its subsidiaries within the Community; whereas, in consequence, a Member State whose legislation is applicable to an undertaking deemed to be a subsidiary must ensure that the latter fulfils all its obligations under this Directive;

Whereas appropriate provisions must be adopted to ensure that the employees of an undertaking within the Community are properly informed and consulted where the undertaking in question is a subsidiary of an undertaking outside the Community;

Whereas steps should be taken to ensure that workers employed by a subsidiary in the Community are kept informed as to the activities and prospects of the parent undertaking and the subsidiaries as a whole so that they may assess the possible impact on their interests; whereas, to this end, the undertaking should be required to communicate to the employees' representatives both general information similar to that which must be disclosed under Directive 83/   /EEC but angled towards the interests of the employees, and information relating more specifically to those aspects of its activities and prospects which are liable to affect the employees' interests;

Whereas steps should be taken to ensure that the employees' representatives are informed and invited to give their opinion in good time before the adoption of any decision significantly affecting the employees' interests and that they are consulted with a view to attempting to reach agreement on the measures to be taken in this context in respect of the employees concerned;

Whereas the management of each subsidiary must be in a position to

ORIGINAL TEXT   AMENDED TEXT

communicate the requisite
information to its employees'
representatives and must have the
necessary powers to conduct the
consultations referred to above in
good faith;
Whereas analogous rules should be
introduced in respect of procedures
for informing and consulting the
representatives of employees
working in the Community in
establishments geographically
separated from the decision-making
centre of the undertaking of which
they form part;
Whereas appropriate penalties
should be imposed by Member
States in the event of failure to
comply with the information and
consultation requirements provided
for by this Directive;
Whereas steps should be taken to
ensure that these requirements can,
insofar as possible, be fulfilled within
the framework of institutions already
established to represent employees
under the laws and customary
practices of Member States;
Whereas the requirement to
communicate information provided
for by this Directive should not apply
to certain information of a secret
character and employees and their
representatives should be required
to maintain discretion as regards
confidential information; whereas,
however, disputes as to the secrecy
or confidentiality of information
should be settled by a tribunal or
other national body;
HAS ADOPTED THIS
DIRECTIVE:

SECTION I
Definitions and scope
Article 1   Deleted and combined with the old
This directive relates to: Article 4 in the new Article 2.
— procedures for informing and
  consulting employees employed
  in a Member State of the

ORIGINAL TEXT   *AMENDED TEXT*

Community by an undertaking
whose decision-making centre is
located in another Member State
or in a non-member Country
(Section II);
— procedures for informing and
consulting employees where an
undertaking has several
establishments, or one or more
subsidiaries, in a single Member
State and where its decision-
making centre is located in the
same Member State (Section
III).

SECTION I—DEFINITIONS AND
SCOPE
Article 1

Article 2
For the purpose of this directive the   For the purposes of this Directive the
following definitions shall apply: following definitions shall apply:
(a) *Employees' representatives*   (a) *Parent undertaking and*
    The employees' representatives   *subsidiary*: an undertaking
    referred to in Article 2(c) of   within the Community is a parent
    Council Directive 77/187/EEC of   undertaking when another
    14 February 1977 on the   undertaking is its subsidiary
    approximation of the Laws of   according to the legislation
    the Member States relating to the   applicable to the parent
    safeguarding of employees'   undertaking and the criteria of
    rights in the event of transfers of   Article 1 of Directive 83/ / ;
    undertakings, businesses or   an undertaking outside the
    parts of businesses([1]):   Community is a parent
(b) *Management*   undertaking when another
    The person or persons   undertaking is its subsidiary
    responsible for the management   according to the Legislation
    of an undertaking under the   applicable to that subsidiary and
    national legislation to which it is   the criteria of Article 1 of
    subject.   Directive 83/ / .
(c) *Decision-making centre*   (b) *Establishment*: an entity,
    The place where the   geographically separate from
    management of an undertaking   but not legally independent of
    actually performs its functions.   the undertaking of which it is a
                                                 part, in particular a workshop,
                                                 branch, agency, factory or
                                                 office.
                                             (c) *Decision-making centre*: the place
                                                 where an undertaking has its
                                                 central administration.
                                             (d) *Management*: the person or
([1]) OJ L 61 of 5.3.1977.   persons responsible for the

ORIGINAL TEXT	AMENDED TEXT
	management of an undertaking under the national legislation to which it is subject.
	(e) *Employees' representatives*: the employees' representatives provided for by the laws or practice of the Member States, with the exception of members of administrative, managing or supervisory bodies of companies who sit on such bodies in certain Member States as employees' representatives.

Article 3
1. For the purposes of this directive an undertaking shall be regarded as dominant in relation to all the undertakings it controls, referred to as subsidiaries.
2. An undertaking shall be regarded as a subsidiary where the dominant undertaking either directly or indirectly,
  (a) holds the majority of votes relating to the shares it has issued, or
  (b) has the power to appoint at least half of the members of its administrative, management or supervisory bodies where these members hold the majority of the voting rights.
	deleted

SECTION II
Information and consultation procedures in transnational undertakings

Article 4	*Article 2*
The management of a dominant undertaking whose decision-making centre is located in a Member State of the Community and which has one or more subsidiaries in at least one other Member State shall be required to disclose, via the management of these subsidiaries, information to employees' representatives in all subsidiaries	1. This Directive relates to procedures for informing and consulting the employees — of a subsidiary in the Community when a total of at least 1000 workers is employed in the Community by the parent undertaking and its subsidiaries taken as a whole; — of an undertaking having in the

ORIGINAL TEXT

AMENDED TEXT

employing at least one hundred
employees in the Community in
accordance with Article 5 and to
consult them in accordance with
Article 6.

Article 8
Where the management of the
dominant undertaking whose
decision-making centre is located
outside the Community and which
controls one or more subsidiaries in
the Community does not ensure the
presence within the Community of at
least one person able to fulfil the
requirements as regards disclosure of
information and consultation laid
down by this directive, the
management of the subsidiary that
employs the largest number of
employees within the Community
shall be responsible for fulfilling the
obligation imposed on the
management of the dominant
undertaking by this directive.

Community one or more
establishments when a total of at
least 1000 workers is employed in
the Community by the
undertaking taken as a whole.
2. When the decision-making centre
of an undertaking is located in a non-
member country its management may
be represented in the Community by
an agent who is responsible for
fulfilling the requirements regarding
information and consultation laid
down by this Directive. In the
absence of such an agent the
management of each subsidiary
concerned in the Community shall be
held responsible for the obligations
arising from Articles 3 and 4.

*SECTION II—INFORMATION
AND CONSULTATION
PROCEDURES*
Article 3

Article 5
1. At least every six months, the
management of a dominant
undertaking shall forward relevant
information to the management of
its subsidiaries in the Community
giving a clear picture of the activities
of the dominant undertaking and its
subsidiaries taken as whole.

1. At least once a year, at a fixed
date, the management of a parent
undertaking shall forward general but
explicit information giving a clear
picture of the activities of the parent
undertaking and its subsidiaries as a
whole to the management of each of
its subsidiaries in the Community,
with a view to the communication of
this information to the employees'
representatives as provided in
paragraph 4. For the same purpose,
the management of the parent
undertaking shall forward to the
management of each subsidiary
concerned specific information on a
particular sector of production or
geographical area in which the
subsidiary is active.

2. This information shall relate in
particular to:

2. This information shall relate in
particular to:

ORIGINAL TEXT	AMENDED TEXT
(a) structure and manning:	(a) structure;
(b) the economic and financial situation;	(b) the economic and financial situation;
(c) the situation and probable development of the business and of production and sales;	(c) the probable development of the business and of production and sales;
(d) the employment situation and probable trends;	(d) the employment situation and probable trends;
(e) production and investment programmes;	(e) investment prospects.
(f) rationalisation plans;	
(g) manufacturing and working methods, in particular the introduction of new working methods;	
(h) all procedures and plans liable to have a substantial effect on employees' interests.	

3. The management of each subsidiary shall be required to communicate such information without delay to employees' representatives in each subsidiary.	3. Where the information provided for in paragraph 2 is brought up to date after the date fixed in accordance with paragraph 1 and communicated in implementation of the relevant legislation to shareholders and creditors, the management of the parent undertaking shall also forward it to the management of its subsidiaries, with a view to its communication to the employees' representatives.
4. Where the management of the subsidiaries is unable to communicate the information referred to in paragraphs (1) and (2) to employees' representatives, the management of the dominant undertaking must communicate such information to any employees' representatives who have requested it to do so.	4. The management of each subsidiary shall be required to communicate the information referred to in paragraphs 2 and 3 without delay to the employees' representatives, with the exception of secret information as defined in Article 7(1). The employees' representatives may ask the management for oral explanations of the information communicated. The management is required to provide such explanations, and, if necessary, to make it clear what information is to be treated as confidential under the terms of Article 7(2).
5. The Member States shall provide for appropriate penalties for failure to comply with the obligations laid down in this article.	5. If the management of the subsidiary fails to fulfil its obligation to communicate the information required to its employees'

ORIGINAL TEXT

AMENDED TEXT

representatives within 30 days of the
date fixed, referred to in paragraph
1, or of the date of communication in
the case of the up-dated information
referred to in paragraph 3, the
representatives of the employees of
the subsidiary may approach in
writing the management of the
parent undertaking. That
undertaking shall be obliged to
communicate the relevant
information without delay to the
management of the subsidiary.
6. The terms of this Article shall
apply equally where the parent
undertaking is at the same time the
subsidiary of another parent
undertaking, unless that undertaking
itself meets the obligations resulting
from this Article.
7. Member States shall provide for
appropriate penalties for failure to
comply with the obligations laid down
in this Article.

Article 6
1. Where the management of a
dominant undertaking proposes to
take a decision concerning the whole
or a major part of the dominant
undertaking or of one of its
subsidiaries which is liable to have a
substantial effect on the interests of
its employees, it shall be required to
forward precise information to the
management of each of its
subsidiaries within the Community
not later than forty days before
adopting the decision, giving details
of:
— the grounds for the proposed
  decision;
— the legal, economic and social
  consequences of such decision for
  the employees concerned;
— the measures planned in respect
  of these employees.

Article 4
1. Where the management of a
parent undertaking proposes to take
a decision concerning the whole or a
major part of the parent undertaking
or of a subsidiary in the Community
which is liable to have serious
consequences for the interests of the
employees of its subsidiaries in the
Community, it shall be required to
forward precise information to the
management of each subsidiary
concerned in good time before the
final decision is taken with a view to
the communication of this
information to the employees'
representatives in the manner
provided in paragraph 3. This
information shall relate in particular
to:
— the grounds for the proposed
  decision;
— the legal, economic and social
  consequences of such decision for
  the employees concerned;

ORIGINAL TEXT   AMENDED TEXT

— the measures planned in respect
of such employees.

2. The decisions referred to in   2. Decisions liable to have serious
paragraph (1) shall be those relating   consequences may in particular
to: relate to:
(a) the closure or transfer of an   (a) the closure or transfer of an
    establishment or major parts   establishment or major parts
    thereof;   thereof;
(b) restrictions, extensions or   (b) substantial restrictions or
    substantial modifications to the   modifications of the activities of
    activities of the undertaking;   the undertaking;
(c) major modifications with regard   (c) major modifications with regard
    to organisation;   to organisation, working
                                             practices or production methods,
                                             including modifications resulting
                                             from the introduction of new
                                             technologies;
(d) the introduction of Long-term   (d) the introduction of long-term
    cooperation with other   cooperation with other
    undertakings or the cessation of   undertakings or the cessation of
    such cooperation.   such cooperation;
                                         (e) measures relating to workers'
                                             health and to industrial safety.
3. The management of each   3. Without prejudice to Article 7(1)
subsidiary shall be required to   the management of each subsidiary
communicate this information   concerned shall be required to
without delay to its employees'   communicate in writing without
representatives and to ask for their   delay the information referred to in
opinion within a period of not less   paragraph 1, with the exception of
than thirty days.   secret information as defined in
                                         Article 7(1), to the employees
                                         representatives, to ask for their
                                         opinion, granting them a period at
                                         least 30 days from the day on which
                                         the information is communicated,
                                         and to hold consultations with them
                                         with a view to attempting to reach
                                         agreement on the measures planned
                                         in respect of the employees. The
                                         provisions of the second
                                         subparagraph of Article 3(4) shall
                                         apply mutatis mutandis.
4. Where, in the opinion of the   4. Where the obligations laid down
employees' representatives, the   in paragraph 3 are not fulfilled,
proposed decision is likely to have a   Member States shall ensure that
direct effect on the employees' terms   employees' representatives have the
of employment or working   right to appeal to a tribunal or other
conditions, the management of the   competent national authority for
subsidiary shall be required to hold   measures to be taken within a

ORIGINAL TEXT

consultations with them with a view to reaching agreement on the measures planned in respect of them.
5. Where the management of the subsidiaries does not communicate to the employees' representatives the information required under paragraph (3) or does not arrange consultations as required under paragraph (4), such representatives shall be authorised to open consultations, through authorised delegates, with the management of the dominant undertaking with a view to obtaining such information and, where appropriate, to reaching agreement on the measures planned with regard to the employees concerned.
6. The Member States shall provide for appropriate penalties in case of failure to fulfil the obligations laid down in this article. In particular, they shall grant to the employees' representatives concerned by the decision the right of appeal to tribunals or other competent national authorities for measures to be taken to protect their interests.

AMENDED TEXT

maximum period of 30 days to compel the management of the subsidiary to fulfil its obligations.
5. The proposed decision referred to in paragraph 1 shall not be implemented before the opinion of the employees' representatives is received or failing that before the end of the period granted according to paragraph 3.

6. Where information concerning a decision within the meaning of paragraph 1 is withheld because it is secret within the meaning of Article 7(1), the management of the subsidiary is nonetheless required, at least 30 days before putting into effect any decision directly affecting conditions of work or employment, to hold consultations with the employees' representatives with a view to attempting to reach agreement on the measures planned in respect of the employees.
7. The terms of this Article shall apply equally where the parent undertaking is at the same time the subsidiary of another parent undertaking, unless that undertaking itself meets the obligations resulting from this Article.
8. Member States shall provide for appropriate penalties for failure to comply with the obligations laid down in this Article.

Article 7
1. Where in a Member State a body representating employees exists at a level higher than that of the

Article 5
1. Where, in a Member State a body representing employees exists at a level higher than that of the

ORIGINAL TEXT	AMENDED TEXT
individual subsidiary, the information provided for in Article 5 relating to the employees of all the subsidiaries thus represented shall be given to that body.	subsidiary, the information referred to in Article 3 relating to the employees of all the subsidiaries thus represented shall be given to that body.
2. The consultations provided for in Article 6 shall take place under the same conditions with the representative body referred to in paragraph (1).	2. The consultations provided for in Article 4 shall take place under the same conditions with the representative body referred to in paragraph 1 if the representatives of the employees whose terms of employment or working conditions are directly affected by the decision agree to transfer their right to be consulted to the higher level.
3. A body representing all the employees of the dominant undertaking and its subsidiaries within the Community may be created by means of agreements to be concluded between the management of the dominant undertaking and the employees' representatives. If such a body is created, paragraphs 1 and 2 shall be applicable.	3. A body representing all the employees of the parent undertaking and its subsidiaries within the Community may be created by means of agreements to be concluded between the management of the undertaking concerned and the employees' representatives. If such a body is created, paragraphs 1 and 2 shall be applicable.
	4. Member States may limit the obligations laid down in Article 3 and 4 to subsidiaries which, in respect of the number of employees fulfil the conditions for the election or designation of a collegiate body representing the employees.
	5. Member States may provide that the information and consultation procedures referred to in Article 3(4) and (5) and Article 4(3) to (6) may take place directly with the employees, without prejudice to the application of the other provisions of this Directive.
Article 9	*Article 6*
1. The management of an undertaking whose decision-making centre is located in a Member State of the Community and which has one or more establishments in at least one other Member State shall disclose, via the management of those	1. The provisions of Articles 3, 4 and 5 shall apply mutatis mutandis to the procedures for informing and consulting the employees' representatives in the undertakings referred to in the second indent of Article 2(1).

ORIGINAL TEXT

AMENDED TEXT

establishments, information to the employees' representatives in all of its establishments in the Community employing at least one hundred employees in accordance with Article 5 and consult them in accordance with Article 6.

2. The management of an undertaking whose decision-making centre is located in a non-member country and which has at least one establishment in one Member State shall be subject to the obligations referred to in paragraph (1).

3. For the purposes of applying this Article, the terms 'dominant undertaking' and 'subsidiary' in Articles 4 to 8 shall be replaced by the terms 'undertaking' and 'establishment' respectively.

2. For the purposes of this Article, the terms 'parent undertaking' and 'subsidiary' shall be replaced by the terms 'undertaking' and 'establishment' respectively.

SECTION III
Procedures for informing and consulting the employees of undertakings with complex structures whose decision-making centre is located in the country in which the employees work.

Article 10
The management of a dominant undertaking whose decision-making centre is located in a Member State of the Community and which has one or more subsidiaries in the same Member State shall be required, via the management of its subsidiaries, to disclose information to employees' representatives in all subsidiaries employing at least one hundred employees in that State in accordance with Article 11 and to consult them in accordance with Article 12.

Articles 10 to 14
Deleted and combined with Articles 2 (1) and 3 to 6.

Article 11
1. At least every six months, the management of a dominant undertaking shall forward relevant

ORIGINAL TEXT   AMENDED TEXT

information to the management of its   *Articles 10 to 14*
subsidiaries in the Community giving   Deleted and combined with Articles
a clear picture of the activities of the 2 (1) and 3 to 6.
dominant undertaking and its
subsidiaries taken as a whole.
2. This information shall relate in
particular to:
(a) structure and manning;
(b) the economic and financial
    situation;
(c) the situation and probable
    development of the business and
    of production and sales;
(d) the employment situation and
    probable trends;
(e) production and investment
    programmes;
(f) rationalisation plans;
(g) manufacturing and working
    methods, in particular the
    introduction of new working
    methods;
(h) all procedures and plans liable to
    have a substantial effect on
    employees' interests.
3. The management of each
subsidiary shall be required to
communicate such information
without delay to employees'
representatives in each subsidiary.
4. Where the management of the
subsidiaries is unable to
communicate the information
referred to in paragraphs (1) and (2)
above to employees' representatives,
the management of the dominant
undertaking must communicate such
information to any employees'
representatives who have requested
it to do so.
5. The Member State shall provide
for appropriate penalties in case of
failure to fulfil the obligation laid
down in this Article.

Article 12
1. Where the management of a
dominant undertaking proposes to
take a decision concerning the whole

ORIGINAL TEXT	AMENDED TEXT

ORIGINAL TEXT

or a major part of the dominant undertaking or of one of its subsidiaries which is liable to have a substantial effect on the interests of its workers, it shall be required to forward precise information to the management of each of its subsidiaries within the Community not later than forty days before adopting the decision, giving details of:

— the grounds for the proposed decision;
— the legal, economic and social consequences of such decision for the employees concerned;
— the measures planned in respect of these employees.

2. The decisions referred to in paragraph (1) shall be those relating to:

(a) the closure or transfer of an establishment or major part thereof:

(b) restrictions, extensions of substantial modifications to the activities of the undertaking;

(c) major modifications with regard to organisation;

(d) the introduction of long-term cooperation with other undertakings or the cessation of such cooperation.

3. The management of each subsidiary shall be required to communicate this information without delay to its employees' representatives and to ask for their opinion within a period of not less than thirty days.

4. Where, in the opinion of the employees' representatives, the proposed decision is likely to have a direct effect on the employees' terms of employment or working conditions, the management of the subsidiary shall be required to hold consultations with them with a view to reaching agreement on the measures planned in respect of them.

AMENDED TEXT

Articles 10 to 14
Deleted and combined with Articles 2 (1) and 3 to 6.

ORIGINAL TEXT	AMENDED TEXT
5. Where the management of the subsidiaries does not communicate to the employees' representatives the information required under paragraph (3) or does not arrange consultations as required under paragraph (4), such representatives shall be authorised to open consultations, through authorised delegates, with the management of the dominant undertaking with a view to obtaining such information and, where appropriate to reaching agreement on the measures planned with regard to the employees.	*Articles 10 to 14* Deleted and combined with Articles 2 (1) and 3 to 6.

5. Where the management of the subsidiaries does not communicate to the employees' representatives the information required under paragraph (3) or does not arrange consultations as required under paragraph (4), such representatives shall be authorised to open consultations, through authorised delegates, with the management of the dominant undertaking with a view to obtaining such information and, where appropriate to reaching agreement on the measures planned with regard to the employees.
6. The Member States shall provide for appropriate penalties in the case of failure to fulfil the obligations laid down in this article. In particular, they shall grant to the employees' representatives concerned by the decision the right of appeal to tribunals or other competent national authorities for measures to be taken to protect their interests.

Article 13
1. Where in a Member State a body representing employees, exists at a level higher than that of the individual subsidiary the information provided for in Article 11 relating to the employees of all the subsidiaries thus represented shall be given to that body.
2. The consultations provided for in Article 12 shall take place under the same conditions with the representative body referred to in paragraph (1).
3. A body representing all the employees of the dominant undertaking and its subsidiaries within the Community may be created by means of agreements to be concluded between the management of the dominant undertaking and the employees' representatives, unless provision is

ORIGINAL TEXT	AMENDED TEXT
made for it by national law. If such a body is created, paragraphs 1 and 2 shall be applicable.	*Articles 10 to 14* Deleted and combined with Articles 2 (1) and 3 to 6.

Article 14

1. The management of a dominant undertaking whose decision-making centre is located in a Member State of the Community and which has one or more establishments in the same Member State shall be required to disclose via the management of the subsidiaries, information to the employees' representatives in all its subsidiaries employing at least one hundred employees in accordance with Article 11 and to consult them in accordance with Article 12.
2. For the purposes of applying this Article, the terms 'dominant undertaking' and 'subsidiary' in Article 10 to 13 shall be replaced by the terms 'undertaking' and 'establishment'.

SECTION IV Secrecy requirements *Article 15* 1. Members and former members of bodies representing employees and delegates authorised by them shall be required to maintain discretion as regards information of a confidential nature. Where they communicate information to third parties they shall take account of the interests of the undertaking and shall not be such as to divulge secrets regarding the undertaking or its business. 2. The Member States shall empower a tribunal or other national body to settle disputes concerning the confidentiality of certain information.	*SECTION III* Secrecy and confidentiality *Article 7* 1. The management of an undertaking shall be authorized not to communicate secret information. Information may only be treated as secret which, if disclosed, could substantially damage the undertaking's interests or lead to the failure of its plans. 2. Employees, their representatives and the experts to whom they refer shall not reveal to third parties any information which has been given to them in confidence. 3. Member States shall ensure that a tribunal or other competent national authority can settle disputes concerning the secret character of any information withheld in

ORIGINAL TEXT

AMENDED TEXT

application of paragraph 1, or the confidential character of the information referred to in paragraph 2.
4. Member States shall provide for appropriate penalties for failure to comply with the obligations laid down in this Article.

3. The Member States shall impose appropriate penalties in cases of infringements of the secrecy requirements.

SECTION V
Final provisions
Article 16
This directive shall be without prejudice to measures to be taken pursuant to Council Directive 75/129/ EEC of 17 February 1975 on the approximation of the laws of the Member States relating to collective redundancies(1) and Directive 77/187/ EEC or to the freedom of the Member States to apply or introduce laws, regulations or administrative provisions which are more favourable to employees.(2)

SECTION IV
Final provisions
Article 8
1. This Directive shall be without prejudice to measures taken pursuant to directive 75/129/EEC and Directive 77/187/EEC or to the freedom of the Member States to apply or introduce laws, regulations or administrative provisions which are more favourable to employees.

2. In implementing this Directive, Member States may lay down special provisions for undertakings and establishments whose direct and main objectives are
(a) political, religious, humanitarian, charitable, educational, scientific or artistic, or
(b) related to public information or expression of opinion.
Such special provision must be limited to that which is necessary to ensure that such undertakings enjoy the freedom to which they are entitled under the national laws to which they are subject.
3. This Directive shall be without prejudice to the application of national laws concerning bankruptcy, winding up proceedings, arrangements, compositions or other

(1) OJ No L 48 of 22.2.1975.
(2) OJ No L 61 of 05.3.1977.

ORIGINAL TEXT

AMENDED TEXT

similar proceedings insofar as these proceedings result from judicial decisions.

Article 9
1. The Member States shall introduce the Laws, regulations and administrative provisions necessary to comply with this Directive not later than 1 July 1987. They shall forthwith inform the Commission thereof.

Article 17
2. The Member States shall communicate to the Commission the texts of laws, regulations, and administrative which they adopt in the area covered by this Directive.

Article 18
Within two years from the date fixed in Article 17, the Member States shall transmit to the Commission all information necessary to enable it to draw up a report to be submitted to the Council relating to the application of this directive.

Article 10
Within two years from the date referred to in Article 9, Member States shall forward to the Commission all necessary information to enable it to draw up a report on the application of this Directive for submission to the Council.

Article 19
This directive is addressed to the Member States.

Article 11
No change.

Index